Marianne Heske

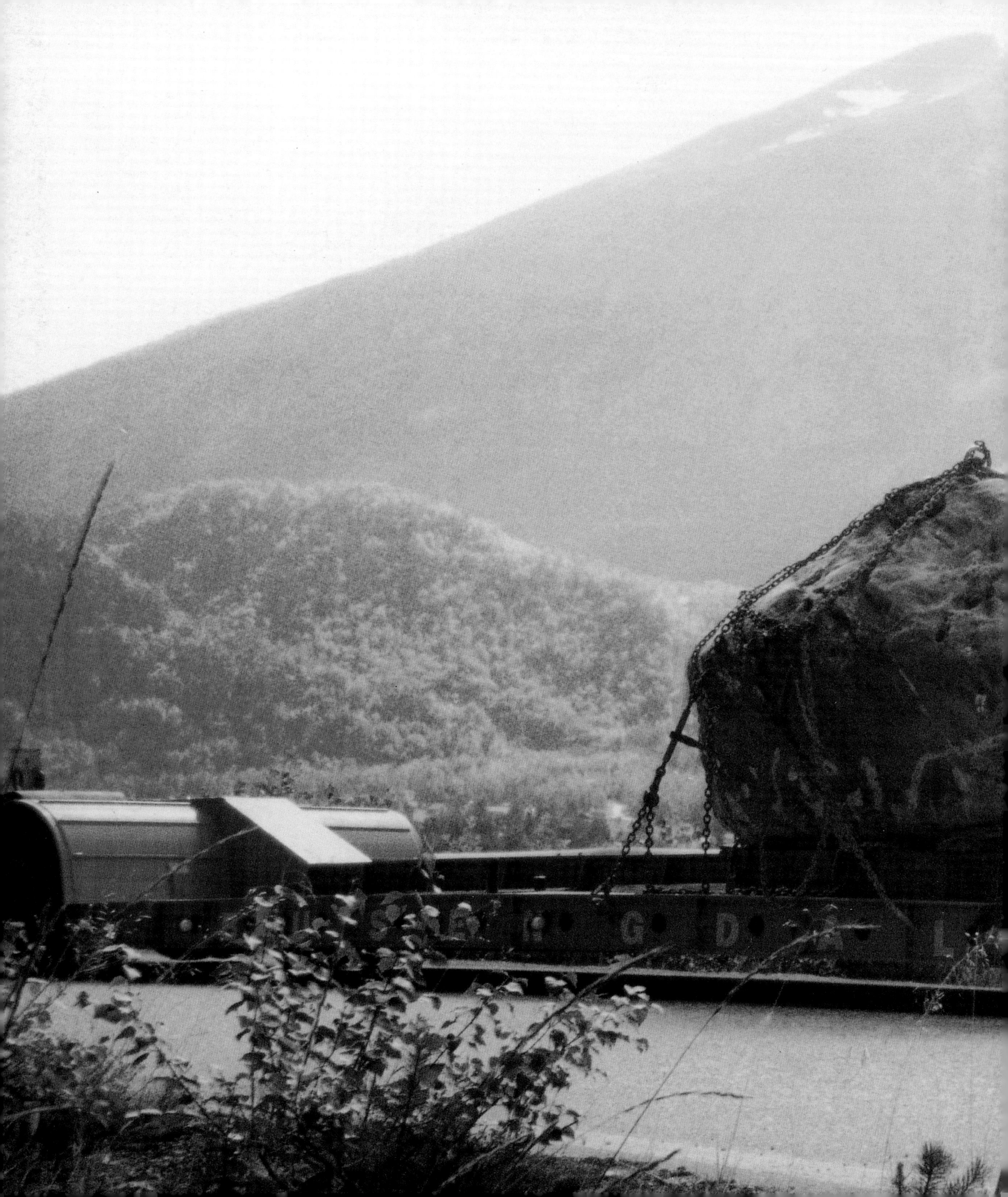

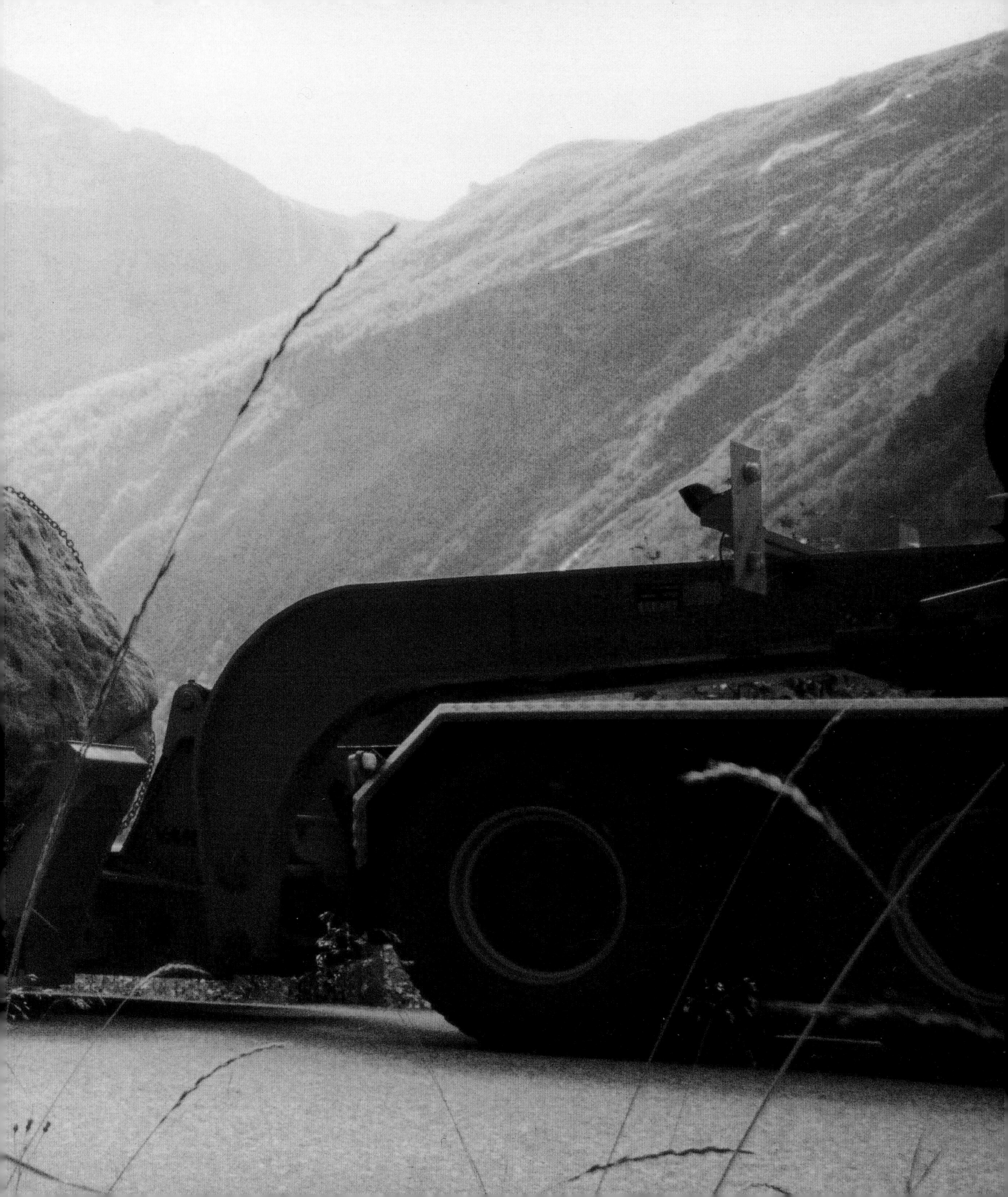

Marianne Heske

edited by Selene Wendt

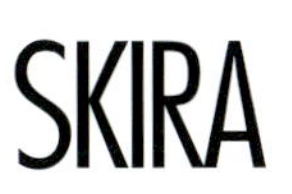 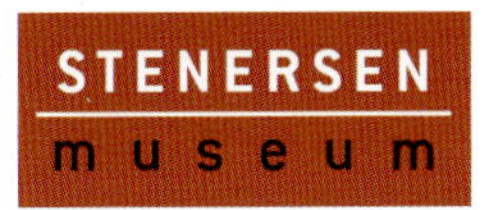

pp. 2-3
Stone Story, Tafjord-Venice.
On the way to Piazzale del
Casino, Lido, 1999. Site-specific
art project.

Editor
Selene Wendt

Editorial Assistant
Lars Toft-Eriksen

Design
Marcello Francone

Editorial Coordination
Emma Cavazzini

Editing
Emily Ligniti

Layout
Sara Salvi

First published in Italy in 2010
by Skira Editore S.p.A.
Palazzo Casati Stampa
via Torino 61
20123 Milano
Italy
www.skira.net

Printed and bound in Italy.
First edition

ISBN: 978-88-572-0851-0
(The Stenersen Museum)
978-88-7624-746-0
(Skira editore)

Distributed in North America
by Rizzoli International
Publications, Inc., 300 Park
Avenue South, New York, NY
10010, USA.
Distributed elsewhere in the
world by Thames and Hudson
Ltd., 181A High Holborn,
London WC1V 7QX, United
Kingdom.

Published on the occasion
of the exhibition

Marianne Heske
Heaven & Earth

The Stenersen Museum, Oslo
4 November, 2010 – 2 January, 2011

Curated by Selene Wendt

Sponsors

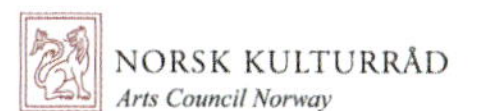

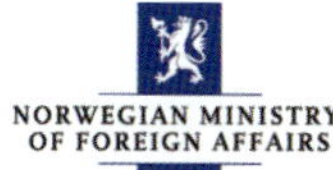

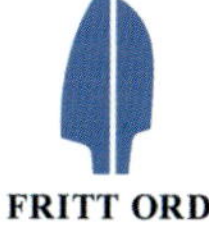

Contents

As the collection of essays in this book conveys, the doll's head is a strong recurring symbol within Marianne Heske's artwork. The power of doll symbolism initially inspired Heske when she came across a box of *papier mâché* doll heads at a flea market in Paris in the seventies. Doll's heads have figured prominently in her work ever since, showing up in lithographs, prints, collages, photographs, video works, installations and sculptures. While the significance and nuances in meaning vary from work to work, doll heads function throughout as a universal symbol of humanity.

The notion that dolls might function metaphorically as a unifying factor between people was a point that she initially made in the photographic series *With and About People,* 1973. While travelling around Europe, Heske asked people to let her photograph them while they posed with one of the Parisian doll heads. The doll as metaphor would soon become part of a significant artistic project, a global exchange that has spanned over decades, bringing Marianne Heske from Norway to Zimbabwe, China and Nepal, and most recently to Kenya.

At the outset, doll heads figured in Heske's investigations of phrenological diagrams, whereby the correlation between the shape of a person's skull and various parts of the brain supposedly indicates certain characteristics of a person. While phrenology today is considered a pseudoscience, it is interesting to see how she played with it in her early works. As the references became less scientific, the doll heads were featured in large-scale installation works and began to take on a life of their own. The tiny heads that populate her works, made from materials such as china, crystal, or stone, bear little resemblance to the original *papier mâché* doll with its ruby red lips and delicately painted eyes. What Marianne Heske found in Paris was a hollow symbol. What has remained interesting through the years is how she turned this symbol into a gender-neutral object, which has provided the basis for an artistic career.

The dolls in Marianne Heske's work are part of a complex art that is all about process and concepts. The dolls are like puppets, devoid of meaning before she determines and changes their context with each new work. The dolls don't change significantly from project to project; in fact they are ostensibly the same, all shaped from the same mould. Made of different materials and placed within different surroundings, they convey different messages that are determined by the context in which they are placed. Just as we are shaped by our surroundings and trapped within our roles, so are the dolls in Marianne Heske's work.

Marianne Heske's use of the doll's head as metaphor is coupled with an ongoing interest in Henrik Ibsen and a fascination with the social themes brought up in *A Doll's House*. While the doll's head generally plays a universal role within Heske's work, it also figures as a very specific reference to and interpretation of *A Doll's House*. For the group exhibition *A Doll's House* (2002), named after Ibsen's play, she created *Take Off*. The work was comprised of a series of colourful, constantly changing light-emitting diodes which led up to and away from a single jade doll's head, logically directing ones thoughts to the idea of take off and landing. The work relates to the possibility of what Nora represents when she leaves her home and family, and the question of what she meets when she reaches her final destination, wherever that might be and whatever it may entail.

Ironically, within the context of Heske's installation, the character of Nora is trapped in the symbol of her role as a doll, the role that she struggled to break free from. The same sort of social and existential issues that defined Ibsen's work are seen to unfold throughout Heske's work, and provide an interesting context for further interpretation and understanding of Heske's artwork.

Heske's use of the doll's head as it specifically relates to *A Doll's House* and the character of Nora

Global Groove, 2010.
Installation detail and
exhibition space. Fort Jesus,
The Gunpowder Tower,
National Museums of Kenya,
Mombasa, Kenya.

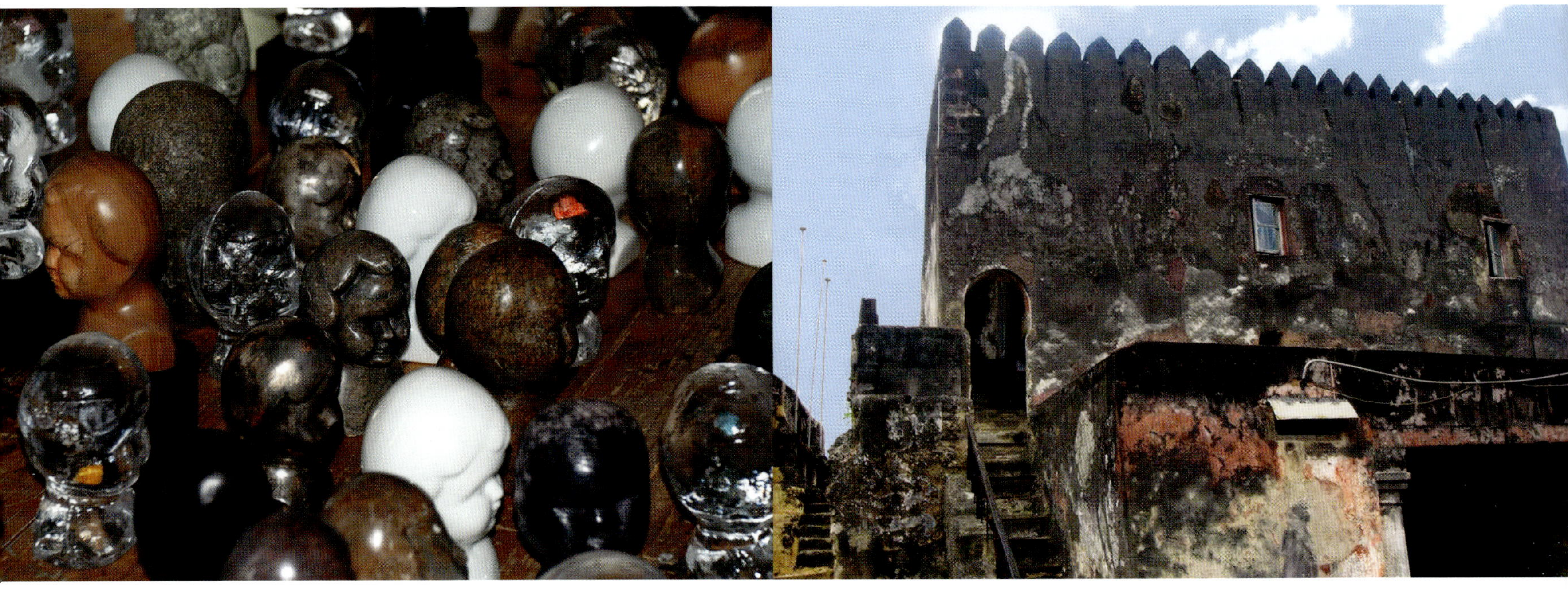

has been thoroughly established through the years. Among the most relevant conceptual similarities between Heske and Ibsen is a shared interest in social structures, power struggles, gender-related themes and identity issues.

While the doll heads used in various projects are physically similar, their significance and roles vary not only from work to work but also from culture to culture. The form itself is pre-determined and definite, yet the possibilities and combinations are endless. Essentially Heske provides a hollow, easily recognizable symbol onto which others can project their own ideas. It is fascinating to see how easily the visual language of her dolls translates from culture to culture, as emphasized in her *Global Groove* project. Throughout her career, Heske has had an interest in bringing her projects to other cultures, so it seems logical that she would also seek to bring her universal symbol of humanity to other cultures. *Global Groove* has developed into a significant work in progress, an artistic journey that has resulted in a dynamic platform for cross-cultural dialogue.

With support from The Norwegian Ministry of Foreign Affairs, Heske has created a truly innovative cross-cultural artistic interchange. Growing from the notion of the fundamental interconnectivity between people from different cultures, the shared understanding of basic archetypes, and the universal symbolism of dolls, the idea has grown into a global project that relates not only to Marianne Heske but to humanity in general. *Global Groove* has facilitated strong artistic ties across geographic borders, linking Norwegian contemporary art practice to Zimbabwe, China, Nepal, and Kenya so far.

The installation work *China from China* includes two thousand white porcelain doll heads, all produced in China. Similar to her *Avalanche* installation, the heads are part of a massive pile that conveys the power of nature over humanity. Many of the heads are broken or damaged, some are intact, and there are small mirrors in which the viewers can see their own reflections, a detail which makes the work resonate on a personal level for each visitor. As if it weren't enough for the viewer to share the same space as the dolls, Heske makes the viewers a part of the installation by including these small mirrors.

Working with local artists around the world, Heske creates doll heads in materials that are specific to each geographic location. She expands the possibilities associated with the doll's head as a visual metaphor by also inspiring artists to create their own interpretations of the doll heads. *Blue* was created in Zimbabwe, shaped from an indigenous stone material. The two hundred heads in *Blue* suggest a mass of people united as one in a cage. A film that captures the delicately fluttering wings of a cobalt blue butterfly is projected onto the doll heads, conveying fragility and evanescence as a powerful counterpart to the mass of heavy, solid stone heads.

Nora's Necklace is another key work that relates directly to the *Global Groove* project. Created in Nepal in collaboration with local artists, it consists of two hundred and fifty doll heads that hang down like a necklace. The heads are plated with gold or silver, in equal quantities, linked together in the shape of a beautiful imaginary necklace. The preciousness and beauty of the materials is offset by the fact that the installation is also a huge knot that symbolises the inner conflict and despair of the human experience.

For her monumental 2006 project *Doll's House*, Heske created a full-scale house that included, what she describes as, thousands of people from all over the world. As inspired as she was to bring her doll heads out into the world and to inspire an ongoing cross-cultural dialogue, she was equally focused on bringing them back to Norway where she would furnish the dolls with a house of their own. The house included five projects: *China from China, Blue* and *Nora's Necklace* from the *Global Groove* project were dramatically featured along with *NN*[1]—comprised of one single head—and her groundbreaking 1993 installation *Avalanche*.

[1] From the Latin term *Nomen Nescio* which translates to Unknown Person. *NN*, 1976.

Marianne Heske's unique approach to repetition has kept her work relevant through the years. The repetitive use of what is essentially the same doll's head, used over and over again, in different materials and within different contexts, is consistently transformed into major installations that signal a lifelong interest in the intricate and overlapping worlds of relational aesthetics, installation art, psychology and philosophy. Repetition is possibly the single most important factor that continues to define Marianne Heske's ongoing projects around the world. The subtle difference between what makes repetition boring and what turns it into pure magic is eloquently defined by art critic Jerry Saltz. In the article *Heaps* and Consequences, which first appeared in the Village Voice in 2006, he wrote, "Repetition is difference repeated within such narrow structures that it opens new possibilities. At its best, repetition conjures what Baudelaire called the "sacred machinery". That's why sometimes when rooms are filled with arrangements of objects, when configurations are fashioned from hundreds, thousands, or even millions of similar things, repetition turns metaphysical, obsession and process become transcendental, and magic happens." Magic is precisely what happens with Marianne Heske's repetitive implementation of dolls.

Within the context of Marianne Heske's work, dolls are used as symbols of something far greater than what first meets the eye. The various groupings, collections, presentations, gatherings, spotlight appearances, crowds, piles, grids, patterns, and crowded rooms featuring the same doll's head in varying forms, conceived in different places around the world, all trace back to their origins. One might think that the Parisian flea market is the origin in question, but when we consider her work as a whole, it is clear to see that the true origin of these symbols of humanity, and the most significant source of inspiration that defines almost all of Marianne Heske's work, is the idea of the power of nature over humanity, as represented in and understood in the symbol of the avalanche—a recurring theme in both her installation and video work since day one. With each and every new installation, Marianne Heske addresses universal themes by creating avalanches that are as improbable, overwhelming, confrontational and surprising as this force of nature. Ultimately, Heske's avalanches reflect overwhelming psychological states of mind and situations of crisis in society.

In his brilliant essay *Marianne Heske or The Art of Relocation,* Nicolas Bourriaud delves beneath the surface of the paradoxical nature of Heske's deceptively simple work. The French scholar, who coined the term relational aesthetics, places Heske's work into what is perhaps its most relevant context ever. He outlines the development of her work from a perspective that not only opens up an entire new level of meaning in her work, it credits Marianne Heske, the Norwegian artist born and raised on the side of a remote Norwegian mountainside, as being at the forefront of international contemporary art practice in addition to being a pioneer of relational aesthetics before the term was even created.

In Lorella Scacco's essay *Ways of Seeing* she touches upon the importance of Heske's *Doll's House* project and discusses Ibsen's ties to Italy as they relate to Heske's work. Perhaps more than any other single project up until that point, *Doll's House* brought together the various aspects of Marianne Heske's different projects, highlighting the subtle underlying messages that unify her work as a whole. The house was more than an artistic framework for her doll heads, it functioned as a utopian structure where conceptual, philosophical and formal aspects all came together in a controlled environment that viewers shared with the doll heads.

It is interesting to note that Heske refers to the doll heads not as sculptural objects but as people, thereby blurring the boundaries between signifier and signified. The project extended beyond being an installation work including doll heads. Heske had created a perfect environment for the protagonists in her life-long artistic drama. The house provided a fascinating context that ultimately emphasized the universality and timelessness of the themes she has addressed throughout her work. By presenting the dolls in a realistic home-like environment and inviting viewers into that domain, Heske further emphasized their conceptual importance as cultural—and gender —neutral objects onto which the other players in her artistic project, the viewers, could project their own meanings and interpretations. Heske not only raised the question of what became of Nora after her dramatic exit in her earlier work *Take Off*, she took the idea further and created shelter, in the form of an actual house with *Doll's House*.

In his essay *A Doll's House from Ibsen to Heske,* Ken Friedman also highlights the distinct thematic correlation between Ibsen's plays and Marianne Heske's artwork. He provides an in-depth analysis of the overriding themes that have been a source of inspiration for Heske through the years. Her fascination with the social, gender and identity issues raised in Ibsen's dramas, and as they relate to the human experience in general, has influenced her entire artistic practice including land art, sound art, photography, video, and performance and installation art. Friedman's emphasis on the importance of the psychological, social and philosophical underpinnings of Ibsen's work provides a highly relevant framework for understanding the depth of her artwork. Ultimately, Heske transforms the intricate drama of human experience, as expressed by Ibsen, into rich visual metaphor in her own work.

Underneath the serious philosophical and theoretical aspects of Marianne Heske's work there also lies a humorous undertone. In a suitably offbeat interview with Marianne Heske and the Norwegian author Jon Fosse, Hans Ulrich Obrist brings out Marianne Heske's playful side. His interview focuses on the unique connection between Heske and Fosse, their shared interest in the house as metaphor, and the complexities of human existence as they play out in literary and artistic narratives that relate to desire, hope, fear and happiness, or what Marianne Heske would define as the struggle of human existence.

Jon Fosse's text *Freedom* was written specifically for this book, and stands out as an open-ended, suitably surreal text among a collection of concisely written essays that document the timelessness of Heske's *œuvre*. Herein lies the essence and complexity of Heske's artwork. Each layer of meaning can be stripped down to the most specific interpretation or expanded to include universal themes that are relevant from culture to culture. The numerous interpretations included in this book widen our understanding of an artistic project that has remained contemporary and fresh through the years precisely because Marianne Heske raises timeless, existential questions without forcing absolute answers on the viewers. In fact, she prides herself on leaving the door open for each individual's own projections and illusions.

Maybe

I think it all started when my father told me, in the hallway in the house in Tafjord, that the scale of our planet in the total universe could be compared with the size of a grain of sand on a big beach.
I was about six years old. I was visualizing the beach of Sola outside Stavanger, where the family had spent the summer. The beaches there were enormous. This picture has probably matured in my mind.
If the planet is so microscopic, what about us, the people inhabiting the planet? And yet we think we are so important. We believe our planet to be the center of the universe: our ego the center of the planet.
Since the beginning of time, people have tried to immortalize themselves in drawings, carvings and through all kinds of efforts to portray themselves, trying to solidify and mirror their existence.
Dolls are one of these expressions.
Puppets and marionettes are inherently empty of meaning, but are given certain roles, projected by the societies in which they are created.
Dolls as such have never been of any interest to me. Likewise, neither video nor technology is of interest to me, except in the sense of being tools to express the human mind and the sensory apparatus.
But I have always had a great interest in metaphors. Being on the move, I have had the possibility of observing people playing their given roles around the world.
My installations reflect these observations.
They are often represented in precious materials like crystal and ageless stone. Maybe symbols

for the human longing of an everlasting life, of everlasting values.
Maybe a rejection of impermanence.
These installations often include projections. These images are video recordings of the cyclic avalanches in Tafjord, a phenomenon which occurs every spring.
Maybe an acknowledgement of impermanence.
Avalanches erupting streams of mosaics down the steep mountain sides.
Beautiful, scary. Uncontrollable.
Yet scientists still try to control our natural surroundings and the nature of the human mind—by measuring, categorizing, counting and analyzing.
Inventing and rejecting theories. Phrenology is one of these attempts.
Housing and houses are another attempt to find shelter and security, protection for outside forces, and forces inside our heads.
I have always been on the move. Maybe that is why I move houses ?
Nomads bring their houses along. Uprooting.
Only the mind is clarity. Always there. Luminous and transparent with its illusions, delusions and projections.
The "Mountains of the Mind" remain after you have left.
 "We are such stuff as dreams are made of."
Although there are billions of stars in the universe all the time.
We cannot see them,
but for a few,
at night.

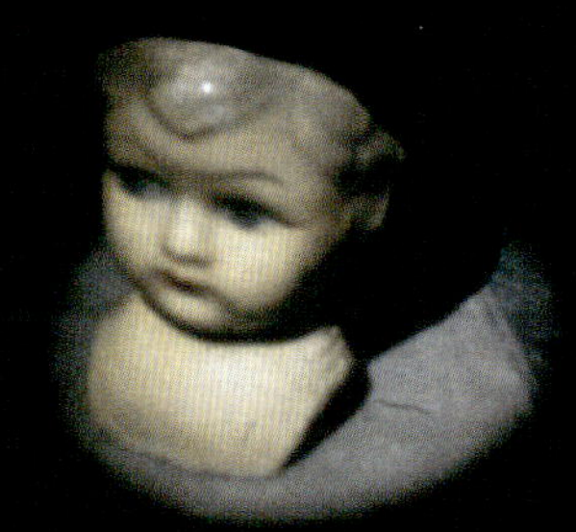

Bijoux, 1972. Assemblage.

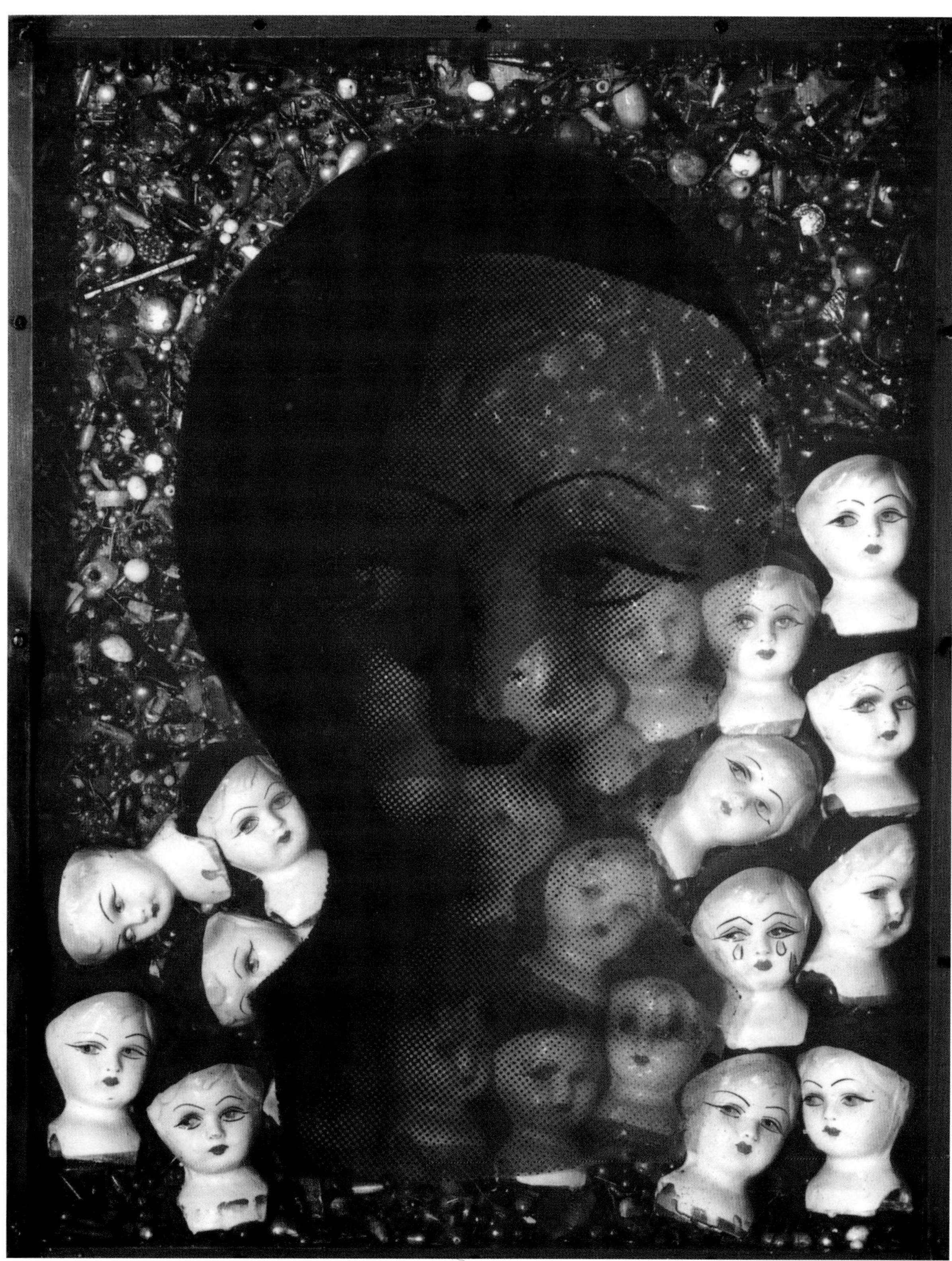

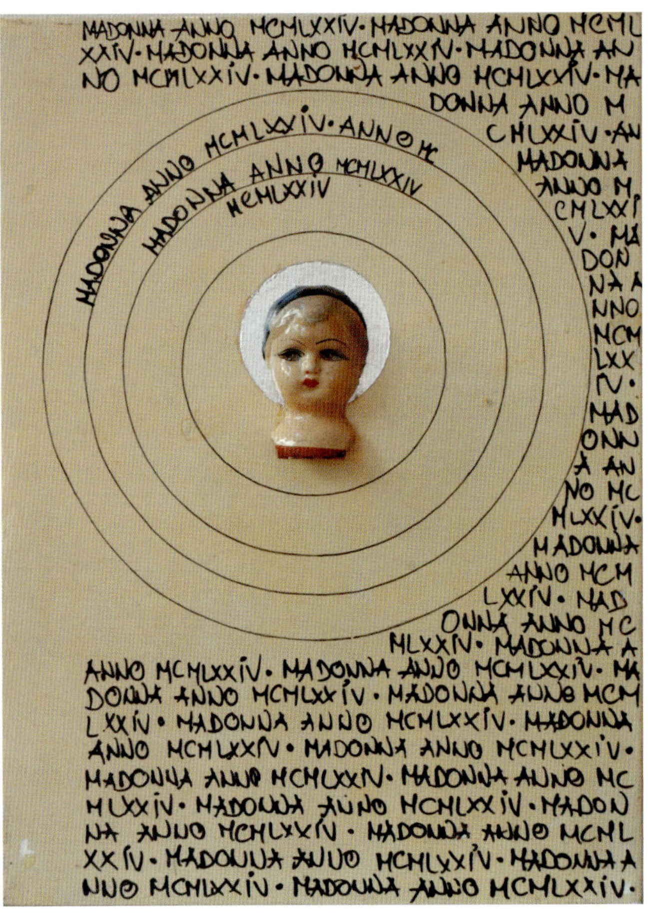

MADONNA ANNO MCMLXXIV · MADONNA ANNO MCML
XXIV · MADONNA ANNO MCMLXXIV · MADONNA AN
NO MCMLXXIV · MADONNA ANNO MCMLXXIV · MA
DONNA ANNO M
MADONNA ANNO MCMLXXIV · ANNO M   CMLXXIV · AN
MADONNA ANNO MCMLXXIV   MADONNA
MCMLXXIV   ANNO M
CMLXXI
V · MA
DON
NA
ANNO
MCM
LXX
IV ·
MAD
ONN
A AN
NO MC
MLXXIV ·
MADONNA
ANNO MCM
LXXIV · MAD
ONNA ANNO MC
MLXXIV · MADONNA A
ANNO MCMLXXIV · MADONNA ANNO MCMLXXIV · MA
DONNA ANNO MCMLXXIV · MADONNA ANNO MCM
LXXIV · MADONNA ANNO MCMLXXIV · MADONNA
ANNO MCMLXXIV · MADONNA ANNO MCMLXXIV ·
MADONNA ANNO MCMLXXIV · MADONNA ANNO MC
MLXXIV · MADONNA ANNO MCMLXXIV · MADON
NA ANNO MCMLXXIV · MADONNA ANNO MCML
XXIV · MADONNA ANNO MCMLXXIV · MADONNA
NNO MCMLXXIV · MADONNA ANNO MCMLXXIV ·

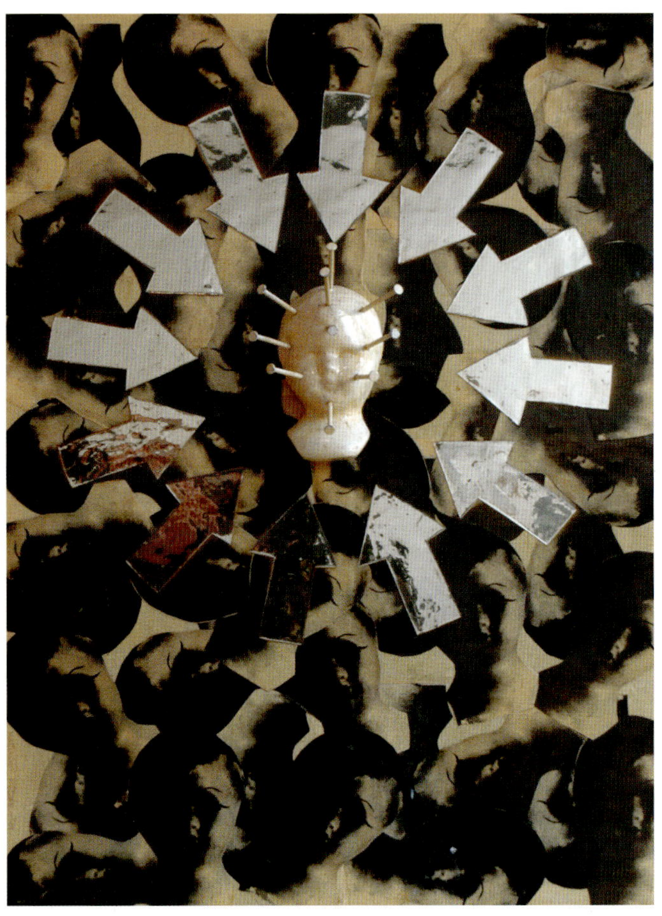

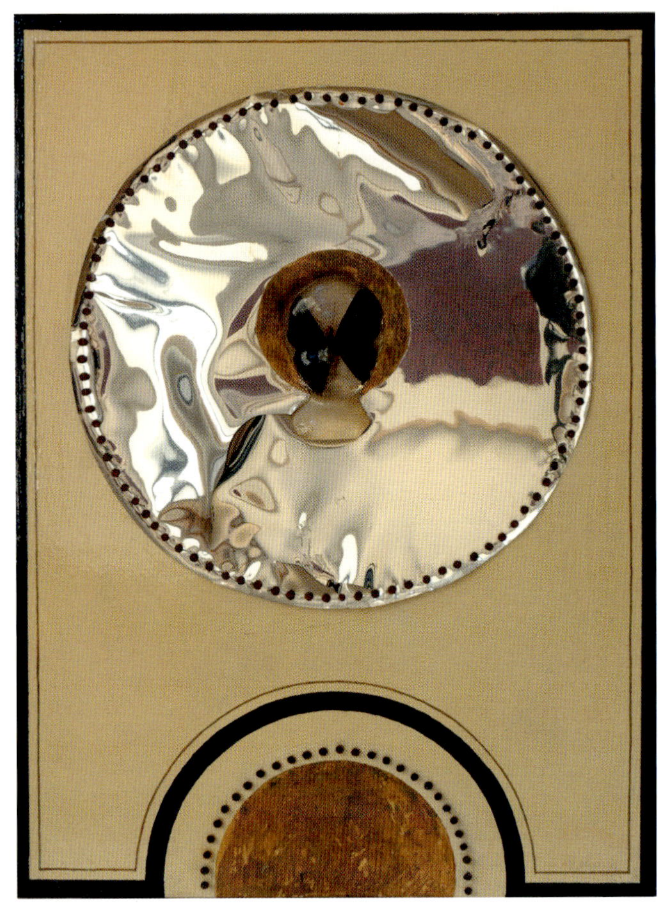

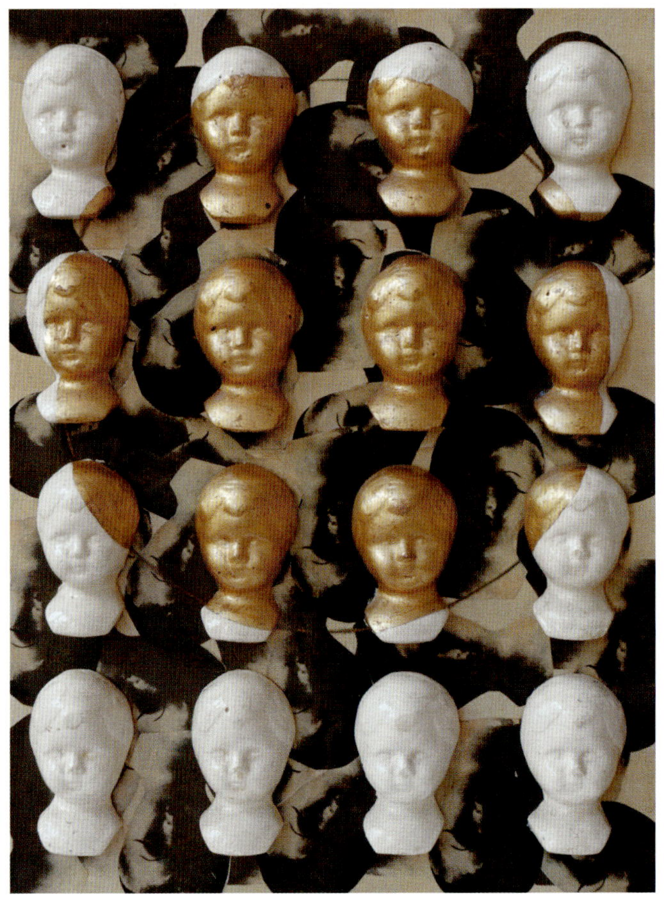

Icon I–V, seventies.
Assemblage.

Madonna, 1975. Triptych,
assemblage.

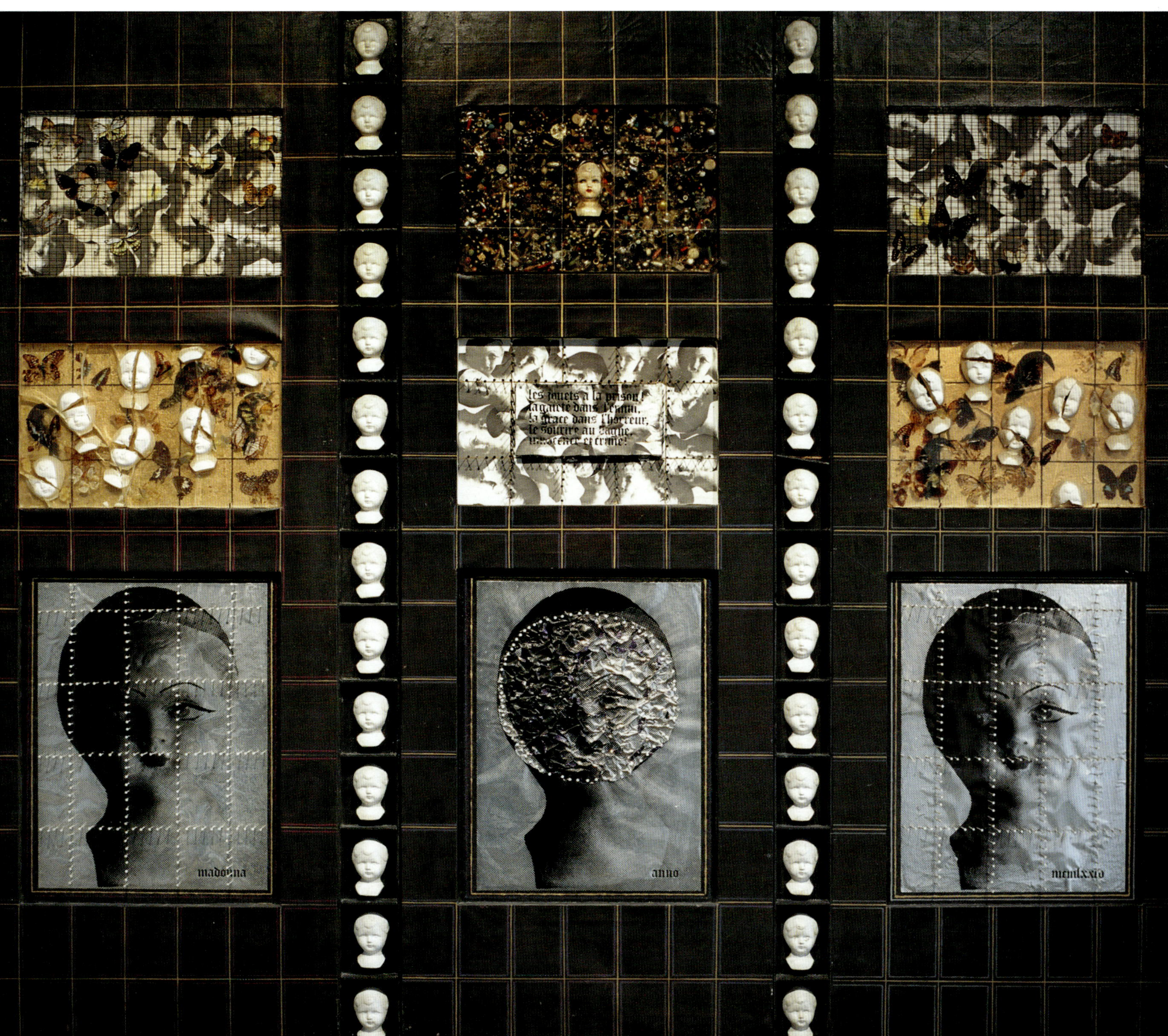

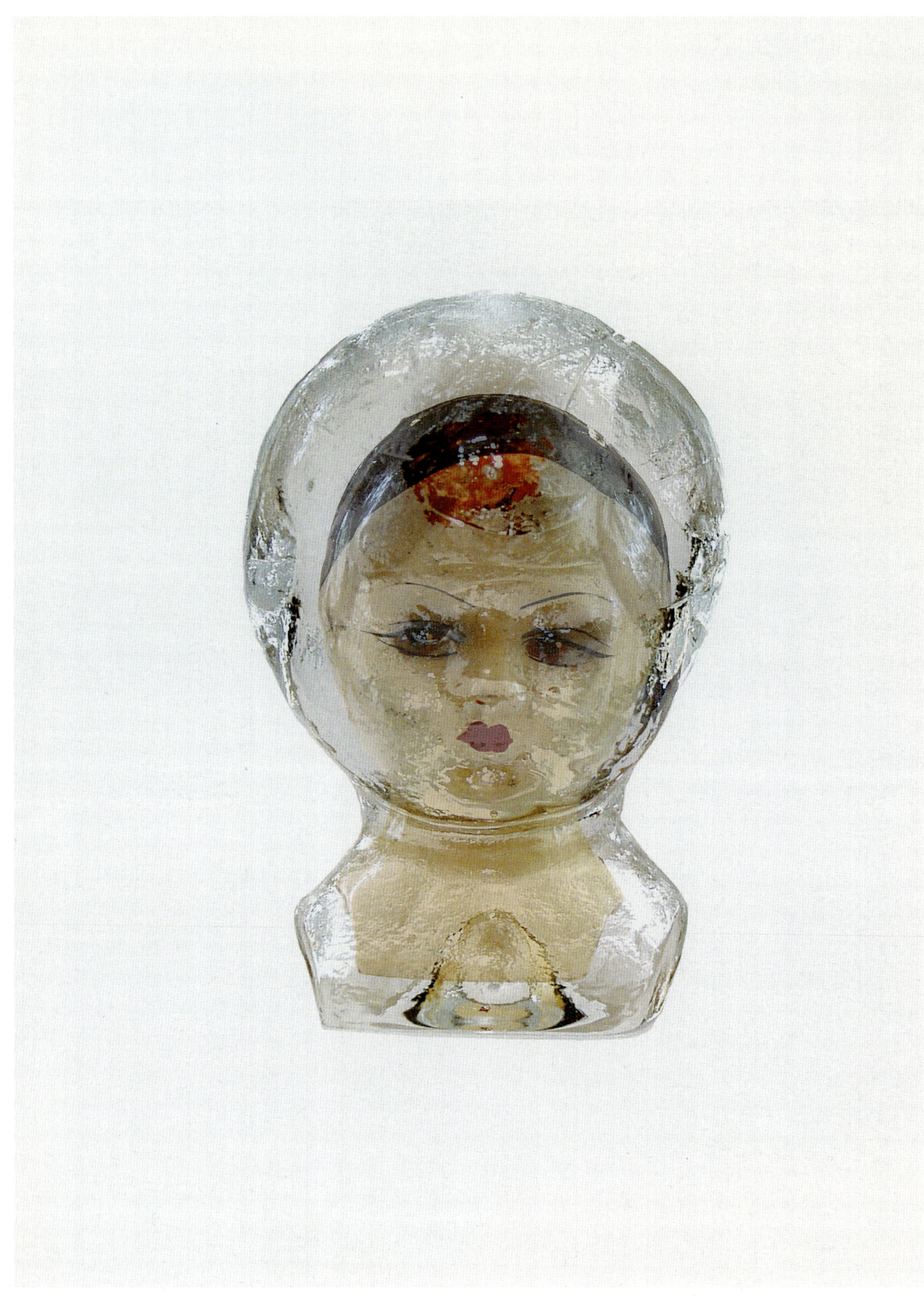

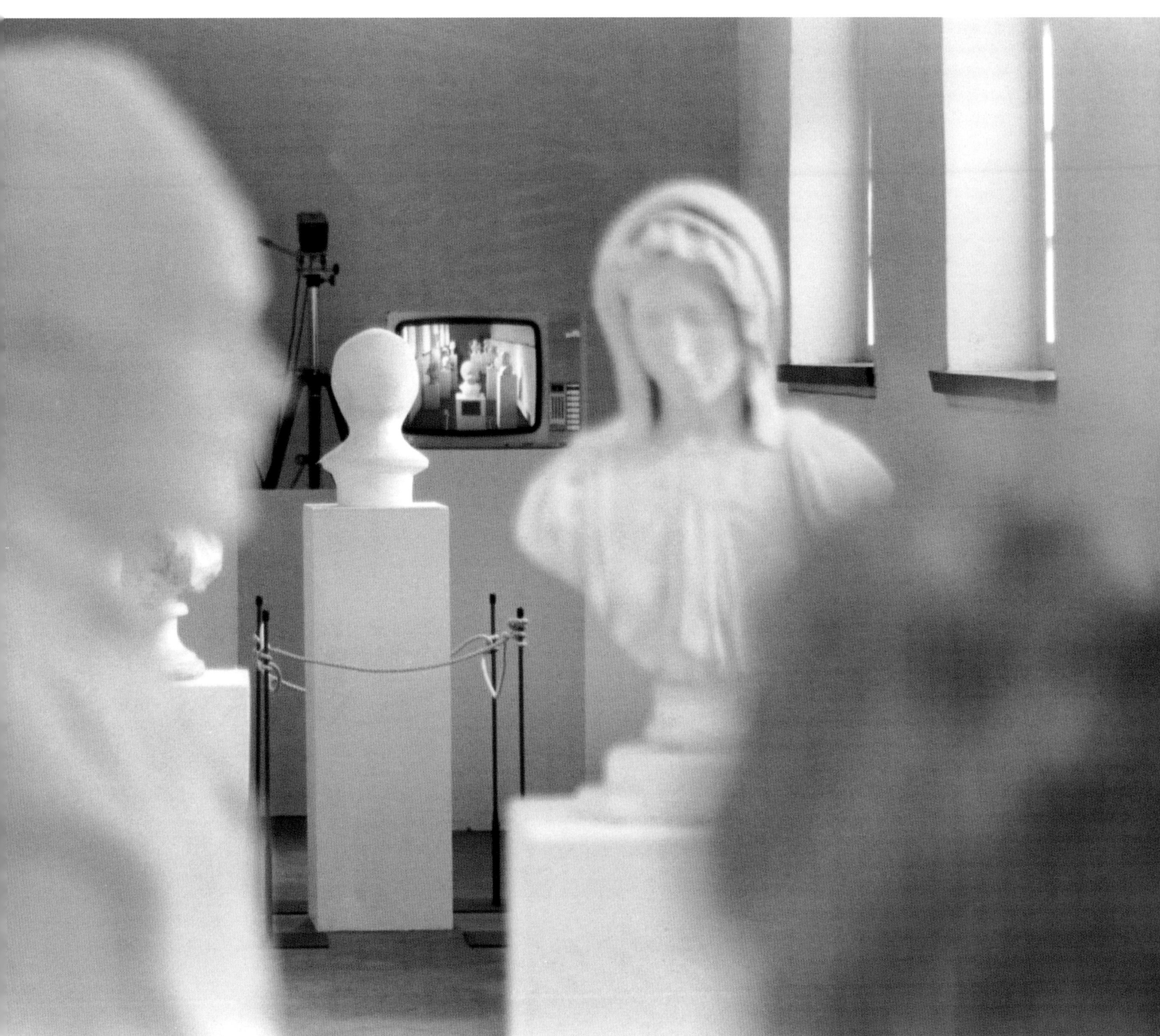

Exhibition poster for
exhibition *+ - 0* at Henie
Onstad Art Center,
Høvikodden, Norway, 2002.

Hall of Fame, 1978.
Installation of plaster busts,
pedestals, surveillance
camera and monitors.
Bonnefantenmuseum,
Maastricht, The Netherlands.

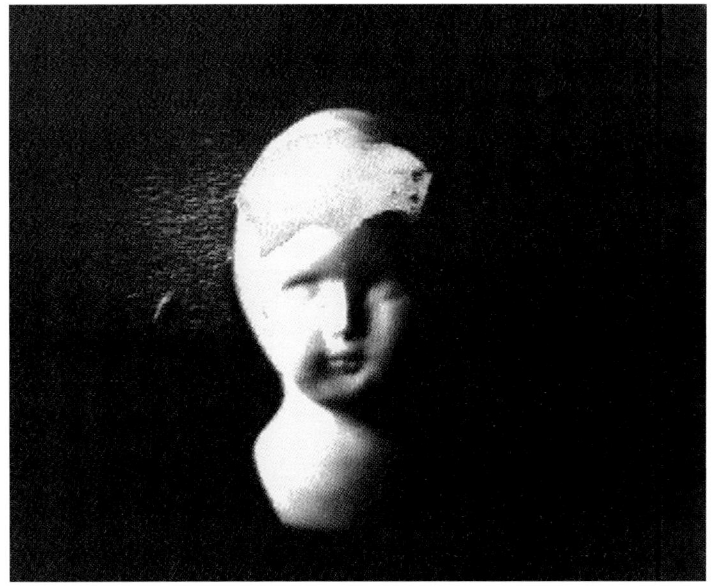
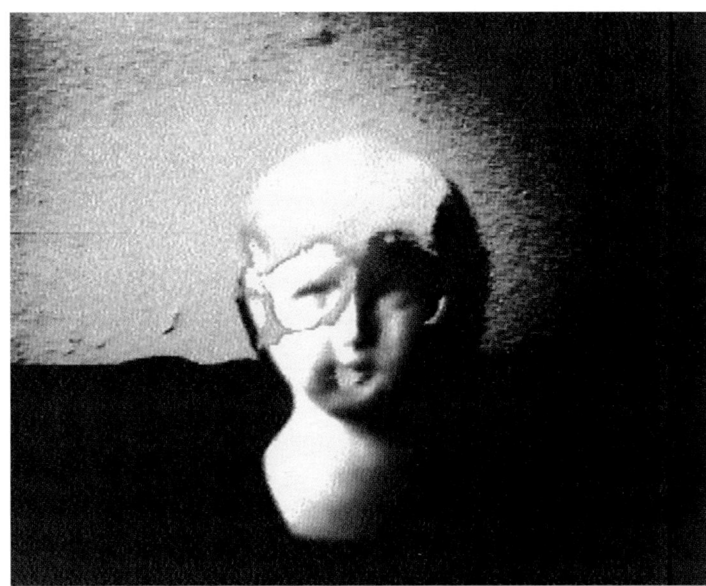
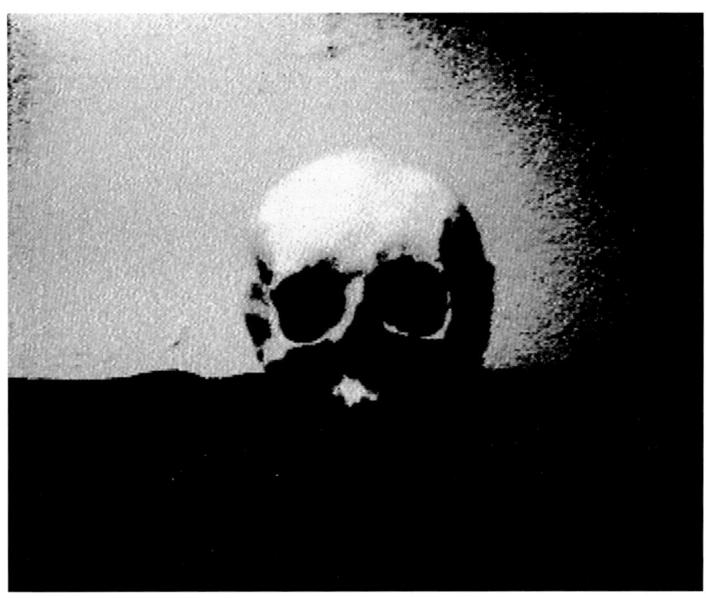

Unreal/Real, 1977. Video stills from "Video Sketch no. 1" in the series *All the World´s a Stage etc. etc.*

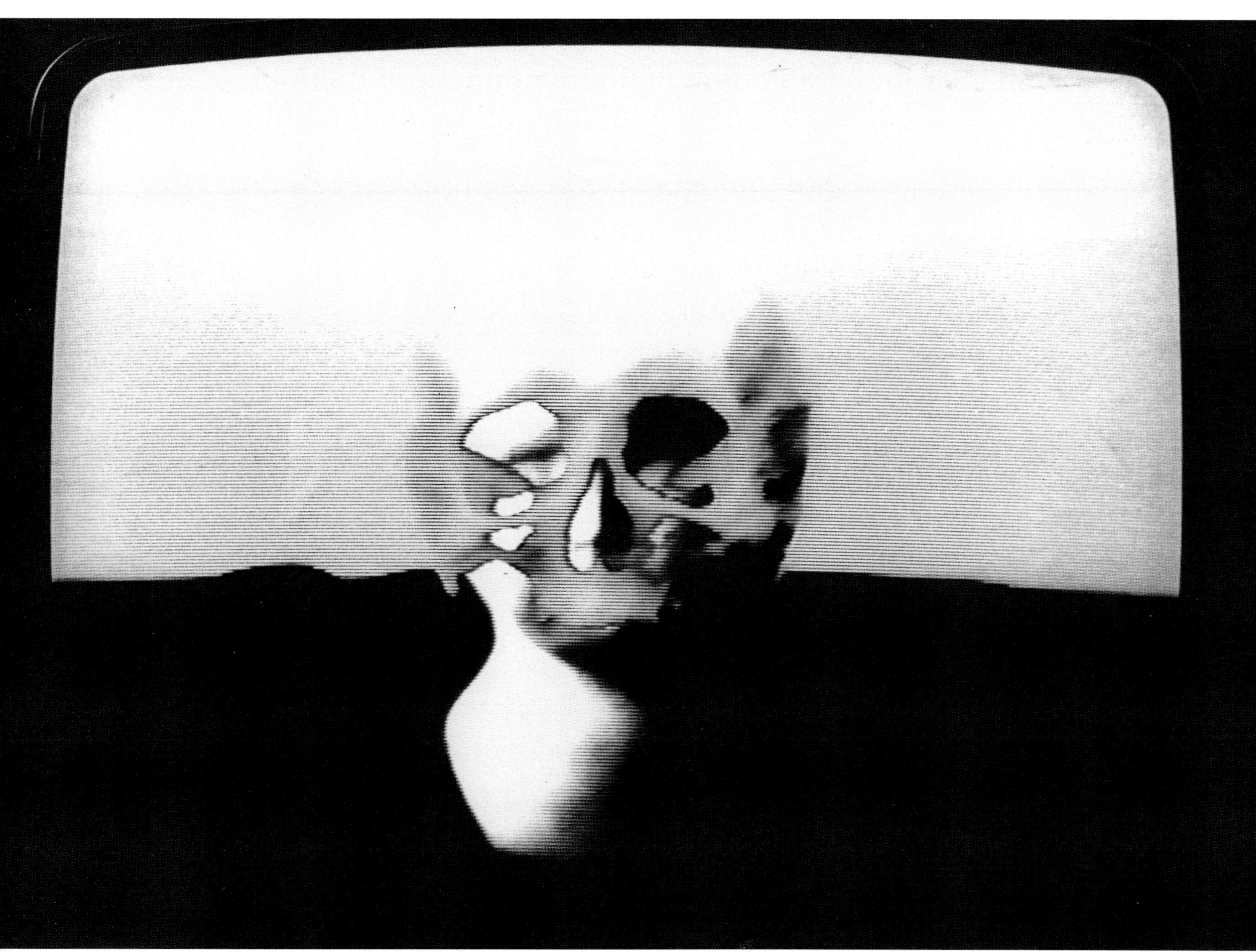

Unreal/Real, 1977. Video still
from "Video Sketch no. 1"
in the series *All the World's
a Stage etc. etc.*

False Face Society Mask,
1976. Video stills.

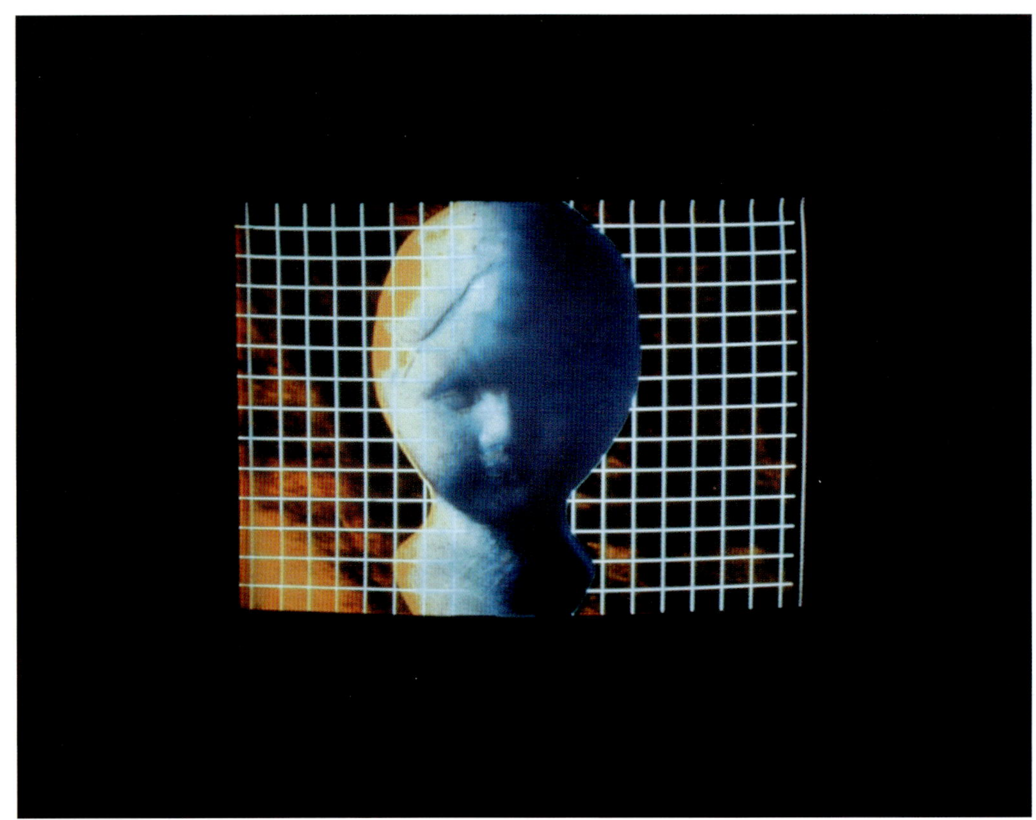

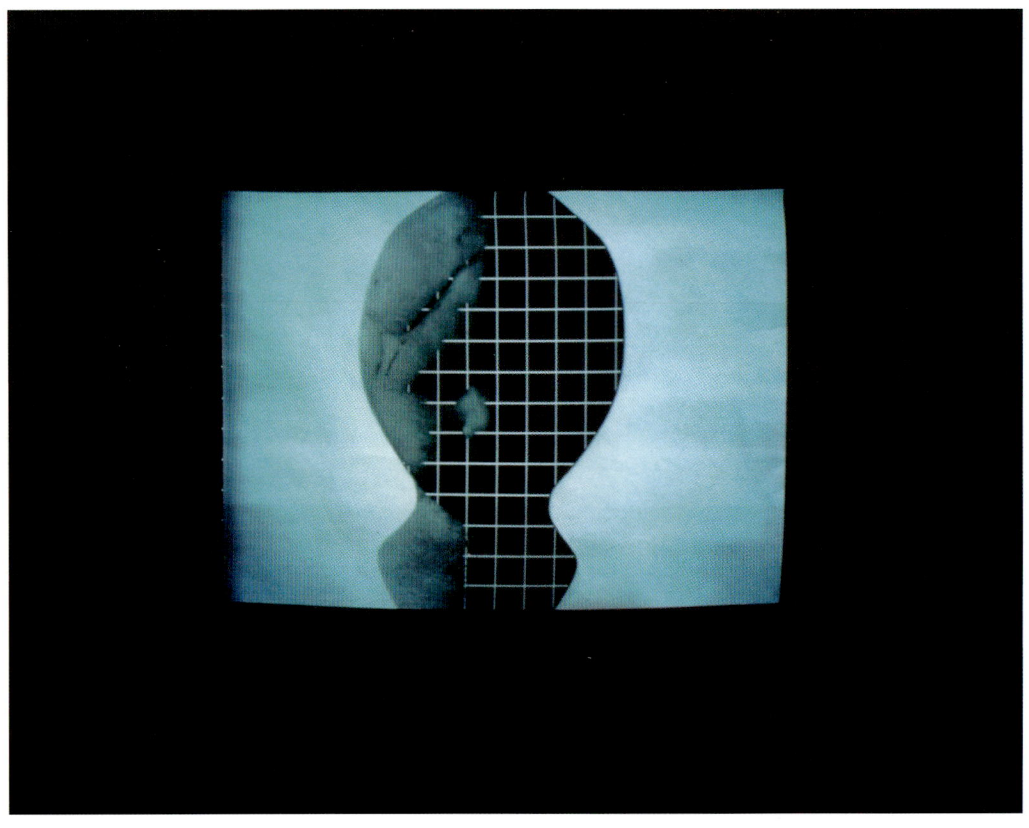

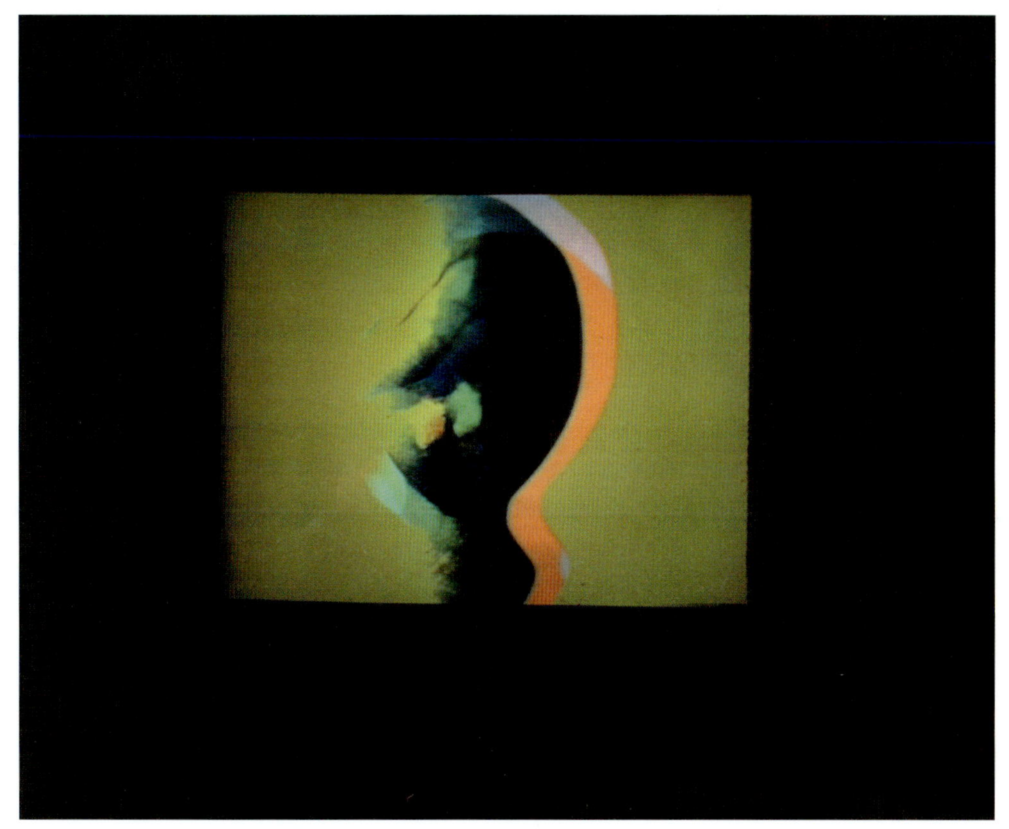

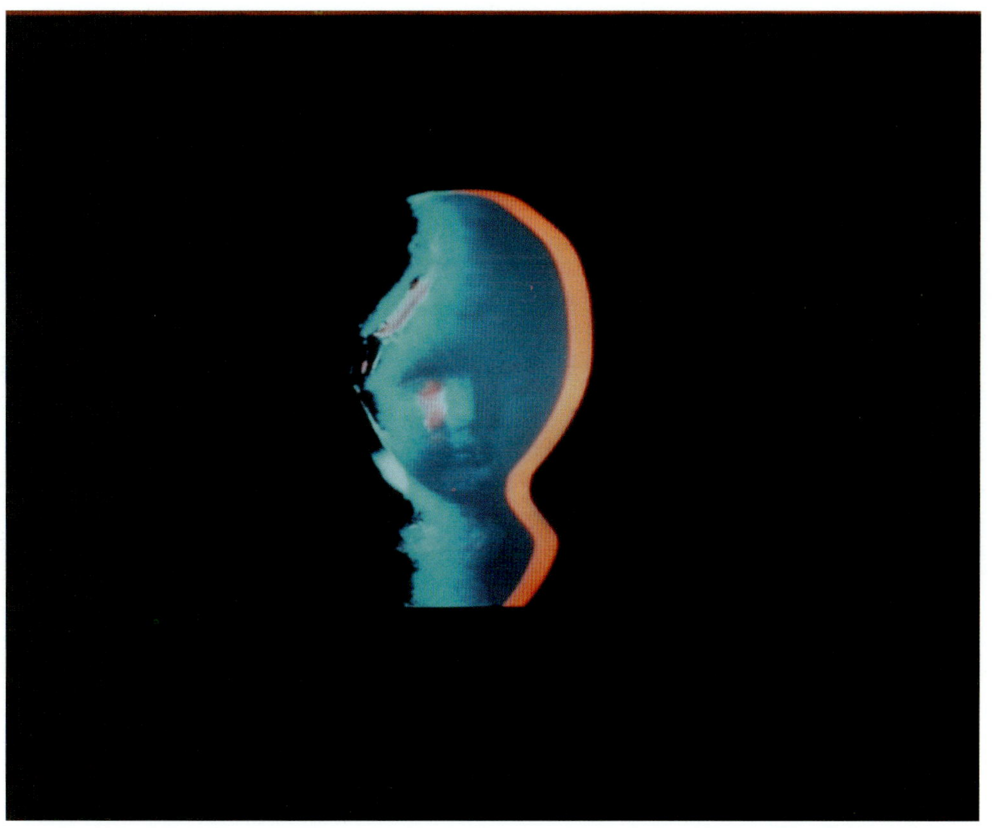

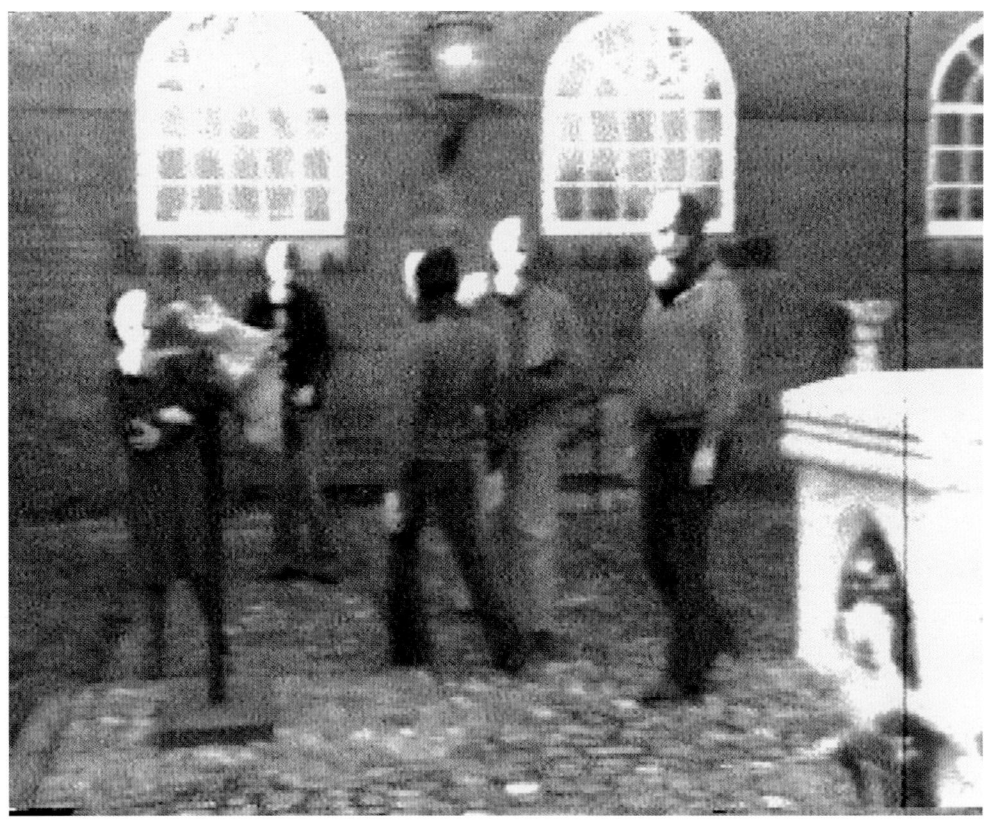

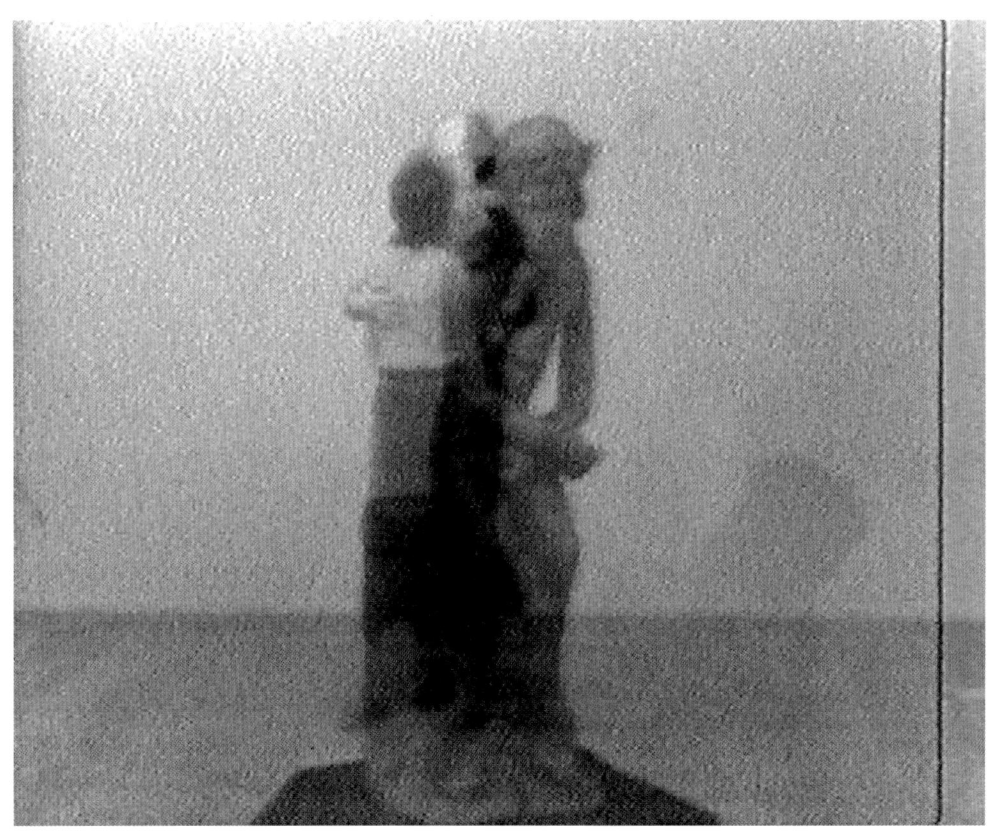

Relating to Art, 1977. Video still from "Video Sketch no. 2" in the series *All the World's a Stage etc. etc.*

Relating to the Sacred, 1977. Video still from "Video Sketch no. 3" in the series *All the World's a Stage etc. etc.*

Relating to Music, 1977.
Video stills from "Video
Sketch no. 4" in the series
*All the World´s a Stage etc.
etc.*

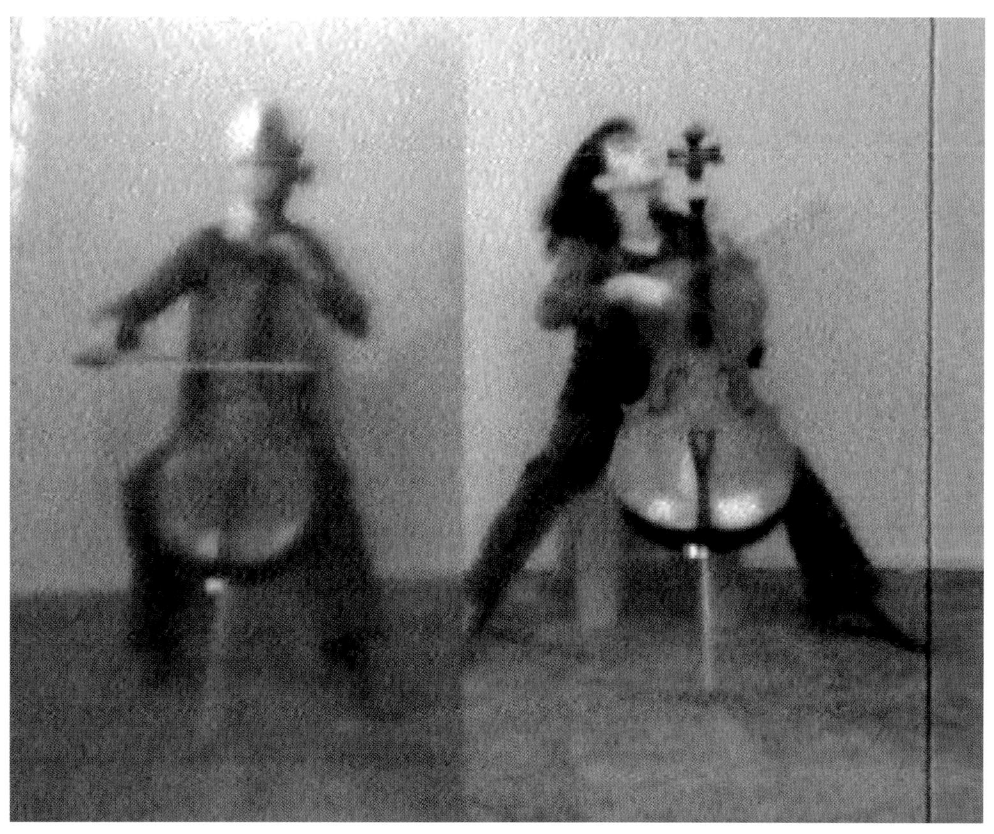

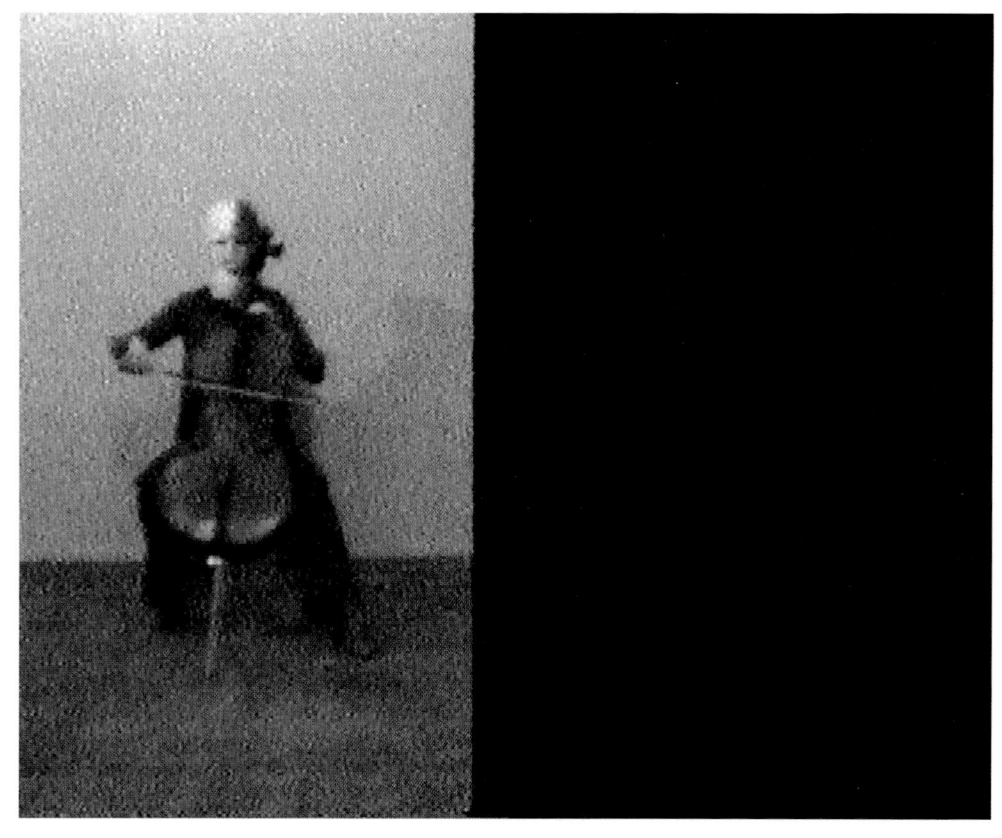

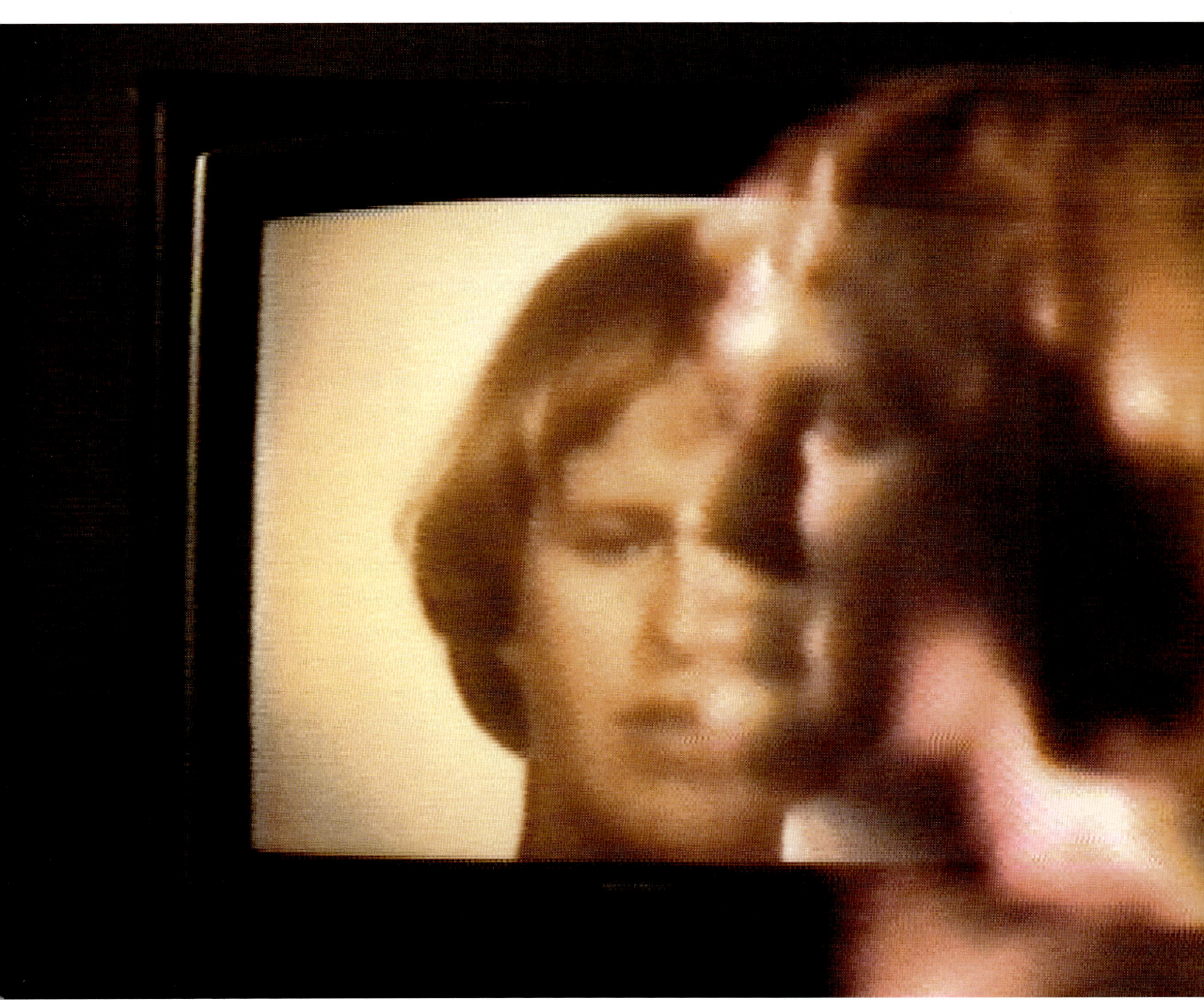

Phrenological Self-Portrait,
1978. Video stills.

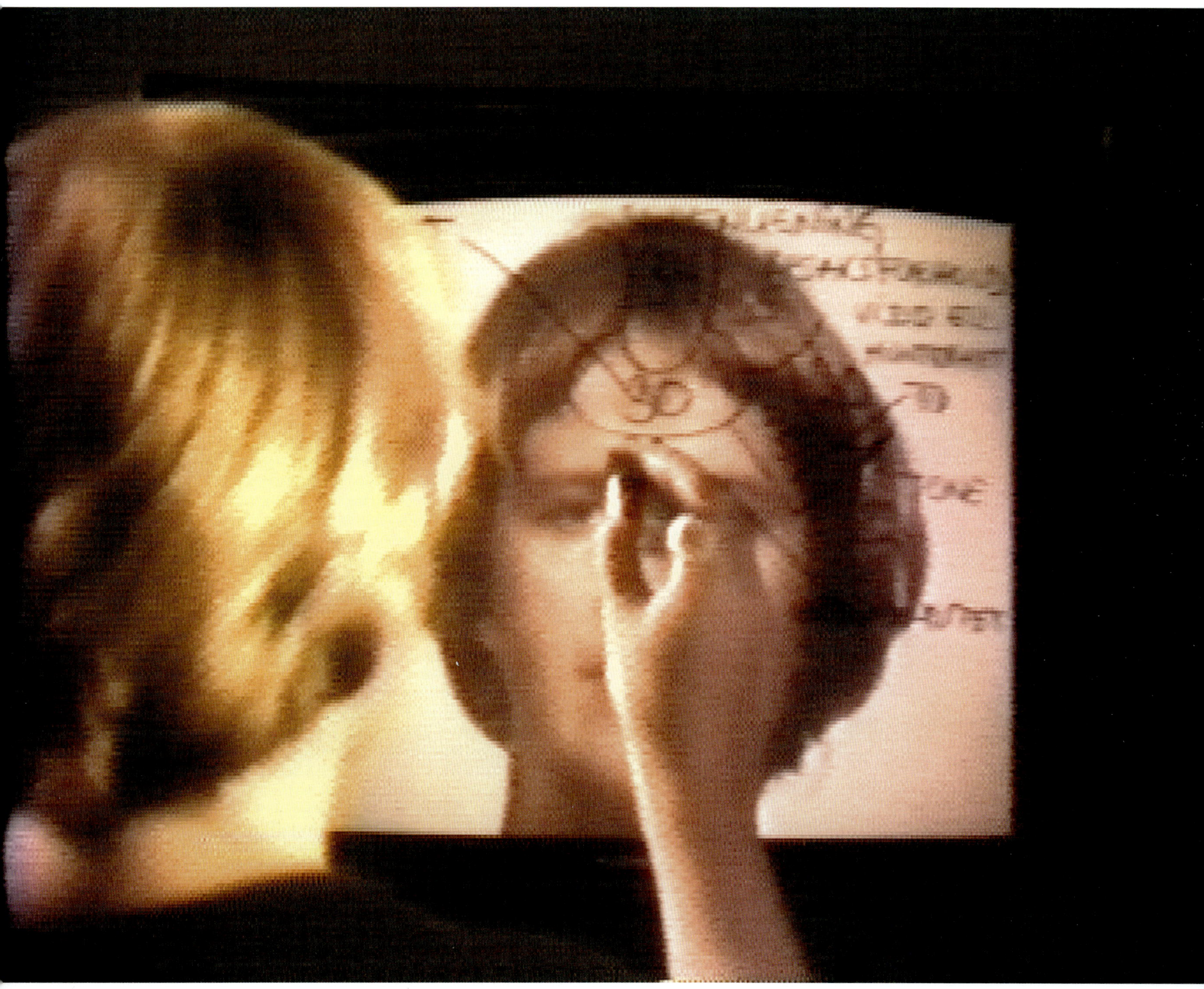

Phrenological Self-Portrait,
1978. Video stills.

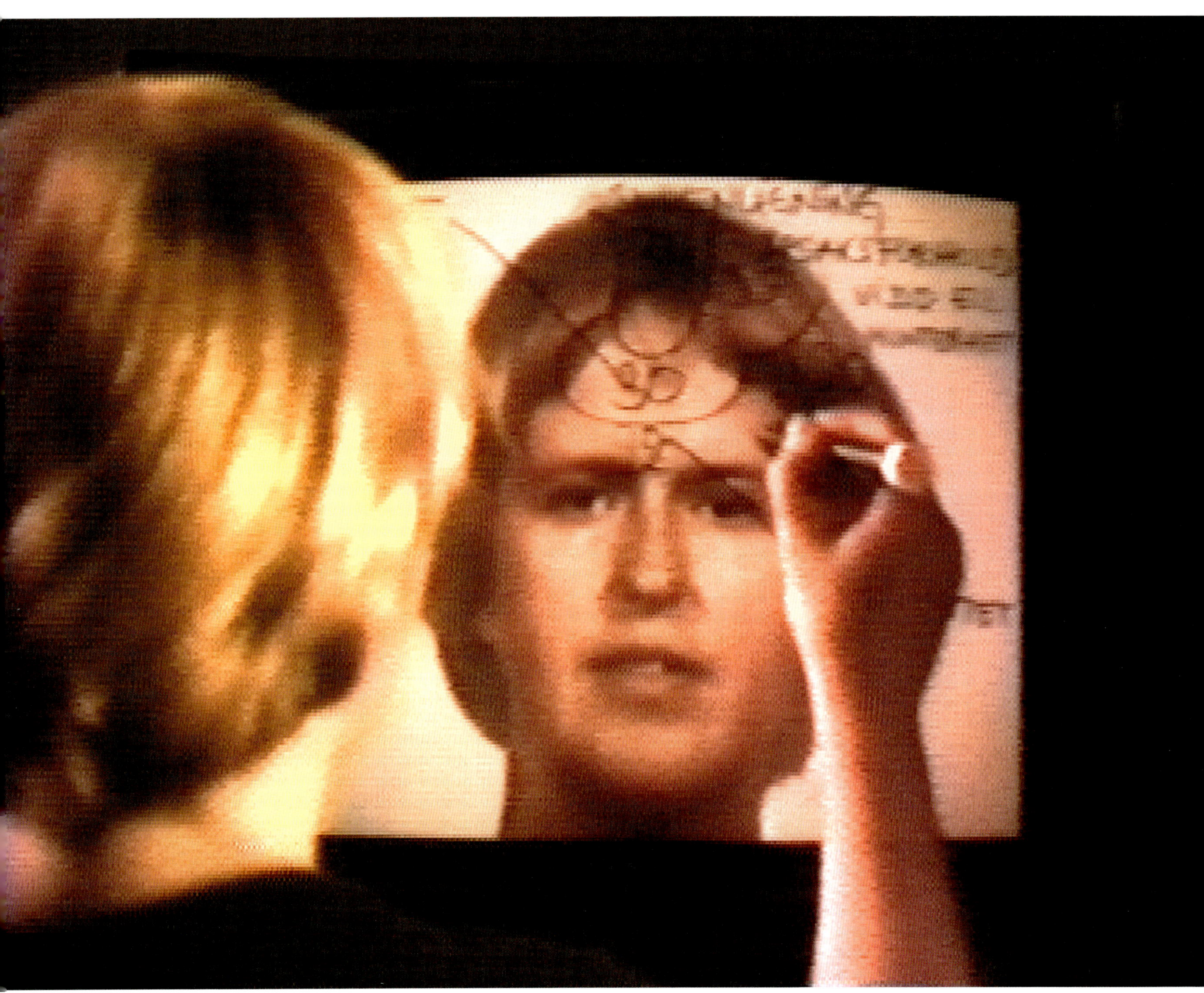

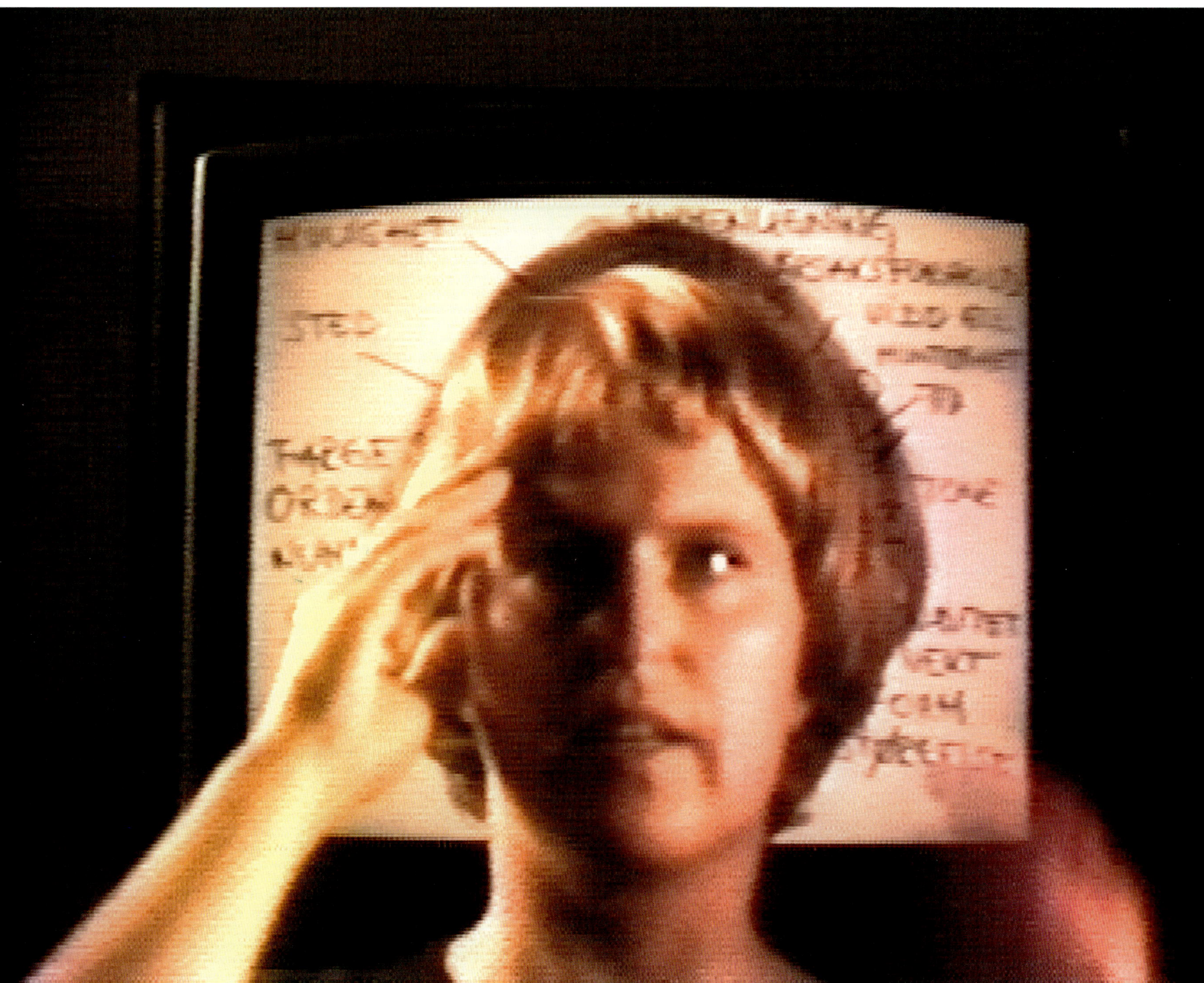

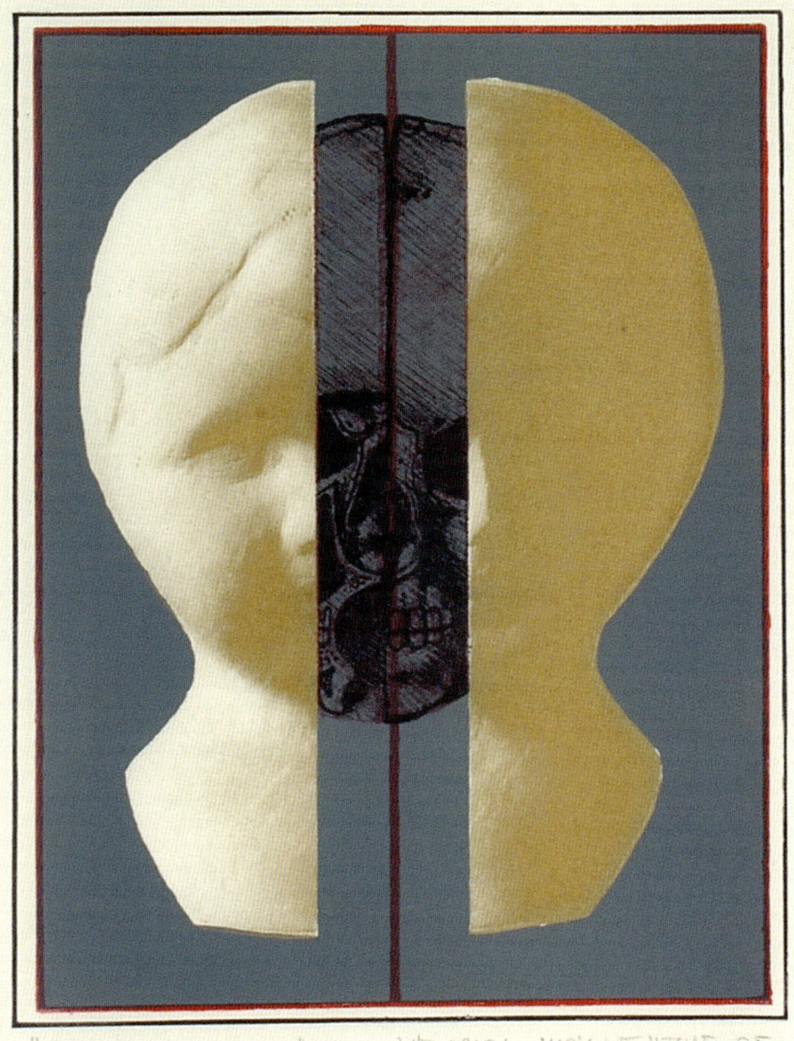

"PORTRETT MED MASKE" I.   "LITOGRAFI". MARIANNE HÆNE -95

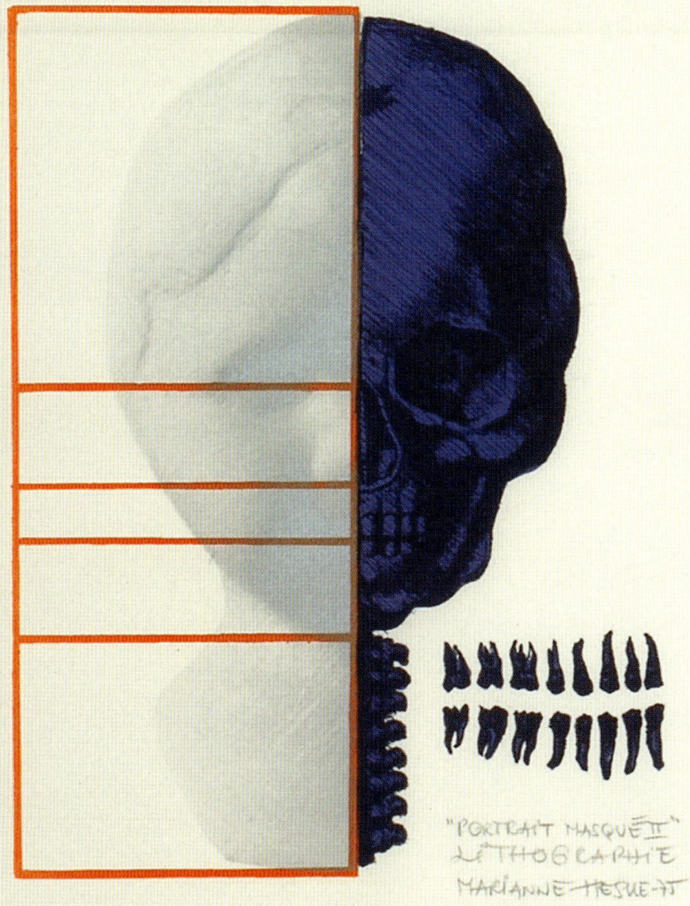
"PORTRAIT MASQUE II"
LITHOGRAPHIE
MARIANNE HESKE 75

Manscape (The Faceless
Face of the Masses), 1976.
Silkscreen and offset print.

In Focus I, 1977. Lithograph.

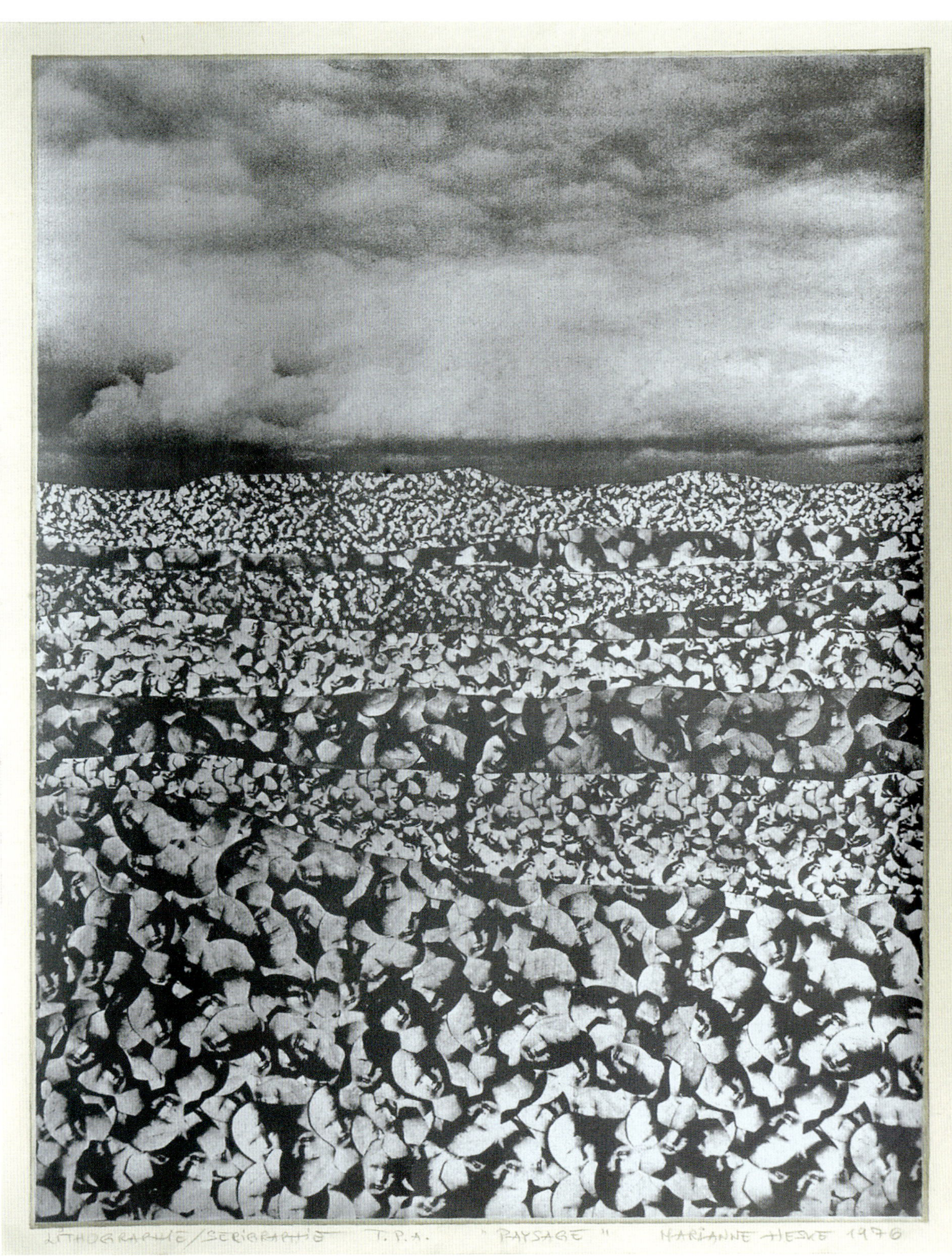

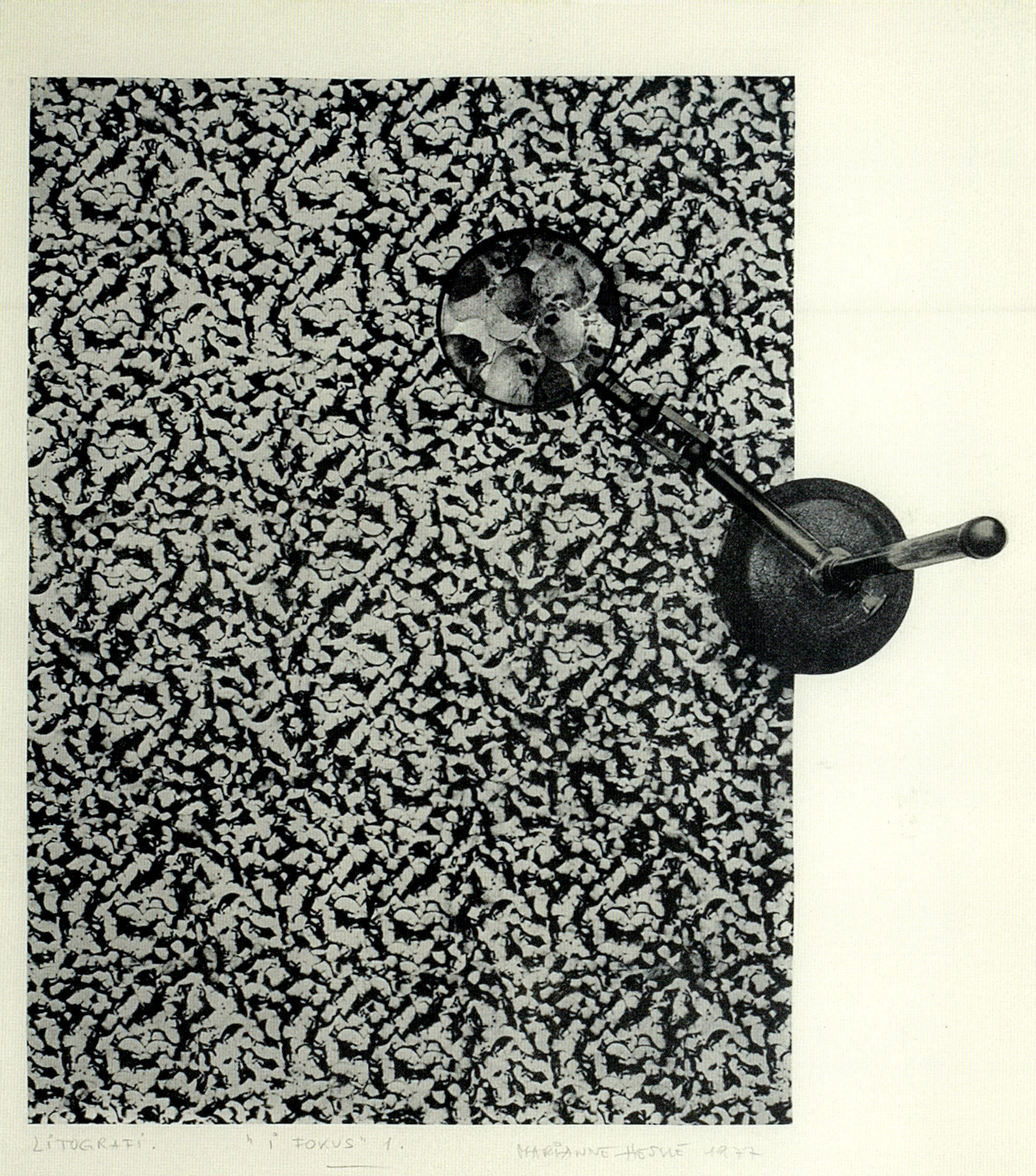

LITOGRAFI.   "i" FOKUS" 1.   MARIANNE HESKE 1977

Dialectical Portrait I, 1976.
Lithograph.

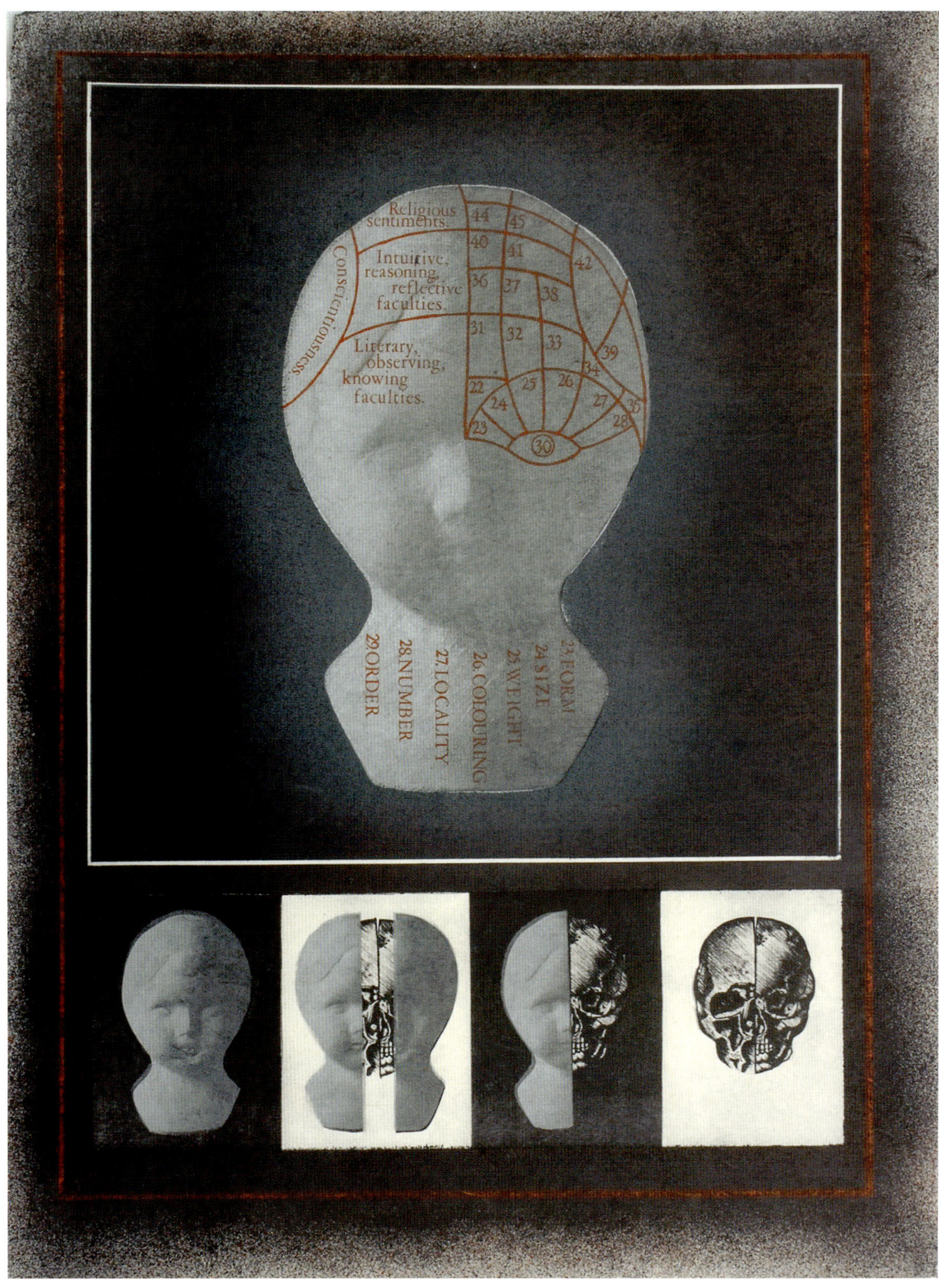

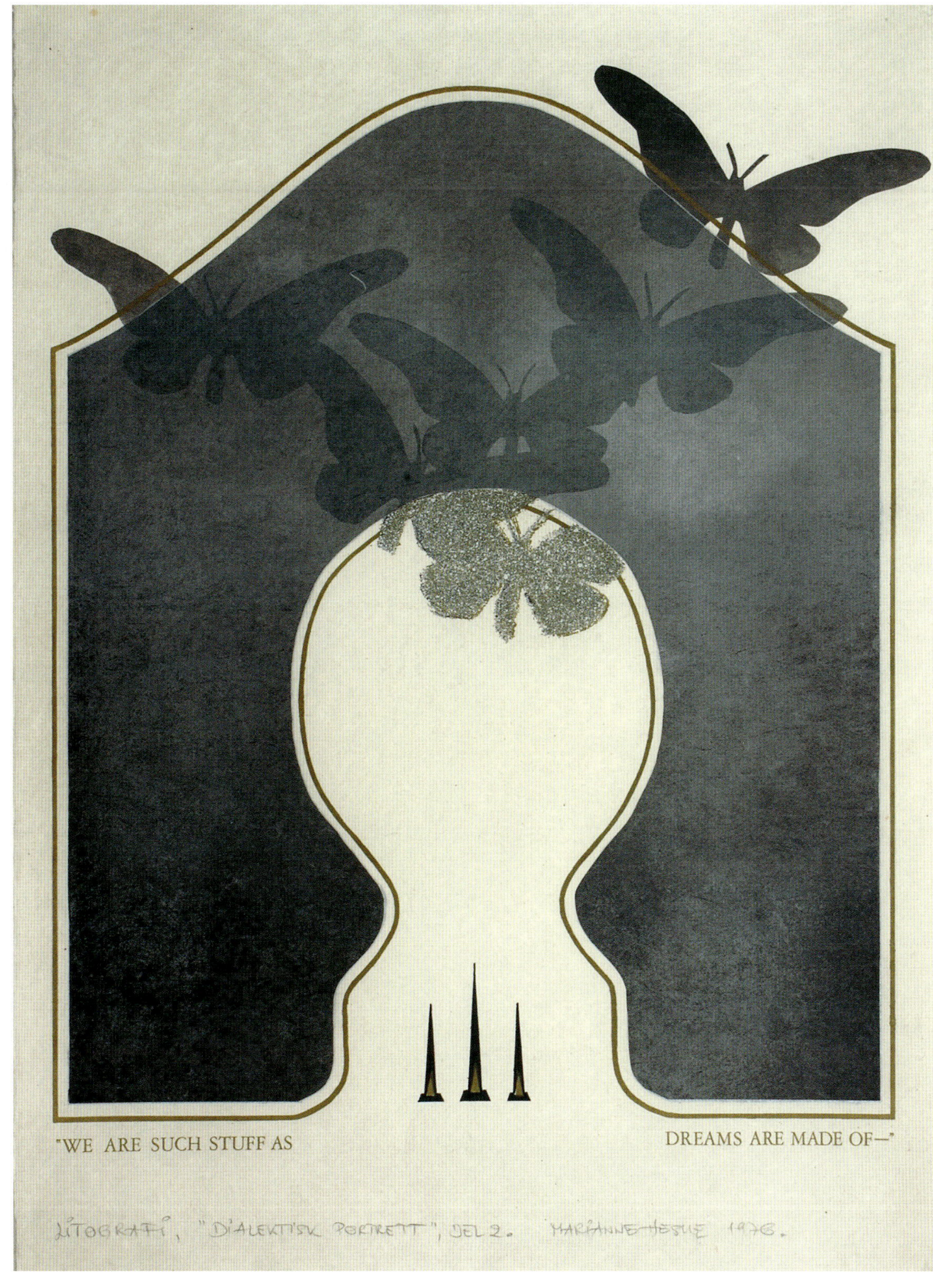
"WE ARE SUCH STUFF AS
DREAMS ARE MADE OF—"
LITOGRAFI, "DIALEKTISK PORTRETT", DEL 2.   MARIANNE HESLIE 1976.

Litho-concept, 1975.
Lithograph.

Peut-on tuer quelqu'un qui est déjà mort?, 1974.
Lithograph.

With and About People, 1975. 16 b/w photographic reproductions from 100 color slides taken on a journey through Europe in 1973.

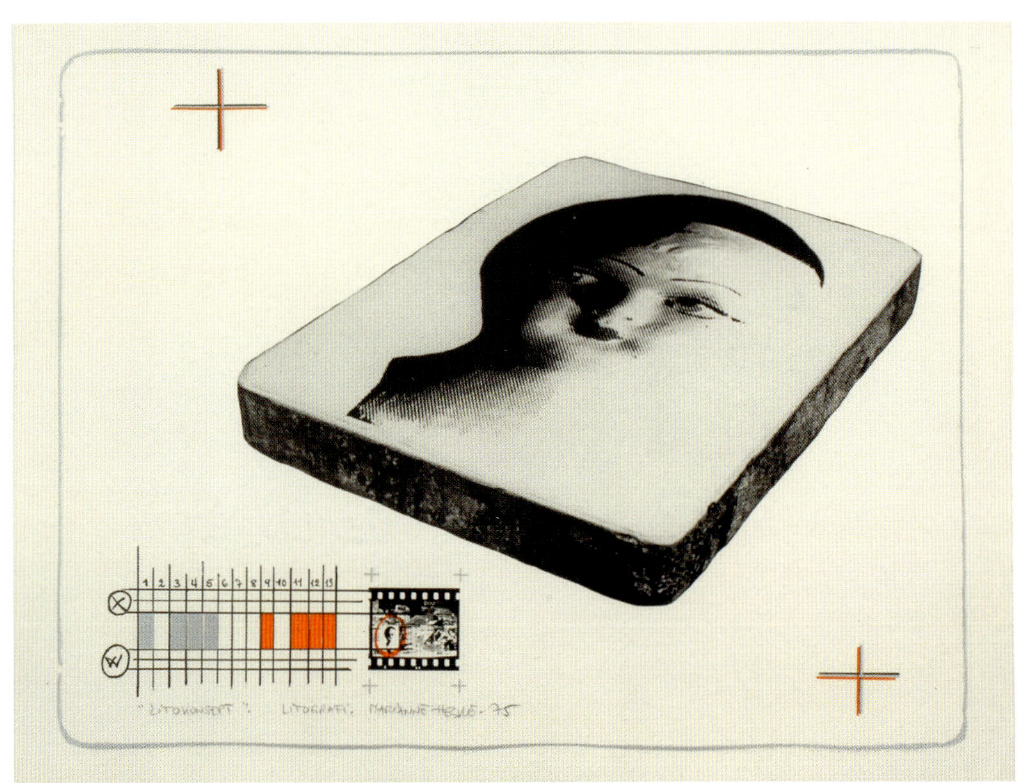

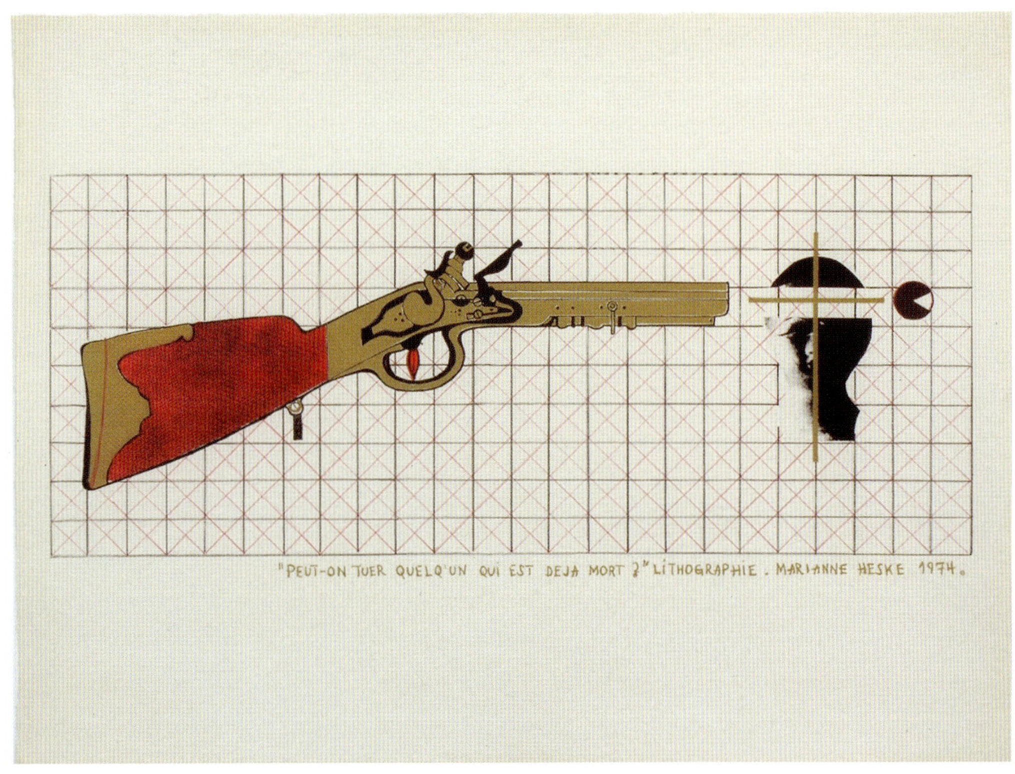

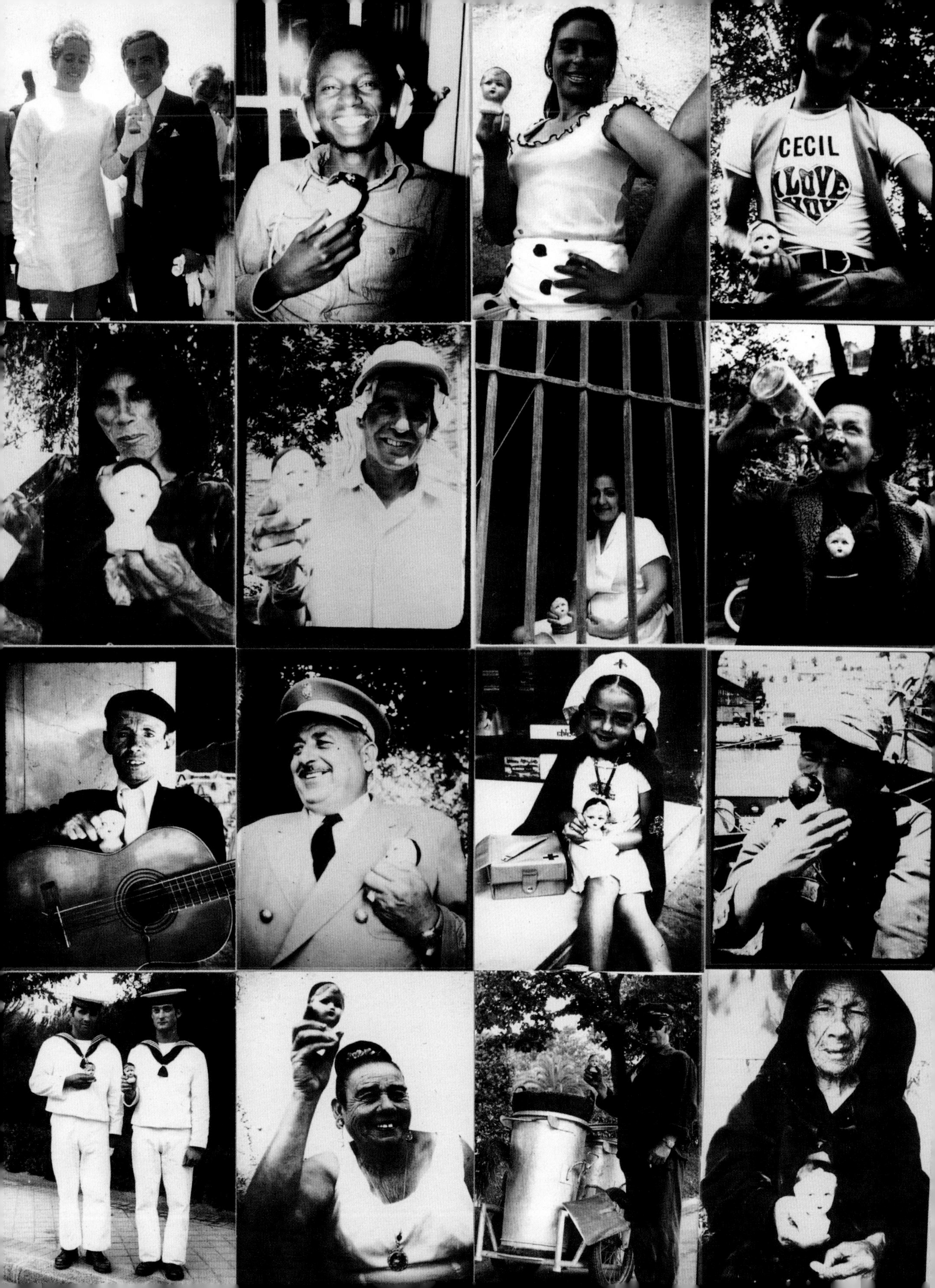

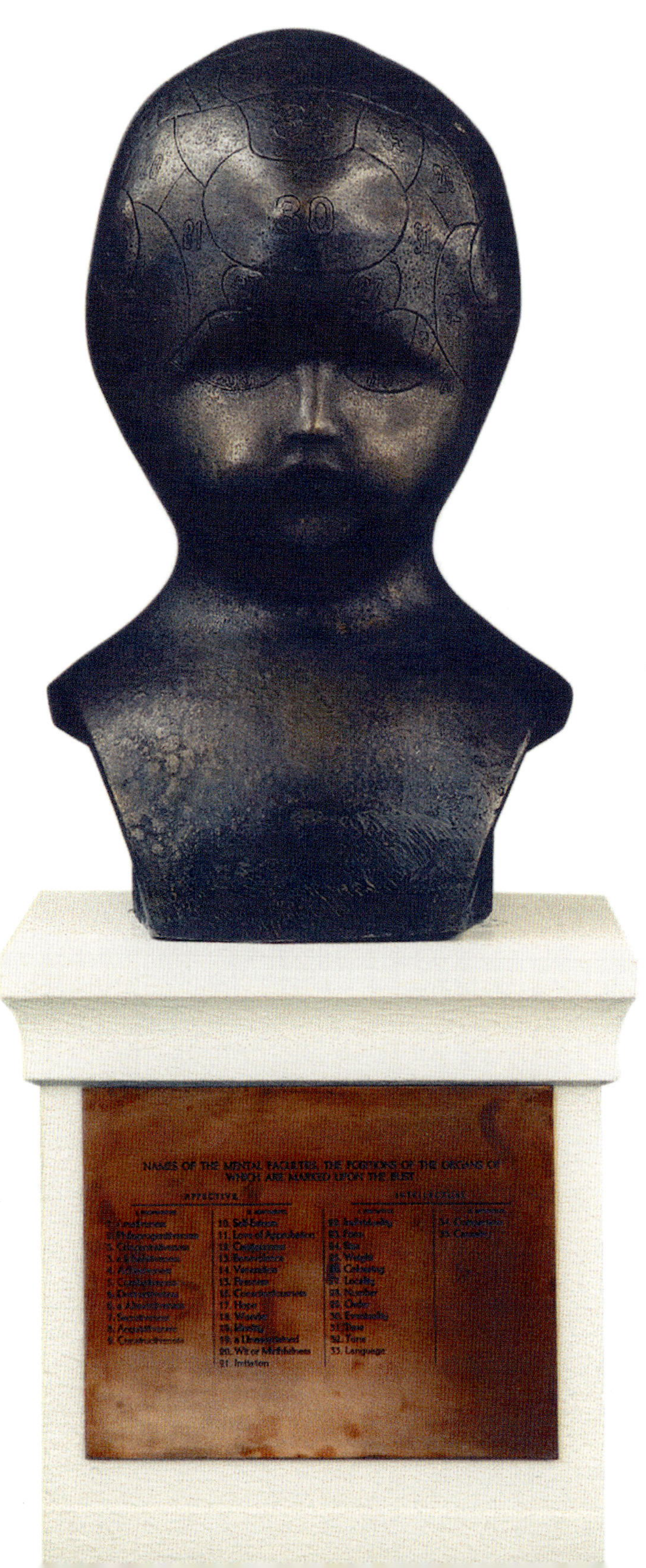

NN, 1978. Installation with phrenology chart.

Medical drawing of the human head. Undated. Wellcome Library of Historical Medicine, London.

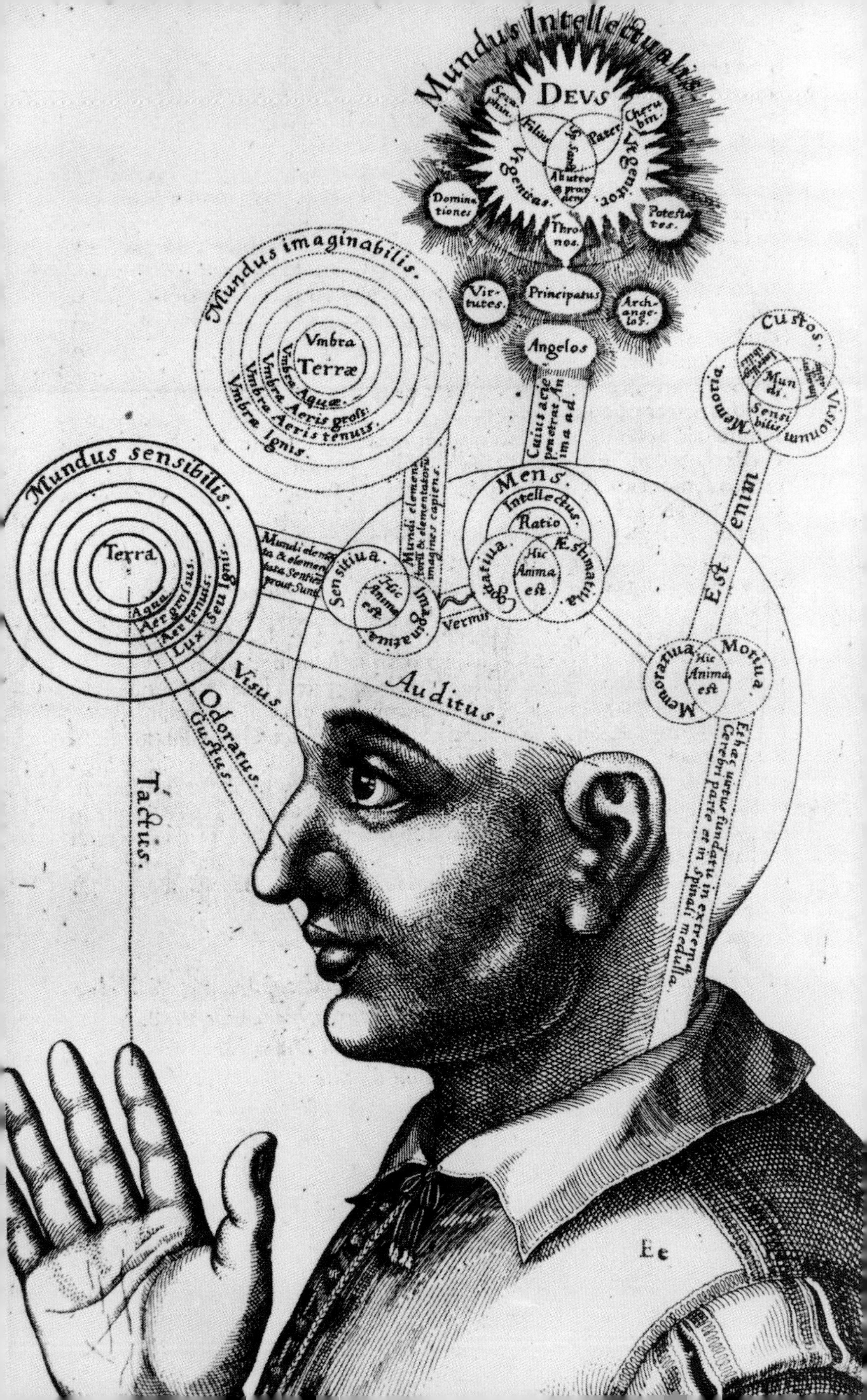

Mundus Intellectualis
DEVS
Seraphim.
Filius
Pater
Cherubim.
Virgenias.
Abuttor à prouidens.
Vt generot.
Domina tiones
Thronos.
Potestates
Mundus imaginabilis.
Vmbra Terræ
Vmbra Aquæ.
Vmbra Aeris grofs:
Vmbra Aeris tenuis
Virtutes.
Principatus
Arch angelos.
Custos, Visionum.
Mundi
Sensibilis
Memoria
Angelos
Cuius acie penetrat Animam ad.
Mens.
Intellectus.
Ratio
Cogitatiua.
Æstimatiua.
Hic Anima est.
Mundus sensibilis.
Terra.
Aqua.
Aer grofsus.
Aer tenuis.
Lux seu Ignis.
Mundi elementa & elementata Sentit prout Sunt.
Sensitiua.
Hic Anima est.
Imaginatiua
Mundi elementorii & elementatorii imagines capiens.
Vermis
Est vna
Memoratiua
Hic Anima est
Motiua
Et hæc vertus fundatur Cerebri parte et in extrema parte et in Spinali medulla.
Visus
Odoratus.
Gustus.
Auditus.
Tactus.
Ee

Demonstration of
phrenological analysis.
Undated photography.
Unknown photographer.

*Notre tête est ronde pour
permettre à la pensée de
changer de direction (F.
Picabia)*, 1978. Installation.
Bonnefantenmuseum,
Maastricht, The Netherlands.

Untitled, 1979. Performance.
Bergen Art Museum, Bergen,
Norway.

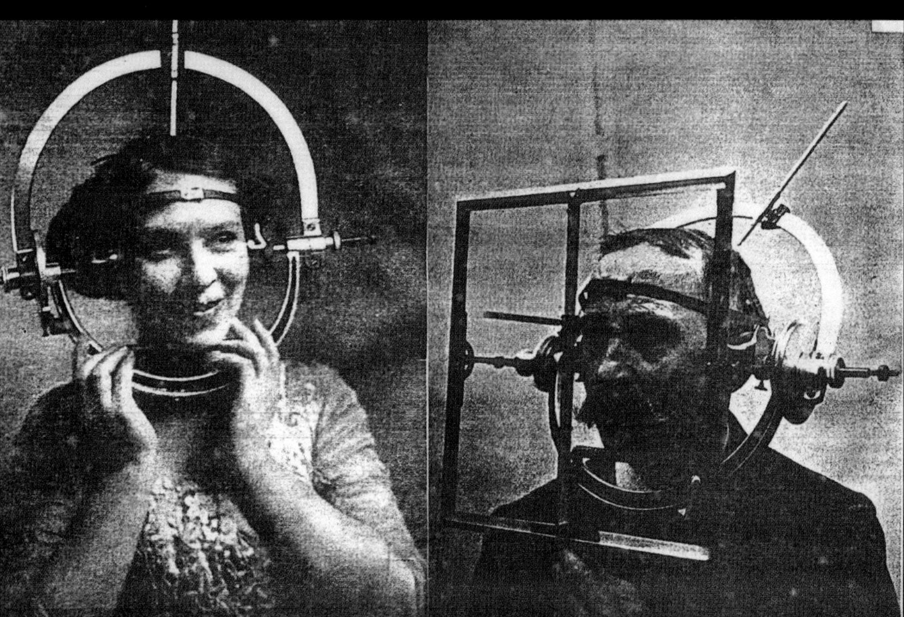

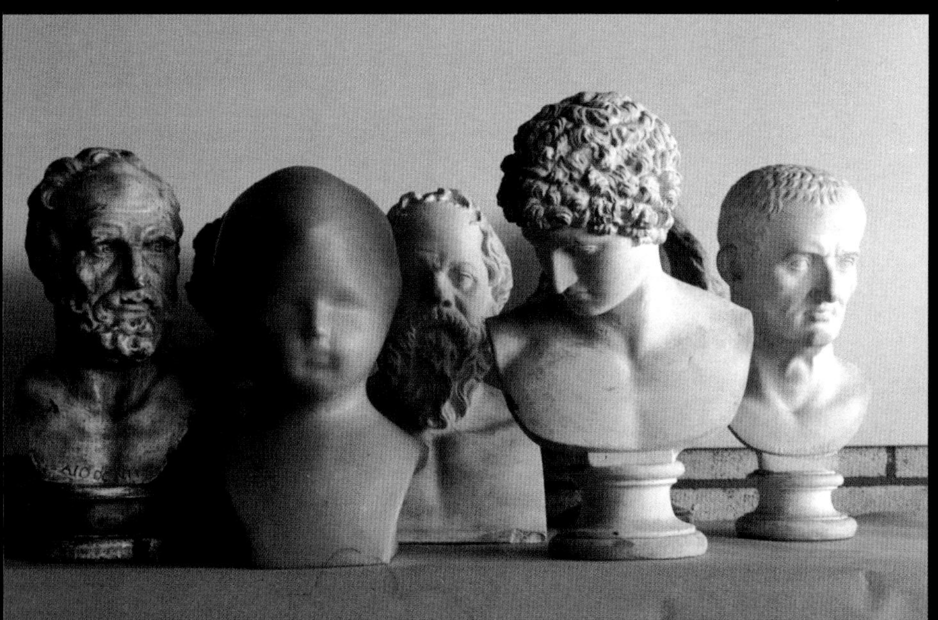

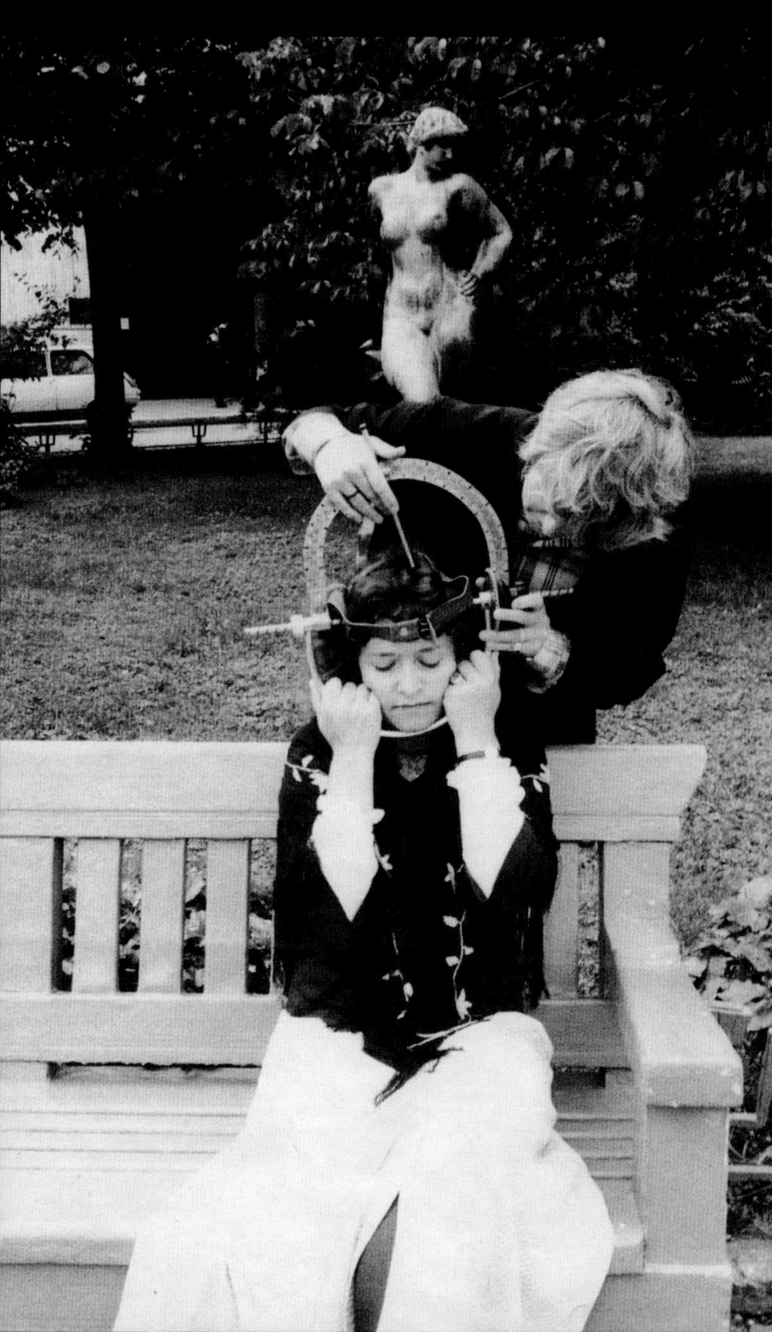

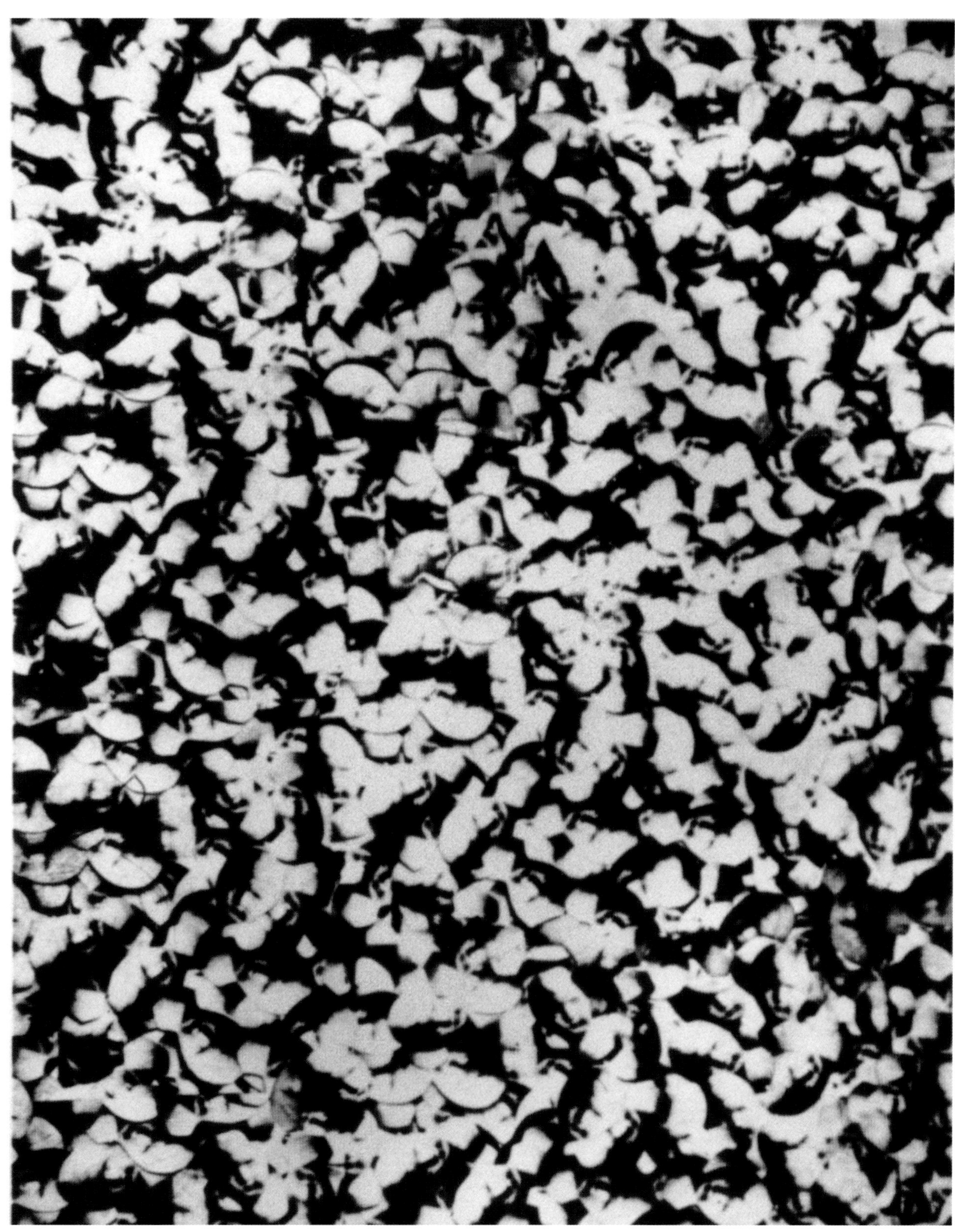

*Manscape (The Faceless
Face of the Masses)*, 1976.
Serigraph and offset print.
Detail.

Nicolas Bourriaud

Marianne Heske or The Art of Relocation

In 1980, after ten years of training in Paris and in London, and then at the Jan Van Eyck Academy in Maastricht, Marianne Heske returned to Norway, where she was born. In the mountains that surround Tafjord, she found a log cabin from the seventeenth century. In a completely isolated location within the overwhelming natural surroundings of the Scandinavian alps, accented by dramatic fjords cut from granite, this mountain cabin was used to store hay, and sometimes used as a makeshift shelter. Although small in scale, the cabin is composed of rough hewn logs placed one on top of the other with a stone foundation at the base; a rough framework constitutes the doorway, and the roof is covered with grass and lichen. On the inside and outside walls, the various occupants of this cabin have whittled their names, or left simple drawings, the oldest of which evoke cave paintings. In short, the cabin that Marianne Heske found, constructed from timber from the surrounding forests, seems at one with the natural surroundings. It almost seems embedded in the mountain like the pine or the birch, the glacier buttercup or the wood anemones in the crevices of the deep, winding inlets of the fjords.

All of this to arrive at this simple observation: to relocate this hut appears to be the least obvious idea. Marianne Heske's project, selected for inclusion in the 1980 Paris biennial, nonetheless involved deconstructing this habitat, piece by piece, and transporting it to the Centre Pompidou in Paris for an exhibition. Anticipating that its users would leave multiple traces of their passage, the Parisian visitors intuitively added their own graffiti to the already existing markings before she dismantled the cabin and returned it to its original destination, one year later.

This project is fascinating due to its complexity: questions regarding displacement, the participation of the viewer, the notion of the ready-made, are all addressed in a very original manner. Ultimately, the intricacies related to art *in situ* are turned inside out,

like a glove. Surprisingly, there is very little written about the Project Gjerdeloa, which seems to have been drowned in the reflux of conceptual art, perceptible from the early eighties, initiated by the "Aperto" section of the Venice biennial, the triumph of postmodern painting. 1980 is a transitional year: the energy of the avant-garde and political activism loses steam. Within this ideological void, postmodernism manifested itself slowly but surely, and with it renewed faith in the image. Since 1977, a new generation of American artists (who would much later be called the "picture generation") attempted to reconcile the criticism of the avant-garde artists of the sixties with the world of "new images" from new media and video, which was becoming more widespread. Cindy Sherman, Barbara Kruger, Sherrie Levine and Dara Birnbaum had their first exhibitions, drawing heavily on this visual universe. The same year, Marianne Heske produced the series *All the World's a Stage etc. etc.* and *Phrenologic Self Portrait*, which explored the power of the video image. Phrenology, the science of the cranial landscape, constituted for Heske a psychological equivalent to her geographical investigations. Phrenology localises in the protrusions and flat areas of a human head the passions and psychological characteristics of the person in question. Heske approaches the earth in the same way as the phrenologists study skulls: in her *video paintings* from the end of the seventies and early eighties, this is the imprint which is the key. The terrestrial crust is the skin, which is read as a text in its entirety. With these works, Heske anticipated the ecologists "Gaïa theory", meaning a perception of the planet as a living being one. Phrenology and video, geography and psychology, mountains and faces are in constant dialogue in Heske's work. Such is the fundamental intuitiveness of her work, the primal scene which will result in other works.

Was she before her time? Yes. Project Gjerdeloa didn't resonate in its time the way it would much later, as it spawned numerous works based on similar ideas of displacement. Outside of Scandinavia, the renowned critic of New Realism, Pierre Restany, expressed the most enthusiasm, and continued to follow closely the development of this artist. Significantly, Restany comments strongly on Heske's own thoughts on the subject of the exhibition at the Centre Pompidou, as noted by Per Hovdenakk: "I knew the hut would be regarded as a hut in Norway, whereas in Paris it would be seen as a manifestation of conceptual art". This is significant because it is the description of the ideological process that proceeds the project, and Restany was particularly interested in these kinds of statements of intent. Restany wrote, "Apart from the seemingly naïve speculation regarding the change of scene and interpretation of an object outside its original context, the artist's attitude reveals a profound analytical capacity. Marianne Heske's gaze is the powerful creator and messenger of a vision centered on the essential relativity of perception. Her gaze is a question mark to realism itself."[1] Realism—touchstone of Restanian thinking. The relationship to the physical environment, and the ability of the artist to transcend it through a radical gesture, are the primary principles of his writing. The fact is that the Project Gjerdeloa represents a striking manifestation, an apparently simple act (displacing an object from one place to another), that could pass today as an important inaugural gesture within art history.

In art, what does this kind of displacement mean? Within the common economical discourse, Michel Henochsberg writes in *Nous nous sentions comme une sale espèce* (*We Felt Like a Dirty Kind*), "the sphere of circulation is akin to the sphere of suspicion. The development of productive forces embodies the 'good sense' of a beneficial economy, while the area of exchanges and money houses all the irregularities and wrongdoings of an unhealthy activity, due to the excesses of certain players on this level, merchants and bankers."[2] Today, shortly after the collapse of the financial bubble, this tendency is again reinforced. *Production* represents good, while trading and its derivatives signals the bad, the world of appearances and artifice. Within history, the merchant takes on the role of the stranger, the wanderer, the hawker who arrives from afar to intrude the community. Contemporary art, victim of this ideological prejudice, suffers from the same bad reputation: the makers of images reassure the public, while those who negotiate art, duplicate it or make a business out of it offend or annoy. Trading is an object of suspicion, as it represents an unwarranted benefit: it represents a gain, it symbolizes exploitation of the producer (capital comes from captial gains levied on the worker's labour). Within twentieth century art, one could say that the space of exchange took precedence over that of production. Thus, when Marcel Duchamp presented a bottle rack and signed it as a work of art, the added-value here was at its maximum, because only the change in status of the object, its displacement, radically modified its value. The artist becomes similar to a merchant, and the work plays on the margins of esthetics in regards to the value of an object. Art is therefore placed on the side of commerce, on the side of negotiation with the viewer, within the context of a visual contract with the viewer. The artist produces relations to the world based on already produced objects, simply displaced by him or her within a context that constitutes the boundary of his or her work.

In 1918 Marcel Duchamp created, based on his intuition of the aesthetics of displacement, the first soft sculpture in the history of art, the *Sculptures de voyage*: "These were pieces of bathing caps, in rubber, that I cut up, that I glued together, and that had no special form. At the bottom of each piece, there was a string that was attached to the four corners; one could change the length of these strings, the possible forms being limitless, that is what interested me. This game lasted three or four years, but the rubber disintegrated and disappeared."[3] Deployment of a flexible material in nomadic ever

[1] Pierre Restany, *Voyage pittoresque*, 1986.

[2] Michel Henochsberg, *Nous nous sentions comme une sale espèce*, Denoël, Paris, 1999.

[3] Marcel Duchamp, *Entretiens avec Pierre Cabanne*, Paris: Belfond, 1967, p. 102.

changing space: Duchamp had invented a new artistic concept, transport. During the sixties and seventies, which relied heavily on Duchampian innovation, displacement is organized in figures. Douglas Huebler, among the pioneers of conceptual art, created forms from experiments with displacement: *42ⁿᵈ Parallel* (1968), was based on mailings between various American towns situated at the location indicated by the title. Rather than produce actual objects, Huebler declared that he prefered to "establish the existence of things in terms of time or place". The artist Alighiero Boetti geographically displaced the process of producing a work by having his works created, from the beginning of the seventies, by Afghan artisans, then by Pakistanis: the relocation of the manufacturing process thereby becomes a significant element within the system of art creation. In the manner of a pilgrim, André Cadere (1934–1978) transported colored sticks of wood, which he arranged within different galleries and art institutions, in other words in locations that would not recognize these objects *a priori* as works of art, places that would reject these works as foreign objects. Cadere's approach can be summarized as a "strategy of displacement": in 1972, invited by Harald Szeemann to Documenta in Kassel, he announced that he would travel there by foot, but in reality he took the train, thereby disrupting his own legend and triggering the wrath of the curator…

Within this historical framework of aesthetic displacement, Marianne Heske stands out as the artist who played with the map of *realism* in her choice of a historical artefact, the painstaking deconstruction of an object, the transport of this object from one country to another, and back again, and finally the transition from utilitarian object to conceptual object. Realism, because the hut in question represents an authentic record about the way of life for a very specific group of human beings who belong to a specific place. Realism, also because its function constitutes the actual subject of the work.

As a mountain shelter, the hut was occupied by individuals who inscribed the traces of their passage on the walls of the hut; later, as a work of art exhibited at the Centre Pompidou, it was seen by visitors who added their own messages to the walls of the hut. Once reintegrated in its original environment, the cabin had acquired the status of a space of encounter between two distinct populations: the mountain hikers of Tafjord, and the Parisian museum visitors. Project Gjerdeloa presents itself as a meeting point, as a relational work before its time. It is not only about the transition of an object from one point to another, more importantly it is about the confrontation between two human groups.

The method employed by Marianne Heske would become a popular form of expression within contemporary art in subsequent decades: to cite only two well- known examples, artists such as Simon Starling or Jens Haaning were seen to use the displacement of objects to generate forms. Yet these two artists, some twenty years later, work within a very different context, marked by economic globalization: from the beginning of the nineties, the pattern of "flow" dominated the global imagination, and it comes in many different forms, from international transport to the transfer of capital, and also including immigration, travel and the internet. The theme of voyage, that permeates Marianne Heske's video paintings just as it does her Project Gjerdeloa, subtly anticipates the problematics of the following decade. Yet until this point Heske was not widely known for this because she neither systematized the procedure in question, nor did she wish to fully exploit its conceptual consequences, opting to remain faithful to the ceremony of an inaugural gesture—applying a systematic gestural spirit onto the figure of the doll, as we will see later on.

Interestingly, *Shedboatshed* (2005) by Simon Starling reproduced the same circularity as what we find in Project Gjerdeloa: in deconstructing a wooden boat on which he traveled to Basel on the Rhine river, the Scottish artist then restores its original shape for an exhibition, before reinstalling it where he had found it. As for the Danish artist Jens Haanning, he also practices this kind of an exchange, or rather the substitution of objects, as a method of creating relationships between diverging realities. Thus a neon tube from an exhibition space in Copenhagen, reappears on the ceiling of the Luther King grocery store in Houston, Texas (*Copenhagen-Texas*, 1999). On another occasion, he exchanges a chair from his gallery with a chair from the *Klub Diplomat*, a place where foreigners gather in Copenhagen. Regular objects are thus displaced and function as reverse ready-mades: the manufactured object doesn't change its status, but constitutes a twinning; it puts two spaces in relation to one another, thus creating a space that becomes the actual form of the work, namely one space between two places, a give and take between two situations, an aspect which one finds in numerous contemporary art works. Rirkrit Tiravanija thus recreated the dimensions of his New York apartment inside the Kunstverein in Cologne, Maurizio Cattelan exhibited at the De Appel Foundation the stolen goods from a burglary that took place down the block, and Pierre Huyghe works on the distance that separates a real experience from a Hollywood fiction. The concrete representation of the distance between remote locations has become a major aspect in contemporary art, and one finds it in an unprocessed state in the Project Gjerdeloa.

Nonetheless it is a simple doll's head from the twenties that she accidentally came across in Paris, that would become a central element in the work of Marianne Heske. For her, this banal and impersonal toy represented the anonymous individual in the era of mass production, and the dialectic between repetition and singularity. *Avalanche* (1993) is another powerful work that symbolizes the infinite fall of bodies in a crowd, while also echoing the essence of her video works, the effect of a tiny detail of the image combined with an overall saturation of colors.

The work still relates to an "extraction of the anti-body of the image" as Pierre Restany wrote. The series *Mountains of the Mind* reveals mental landscapes filtered by the effects of video, which confirms the mountain form as the exact inverse of the infinite and sudden downfall symbolized in the installations that Heske has created with the heads of dolls. Singular, overpowering blocks of solarized color, the Heskian mountains create an absolute, thus an antidote to the social pixellization of the dolls. The installation *Avalanche* reveals color that is disseminated and defracted, whereas the filmed mountains in video form affirm the concentrated color, pushed to the limit. The individual, in order to resist social serialization, must become a rocky peak, a solid mass.

As far as the artist is concerned, she presents herself as this miniscule habitat, in the heights of Tafjord, which puts into play a give and take between these two worlds.

Translated from French by Selene Wendt.

And what does it mean, then, to be a poet?
It was a long time before I realized that to be a poet
means essentially to see.
(Henrik Ibsen, 1874)

In a letter to the author Bjørnson written in 1867, Ibsen asserted that "My plan is to become a photographer. I will have my contemporaries pose before my lens, one by one . . . I will not spare the baby in the mother's womb, nor even let a thought or feeling hidden in a person's utterances pass whenever I find myself in the presence of a spirit which deserves to be reproduced." If this declaration can be interpreted as the birth of modern bourgeois theatre, the comparison with a reproductive technique such as photography is fascinating. From its origins in 1839, photography had become the cutting edge of technology, the "contemporary" medium to portray the reality of the time. It brought many things to light that had previously never even been perceived, let alone seen. Ibsen's marked visual sensitivity would have drawn him to the new photographic techniques.

In 1973, Marianne Heske travelled around Europe with her camera. Over one hundred of her photographs were collected in a project entitled *With and about people*, showing a wide spectrum of people photographed with a doll's head supplied by the artist. Each photograph is part of an interpretive "game" and this way becomes part of the same creative process. The result was a cross-section of personalities. According to Jorunn Veiteberg: "At the same time they fill their social role as prostitute, housewife, judge, drunk man, immigrant, religious woman, etc., even as they play the marionette for the artist."[1]

Ibsen's walks around Rome were often dedicated to antique art, such that he was moved to say that "the Vatican and Capitolino Museums are like home to me". When he discovered the sculpture of *Melpomene*, the Muse of Tragedy, in the Vatican Museums, this proved to be a moment "charged with revelation" as it exposed "the essence of Greek tragedy". "That indescribably sublime joy, so clear and calm in her expression, her head encircled by a rich crown of leaves, a *je ne sais quoi* that is divinely bacchanalian and delirious, the eyes that look inwards but at the same time traverse and prevail over all that is put before them—it sums up Greek tragedy perfectly."[2] Most of all, Ibsen was interested in "that in beauty which remains eternal"[3], referring to the classical concept of identifying form with life which would be revisited in *When We Dead Awaken* (1899), in which the protagonist, Rubek, is a sculptor who considers his statues to be his children.

In Marianne Heske's *Hall of Fame* installation (1978), you are confronted with classical art and led to consider the role of art and the model in history. The artist mounts the doll's head on a plinth and places it between copies of busts of Greek philosophers and historical figures. In the same room, a video camera records the visitors who can be seen on two television screens, in turn becoming part of the exhibition. The monitors display a simultaneous image and a delayed image, thus disorientating the visitors' perceptions, in the same way that the modern icon does in among the antique busts.

Henrik Ibsen was a point of reference for Italian culture in the early twentieth century, both in academia as well as for authors such as Pirandello and D'Annunzio. In 1943, Savinio published both *Vita di Enrico Ibsen (The Life of Henrik Ibsen)*, the central theme of which is women and feminism, and *Casa "La vita"*, the title of which reflects the famous Ibsen drama. The Norwegian dramatist's stay had profound effects in Italy; his time in Rome was also important in the writing of *A Doll's House* (1878–79). His participation in the Scandinavian Circle of Artists and Scientists in Rome gave the background to the ideological structure of Nora's conflict.[4] In 1879, the hypocrisy of male society members caused him to propose that women should have the right to vote in the Circle. The initiative was successful and led to the

---

[1] J. Veiteberg, "A stage for art", in *Marianne Heske, To Whom it may concern*, exhibition catalogue, The National Museum of Contemporary Art, Norway, 2002, p. 25.
[2] Letter from Ibsen to Bjørnson, 28 January 1865, published in S.M. Nilsen,
L. Reznicek, *Ibsen in Italia*, Oslo-Rome: Biblioscandia, 1987.
[3] Ibidem.
[4] Cfr. in *Ibsen in Italia*, cit.

full equality of men and women in the Circle. Just a month later *A Doll's House* was published.

The issue of the role of women in society returned to prominence a century after the publication of *A Doll's House*. In 1976, under the slogan "Reclaim the Night", 26,000 women descended on the piazzas of Rome to claim the right to the existence of a feminine identity that was not a reflection of masculine values. At this time, Marianne Heske was living in Paris where the same tensions of the era were apparent. The head of a 1920s doll, unearthed in a local flea market, became the protagonist of her work. The artist drew up the following mental equation: "Greta Garbo = Doll = Marianne Heske = No one"[5], taking her work in two directions. In one way, her image of the doll's head inside a bird's cage reflected ideological struggles in which an imprisoned bird was a metaphor for women's experience in art in the seventies, as in the lithograph *Doll Pondering Risky Ideas* (1975); in another way, the concept behind the mass-produced doll transformed it into a symbol of humanity, a representation of the anonymous individual immersed in the masses. This led to *NN* (1978), a bust of an unknown person. This Latin abbreviation means "nameless". Using a range of media, from photomontages to video and from engraving to installations, the artist then linked the doll's head to drawings of skulls and behavioural classification systems, inspired by the theory of phrenology.

Halvdan Koht, a biographer of Ibsen, observed that: "One day in Oslo, Erik Werenskiold came across Ibsen walking very slowly in the street examining some new houses with intense concentration. 'Are you interested in architecture?' he asked. 'Of course,' replied Ibsen, 'it is my trade.' He considered his works to be architectural constructions."[6]

Marianne Heske's *Doll's House* is an architectural construction that, according to the artist, "houses thousands of people from all over the world." Everyone can identify with one of the thousands of dislocated doll heads inside the building, whether in the form of sculptures, installations or projections. What better symbol to represent the masks that we all wear in our dealings with others?

The doll's head is in fact a metaphor for the individual and the different roles that we assume in society every day. This metaphor is taken further by Marianne Heske's installation: the house becomes a theatre and the inhabitants recite their scripts like actors, inspired by Ibsen's famous work. Towards the end of *A Doll's House*, Nora exits the stage, withdrawing to her room saying "I'm taking off my fancy dress". These words reveal the symbolism. Nora wants to be released from her destiny as an eternal plaything, an object at her husband's disposal. Marianne Heske's *Doll's House* returns to this metaphor as a contemporary, universal theme which encourages reflection on the extraordinary cycle of life and the conditions of human existence.

The idea of travel is another *leitmotiv* in the poetical work of Marianne Heske. In 1980, the *Gjerdeløa Project* transferred a hut from Norway to the Centre Pompidou in Paris, while in 1999 *Stone Story* undertook the transit of a 17-tonne stone from the mountains of Norway to Venice's Lido. With these projects, the artist explored the significance of the work in terms of the concept and context in which it existed, irrespective of its form. The work followed an itinerary of exhibitions to stimulate and at the same time welcome different interpretations, or even better, new ways of seeing.

In *Peer Gynt* in 1867, Ibsen wrote: "Monsieur Ballon: You are Norwegian? Peer Gynt: Yes, by birth, but here, in my heart, 'the world' is my country!"

[5] Cit. in J. Veiteberg, *op. cit.*,
p. 18.
[6] Cit. in A. Savinio, Vita di Enrico Ibsen
(written in 1943), Milan: Adelphi, 1979.

A Doll's House

There it is: a quiet house built on a model of Palladian proportions. This is a classic house echoing the Renaissance villa, the echoes reaching back across time to the Greek and Roman models of an idealized past. This house is life sized. It is nevertheless a doll's house. The model house hints at the lives inside. A doll's house represents toy worlds. We think of these as lovely worlds, charming, radiant with the joy and pleasures of childhood. This is hardly so. Anyone who remembers the real world of childhood remembers a world of jealousies, cliques, and gangs. Just as the toy world of the doll's house socializes little girls to the adult life to come, the social worlds of childhood prepare us for a life of difficulty and deception. The worst of these deceptions are those by which we deceive the self. In this world, the tranquil façade of daily experience hides a darker world beneath.

Ibsen's title for his play captured both levels of reality in stark and terrible ambiguity. When H. F. Lord first translated *Et Dukkehjem* into English, she understood the risk of using a title that might as easily deceive readers as inform them. To avoid this, she titled her translation *Nora*. "The play now given to us as *Nora*," she wrote, "is called in Norwegian *Et Dukkehjem*. To a public unused to Ibsen's surprises, *A Doll's House* is a misleading title."

For Ibsen, it may be that all houses were doll houses. They represented the public façade of perfect life while covering the despair and imperfection of an inner world. Both worlds are social. In one, we act our idealized image of a self. In the other, we live as a self, tormented and disturbed by those who know us best, even as we torment and disturb them.

For the centennial anniversary of Henrik Ibsen's death, artist Marianne Heske explored the world of the doll's house in a series of five major works, presented as a large-scale installation in a single house. Each of these five projects involves work based on a doll's head that Heske found many years ago in Paris. This fact and the presentation in a model house gives rise to the metaphor of the doll's house, itself the title of Ibsen's best known and most influential work.

Heske describes her relation to the Selvida House, saying: "The architectural principle of the golden section in this house supports and emphasizes the installation. The harmonious scale of the building offers a shelter. The interior deals with human conflict and emotional projection embodied in Ibsen's play, *A Doll's House*."[1]

The Age of Ibsen

Henrik Ibsen endowed his work with a quality unseen since Shakespeare by generating enduring significant symbols. Philosopher and sociologist George Herbert Mead developed the concept of the significant symbol to describe the process of acculturation, the way that societies shape the context of belonging.[2]

Significant symbols emerge at the meeting point of emotion and intellect. In social and psychological terms, what makes a symbol significant is that it functions both intellectually and emotionally. Both dimensions are equal, or nearly so, enabling significant symbols to create existential and experiential meaning as well as abstract, cognitive meaning. They can evoke emotional experiences, complex memories, feelings, and even body states while conveying ideas. These symbols are significant because they are meaningful in the deepest existential sense, connected to ethical and moral values as well as to emotional power.[3]

In the years between Shakespeare and Ibsen, theatre was a matter of set pieces that we can hardly recognize today. In a sense, theatre was divided between two kinds of presentation: an intellectual theatre of abstract representation and a popular theatre of comedy and melodrama. Rarely did the full scope of human life come forward on stage, at least not in any sense wider than the agreed complex of meanings visible to the audience for whom a given playwright produced his work.

Ibsen's approach to theatre came at a moment of great change in European affairs: cultural, social, scientific, and technological. During the years of Ibsen's

[1] Conversation with the artist, November 21, 2005.

[2] George H. Mead, *Mind, Self, and Society. From the Standpoint of a Social Behaviorist*. Edited, with an introduction, by Charles W. Morris. Chicago: University of Chicago Press, 1934, pp. 71-72, 89-90.

[3] My renewed interest in significant symbols began in a series of conversations with theologian Ditte Mauritzon Friedman, a doctoral research fellow at Lund University. Her exploration of spiritual symbols in contemporary film builds on Mead's concept of the significant symbol. Our conversations brought me back to George Herbert Mead's work, and to concepts that were crucial to my own research in the sociology of art during the 1970s. Mead's ideas, along with those of John Dewey and C. S. Peirce, have been the focus of renewed attention in many fields. See, for example, Hans Joas, *G. H. Mead. A Contemporary Re-Examination of His Thought*, Cambridge, Massachusetts: MIT Press, 1997.

life, philosophy gave rise to the new fields of psychology, social psychology, and sociology. Mead's life (1863-1931) began shortly after Ibsen's (1828-1906), and Mead's work explored the world that Ibsen was among the first to portray in realistic terms.

Bjørn Hemmer describes Ibsen's greatness as a function of Ibsen's ability to capture the tragic scale of human life. Hemmer writes that "the tragic life feeling itself . . . gives Ibsen's drama its special character, the experience of missing out on life and plodding along in a state of living death. The alternative is pictured as a utopian existence in freedom, truth, and love—in short—a happy life. In Ibsen's world the main character strives toward a goal, but this struggle leads out into the cold, to loneliness. Yet the possibility of opting for another route is always there, one can chose human warmth and contact. The problem for Ibsen's protagonist is that both choices can appear to be good, and the individual does not see the consequences of the decision."

A terrible choice lies at the heart of great modern drama. The world seems to allow all choices. In reality, it allows quite few. "The tragic element in Ibsen's perspective," writes Hemmer, "is that for the type of people that concern him, this seems to be an insoluble conflict. Yet this fact does not exonerate them from the responsibility for their own decisions."[4]

Harold Bloom argues that Ibsen's greatness has little to do with the "social energies of his age"[5] and everything to do with his devotion to his own gifts. I disagree with this assessment: it was the nature of Ibsen's age to focus on the human challenges that all women and men face, and Ibsen set these modern figures on stage in their full existential quality.

Bloom nevertheless perceives this quality. His chapter on "Ibsen: Tolls and Peer Gynt" concludes his section on the democratic age, and it sets Ibsen apart as the only dramatist of the era.[6] Bloom understood the theme as well, and he links it with existential philosophy and psychology, writing that "Kierkegaard, who had a strong if oblique effect on Ibsen, distinguished between two great despairs: that of having failed to become oneself, and the greater one of having indeed become oneself."[7]

A deep understanding of human psychology forms the vital link between Kierkegaard, Ibsen, and Mead. According to Ernest Becker, Kierkegaard was the first modern psychologist. Becker argues that Freud's work and writings finally made it possible to understand Kierkegaard.[8] Bloom ends the democratic age with Ibsen, using Freud to open what he labels the chaotic age. The social energies emerging at the turn of the century divided two aspects of an era.

A Poet of the Mutable

The Western Canon honours only three playwrights with chapters of their own. These artists use more than the power of words to achieve canonical status. What elevates them is an ability to understand and capture human experience. Their work reflects life in a way that enables us to recognize ourselves and to respond. Bloom notes, "The peculiar magnificence of Shakespeare is in his power of representation of human character and personality and their mutabilities."[9] Samuel Johnson's praise of Shakespeare applies to Ibsen: "above all writers, at least above all modern writers, the poet of nature, the poet that holds up to his readers a faithful mirror of manners and of life."[10] I have discussed Shakespeare, Sophocles, and Ibsen using similar examples and phrases, often for the same reasons.[11] While words are powerful, they are bound by the medium in which we find them, caught in the context of their time, "since brass, nor stone, nor earth, nor boundless sea, but sad mortality o'er-sways their power" (Sonnets LXV: 1-2). Like Shakespeare, Ibsen's power is based on more than his rhythm and language. It is built on his eye for human behaviour, his ability to capture and reflect human experience.

Ibsen created a new kind of theatre to engage the intellect and emotions in a new and deeper way than drama had yet achieved. Ibsen's theatre was controversial because it approached the drama of

[4] Bjørn Hemmer, 2006. "'The Dramatist: Henrik Ibsen.'" *Henrik Ibsen Link Page.* URL: http://www.mnc.net/norway/Ibsen.htm Accessed 21 January 2006 January 21. ([Unpaged)]

[5] Harold Bloom, *The Western Canon. The Books and School of the Ages.* London: Macmillan, 1995, p. 352.

[6] Bloom, *op. cit.*, pp. 350–367.

[7] H. Bloom, *op. cit.*, p. 352.

[8] Ernest Becker, 1973. *The Denial of Death*, New York: Free Press, 1973, pp. 67–68.

[9] H. Bloom, *op. cit.*, p. 63.

[10] Samuel. Johnson, *Samuel Johnson on Shakespeare.* Edited with an introduction and notes by H. R. Woudhuysen, London: Penguin Books, 1989, p. 122.

[11] Many authors have discussed the rebirth of a tragic vision in Ibsen's work, noting his ability to give shape to tragic understanding in a new form. See, for example, Richard B. Sewall, *The Tragic Vision*, New Haven: YaleUniversity Press, 1980 (1959).

human experience by dealing with controversial topics. It was shocking because it engaged human experience in a new way. It created and made use of significant symbols.

This can be attributed in part to Ibsen's powers of representation. In part, it is the result of Ibsen's skillful development of character, scene, and action. Ibsen's narrative seems real because his plays seem to trace the genuine and natural development of events. He adjusts them for dramatic effect, but he never violates our human sense of what is natural. Nothing is forced. All grows in natural order. Woody Allen's description of the dramatic development of a joke applies to Ibsen's narrative development, ". . . what's great about a great joke is the straight line. The straight line is what makes one guy's joke better than another guy's joke, because an unforced straight line leads you to a bigger payoff. A forced straight line triggers the audience just a little bit. You don't do a straight line just because it leads to a punch line. You do a straight line because it's the correct line at the time and then you make the joke off it; then the joke is good."[12] Just as a good joke can catch us unaware by virtue of surprising realism, so Ibsen's work embraces our perception of a natural order that lends itself to what Peter Berger and Thomas Luckmann famously termed "the social construction of reality."[13] Ibsen builds on what we know and feel. He uses his art to extend, elaborate, and enrich our perceptions from the outside in.

The Northern chill of Ibsen's measured observation looks back to another Nordic tradition, the Icelandic sagas. The family sagas and district sagas told heroic tales about ordinary heroes. In their time, the landholders of medieval Iceland played the community roles of Ibsen's bourgeois heroes. We meet them as living women and men in an age of florid, stylised literature and drama. These stories, like Ibsen's, show how our choices trap us, propelling us forward to a future we do not imagine in the act of choosing. Knowledge is the key, the knowledge of what we cannot know. This reminds us continually that

knowledge and information are different. Knowledge is embodied and applied, requiring the attributes of emotion, ethics, and value that distinguish significant symbols from the purely cognitive symbols of information.

Kierkegaard's discussion of the pilot's work reminds us that information becomes knowledge only when it is embodied, and changes yet again when applied. "Let us imagine a pilot, and assume that he had passed every examination with distinction, but that he had not as yet been to sea. Imagine him in a storm; he knows everything he ought to do, but he has not known before how terror grips the seafarer when the stars are lost in the blackness of night; he has not known the sense of impotence that comes when the pilot sees the wheel in his hand become a plaything for the waves; he has not known how the blood rushes to the head when one tries to make calculations at such a moment; in short, he has had no conception of the change that takes place in the knower when he has to apply his knowledge."[14]

The power of Ibsen's drama is its ability to encourage direct, personal engagement with great issues. This is an existential challenge. It opens a world of judgment and feeling as well as a world of fact. An artist who confronts Ibsen must be prepared to struggle.

Marianne Heske's Doll's House

Marianne Heske's *Doll's House* has several dimensions. On one level, the house is an installation. It is a work of art in five parts, each relating in some way to a dimension of Henrik Ibsen's work.

Conceived as a contribution to the Ibsen Year in 2006, the artist created this work as a conversation with the great Norwegian playwright who died over a century. The doll's house itself was installed in a prefabricated house of lightweight concrete built by the Selvaag Group, the renowned Norwegian house-building company. The house itself was built on a neo-Palladian model. Heske was attracted to the house for many

[12] Eric Lax, *Woody Allen. A Biography*, London: Vintage, 1992, p. 97.
[13] Peter Berger, Thomas Luckmann, *The Social Construction of Reality*, New York: Doubleday, 1967.
[14] Søren Kierkegaard, *Thoughts on Crucial Situations in Human Life*. Translated by David F. Swenson, edited by Lillian Marvin Swenson, Minneapolis: Augsburg Publishing House, 1941 (1845), pp. 35–36.

reasons. According to Heske, the Selvida House "has the architectural principle of 'the divine proportion.' It can support and emphasize my exhibition." Within the harmony of the most symmetrical house, we find the turbulent asymmetry of human conflicts, the struggle of intellect and emotion, the daily disaster of human experience. The symbol of the Doll's House functions on many levels.

While the house reminds us of Nora and her struggle for freedom and authenticity, the title of Nora's play reminds us that we live in a constructed world, playing the roles that life assigns us. Sometimes we choose the roles we play. Sometimes we are trapped within them. Sometimes we choose a role only to discover that it is a trap. Dolls and doll houses are toy worlds, built for children. They are toys with a purpose, and youngsters use these toys to shape dreams of a future life. It is only later, when we have embarked on life that we find the life we dreamed of is at its most difficult in the moment we realize our dreams.

Nora's despair is a shift from the lesser despair of not willing to be oneself to the greater despair of willing defiantly to be oneself.[15] To be—*that* is the question for Ibsen's troubled heroes. In being, in becoming themselves, they experience the greater of the two despairs. Their choices condemn them to the bleak loneliness of self and memory in time, a sickness that Kierkegaard's identifies as the sickness unto death in his psychological masterpiece of that title.

Albert Camus speaks of the loneliness of self in *Caligula*. In Act II, the Emperor addresses Scipio saying, "One is never alone. Always, we are attended by the same load of the future and the past. Those we have killed are always with us. But they are no great trouble. It's those we have loved, those who have loved us and whom we did not love; regrets, desires, bitterness and sweetness, whores and gods, the celestial gang! Always with us!"[16]

These are durable issues in human experience. Despite the fact that the artist seeks innovative media, Heske feels that her work is old-fashioned. The role of time and social awareness in Heske's work has often been misunderstood, precisely because of the tension between old ideas and modern media.[17]

A Doll's House was conceived as an installation in five parts. The first part, *Avalanche*, is made of one thousand and one doll heads cast in crystal glass. Within each head, the artist implanted a piece of crystal each with a different colour and shape. Heske sees these as "the reflection of a private inner life locked within a social world." However, this social world takes place against the larger scale of nature and the physical world. On the wall of the installation, there was a video painting of an avalanche sandblasted onto an immense aluminium panel.

Heske found the doll's head that she has often used in a Paris flea market forty years ago. Each head in this installation is based on that original model. This head has been the basis of many works since then: as single pieces, as multiples, in an ever-changing variety of materials and colours, while always in the shape of the first doll's head. Some of these installations—like *Avalanche*—gather thousands of the heads. This is also the case for *China from China*.

China from China was based on two thousand white porcelain doll heads. The porcelain heads for this project were manufactured in China. The installed heads are gathered in a mass much like the gathering in avalanche or the remnants of an earthquake. Some heads are whole. Some are broken. Small mirrors are scattered through the mass, allowing the public to see itself in the reflections.

The late Pierre Restany described Heske's fascination with these doll heads, and the riddle of single heads in massive groups: "A tangible metaphor expresses this quantitative awareness of the human context: the uniform mass, a sea made up of balls, the heads of glass dolls. For Marianne, the quantitative phenomenon encompasses the addition of individual particularities. According to Arman, a head and a thousand heads are two different things, but the relationship established between part and totality does

[15] Søren Kierkegaard, *The Sickness Unto Death (with Fear and Trembling)*. Translated by Walter Lowrie, Princeton: Princeton University Press, 1968 (1849), pp. 146–150, 180–207.
[16] Albert Camus, *Caligula and Three Other Plays*. Translated from the French by Stuart Gilbert, New York: Vintage Books, 1958.
[17] Ken Friedman, "'Om Heskekunst og annen kunst'", *Morgenbladet*. Translated into Norwegian by Bente Dahl, 1994.

not destroy the starting point, the initial identity. The artist is perfectly aware of this. She has often said that since 1971, in Paris, she has been obsessed by dolls' heads, by their bulging eyes and rosebud mouths, to the point of making huge photographic enlargements of them which turn the galaxy from its milky way."[18]

Heske's doll heads always startle me. They are a diametrical contrast to the panoramic austerity of Heske's video works. Using video, Heske found a way to translate light images directly from video monitor to canvas without intervention. This imbues her work with several significant qualities. Foremost among these is the fact that Heske works directly with light on tape. This is a direct medium, at least as direct as any technological engagement can be, and far more direct than painting the same thing. This work is close to nature. In contrast, the doll heads are visibly artificial.

The stylised quality of the original doll's head that Heske found in that Paris flea market has a quality that always disturbs me. It has much to do with the style. It is the head of a pre-feminist, objectified woman, nearly the opposite of Ibsen's strong, self-conscious women. They are the opposite of their predecessors, the great women of the sagas, complex, heroic figures with a sense of self, objects to none other. The doll heads represent women who stay home to play the role of Torvald Helmer's little, bustling squirrel.

One must ask the existential question here, Kierkegaard's question. Kierkegaard asks what it is to be healthy in an existential sense. He argues that existential health is always dialectical. While Kierkegaard's philosophical argument has a theological foundation, he speaks to existential psychology in discussing the dialectics of health—a health rooted in his vision of the human being as spirit. Kierkegaard distinguishes the dialectics of spirit, effectively the dialectics of self, and he opposes it to the undialectical immediacy of a human being conceived as the synthesis of body and soul.[19] The problem is clear. The dialectics of self require us to take a position of self-hood. In this dimension, the objectified woman represented by the doll head is body alone, an object to the others who use her and determine her life.[20] The head is the patient. Dr. Ibsen prescribes the cure.

Heske looks at these heads with sympathy, though. She sees them as actors in the greater drama of life. "In this installation," she says, "a cast of thousands meet to form societies where they play roles, like actors on a stage. Each installation is a play, dealing with a wide range of psychological, social, and political issues."[21] For Heske, the panorama of human life takes place on a scale as large as the world of mountains, rock, and snow that formed the basis of her video projects. This large, somewhat impersonal vision is almost Buddhist in its conception of life, a theme that emerges in *Nora's Necklace*.

Nora's Necklace was made in Nepal. It consists of two hundred and fifty doll heads hanging from the ceiling of the Doll's House in the form of a chain necklace. Half of the heads are plated in real gold. Half are plated in silver. The chains form a huge knot, a symbol of the entangled dualism of humanity.

This piece raises a double dialectic. We see the first dialectic in the light of Kierkegaard's opposition between the human being as spirit and as self against the idea of a human being as the synthesis of dualisms, body and soul, mind and emotions.[22]

This is a critical issue in life and in art. Two centuries before Mead developed the concept of the significant symbol, Friedrich Schiller wrote, "Our psyche passes . . . from sensation to thought via a middle disposition in which sense and reason are both active at the same time . . . This middle disposition, in which the psyche is subject neither to physical nor moral constraints, and yet is active in both these ways . . . we must call . . . aesthetic."[23]

This grand, almost impersonal vision reflects the Buddhist concepts visible in the work of Heske's friend and colleague, Nam June Paik. One of the reasons Paik enjoys Heske's video work is its direct, natural quality. Paik's own work is always direct. His early, Zen-inspired work was particularly direct and pure. Video began, in

[18] Pierre Restany, 1995, *Marianne Heske*, Sao Paulo: XXIII Biennal de Sao Paulo. URL: http://www1.uol.com.br/bienal/23bienal/paises/ipno.htm Accessed 4 January 2006.

[19] Kierkegaard, *The Sickness Unto Death*, cit., p. 158.
[20] Kierkegaard, *The Sickness Unto Death*, cit., pp. 155–161.
[21] Conversation with the artist, 21 November 2005.

[22] Kierkegaard, *The Sickness Unto Death*, cit., p. 158.
[23] Friedrich Schiller, *On the aesthetic education of man*. Edited and translated by Elizabeth M. Wilkinson and L. A. Willoughby, Oxford:

Oxford University Press, (1794), 1983, p. 82. I am grateful to Prof. Pierre Guillet de Monthoux of Stockholm University and Copenhagen Business School for bringing this passage to my attention.

fact, when Paik used big magnets to scramble a standard broadcast image on television screens. This was simple kitchen physics. Light is photons. Television paints the screen with electrons shot from an electron gun. Paik's magnets deflected electrons, so the electron gun could not shoot straight. Paik started his career by playing with light, and I think he saw the same spirit as in Heske's work.[24]

Heske shares another quality of vision with Paik, a large-scale of vision of human action within nature. Paik's large-scale television and network projects linked thousands of people at different places around the world in the panorama of passing time. Heske's large cast of doll heads represents an equally large and impersonal world, a world of personalities joined in the stream of history.

This leads to the second dialectic by creating a natural opposition between the intense, personal quality of Ibsen's characters and the larger forces of society and culture. In doing so, it asks us to reflect on personhood and social forces in their twinned aspects of individual development and the socially embedded— socially created—self.

The last two works of the five reinforce these twinned polarities.

Blue was made in Zimbabwe using two hundred hand-carved doll heads in precious stone. These heads represent a unified culture, standing together in massed ranks. The two hundred heads suggest the military ranks of soldiers in the gathered presence of tribesmen and women. The question is whether culture traps us or liberates us. A video camera projects the wings of a huge, blue butterfly fluttering above the crowd of heads to suggest both possibilities.

The last work is titled *NN*, a standard abbreviation for "no name." This is a half-meter tall bronze doll's head mounted on the plinth. The head was made in Holland and Norway, engraved with the 35 human psychological faculties described by phrenology. A real human skull rests on a second plinth.

Heske sees her symbolic society of massed dolls as thousands of inhabitants from all parts of the world. The heads do come from all parts of the world. They are made in Europe, Africa, and Asia. However, they come together in a single place, summoned by a single hand, representing both the single self and the social context. *NN* —the one single head—captures the individual quality of confrontation, the final statement of self, the heroic, decisive self of Ibsen's characters who stand over and against the world of social character.

If no choice is empty, if every choice is made with a hope of some kind, all choices reach the same end. Heske announces this in the second skull, the real skull. Dürer might have made such an installation had he been an artist of the early twenty-first century.

The presence of a real skull in a work of art awakened a sense of horror in me for ethical and theological reasons. Looking past my personal dread, I can see it as one may see the skulls piled high in a monastery, voices with a message. In this sense, Heske's second skull is a messenger, arguing for the dialectical unity that rises above the dual themes on which this house is built. These dual forces touch at every point on the tension between the social forces of the modern age and the women and men who live it:

"Our age reminds one very much of the disintegration of the Greek state. Everything continues, and yet there is no one who believes in it. The invisible spiritual bond that gives it validity has vanished, and thus the whole age is simultaneously comic and tragic: tragic because it is perishing, comic because it continues. For it is still always the incorruptible that bears the corruptible, the intellectual-spiritual that bears the physical. And if it were possible to imagine that an inanimate body could still perform the usual functions for a little while, it would be comic and tragic in the same way."[25]

This is the comedy of life, and its tragedy. We wait to meet each other behind the calm, perfect façade of the doll's house. Here, too, each of us waits to meet— and make—a self.

---

[24] Friedman, *op. cit.*
[25] Søren Kierkegaard, *Or (Kierkegaard's Writings, IV, Part II: Either/Or: Part II.)* Edited and translated by Howard V. Hong and Edna H. Hong. Princeton: Princeton University Press, 1988 (1843), p. 19.

Doll heads, undated.

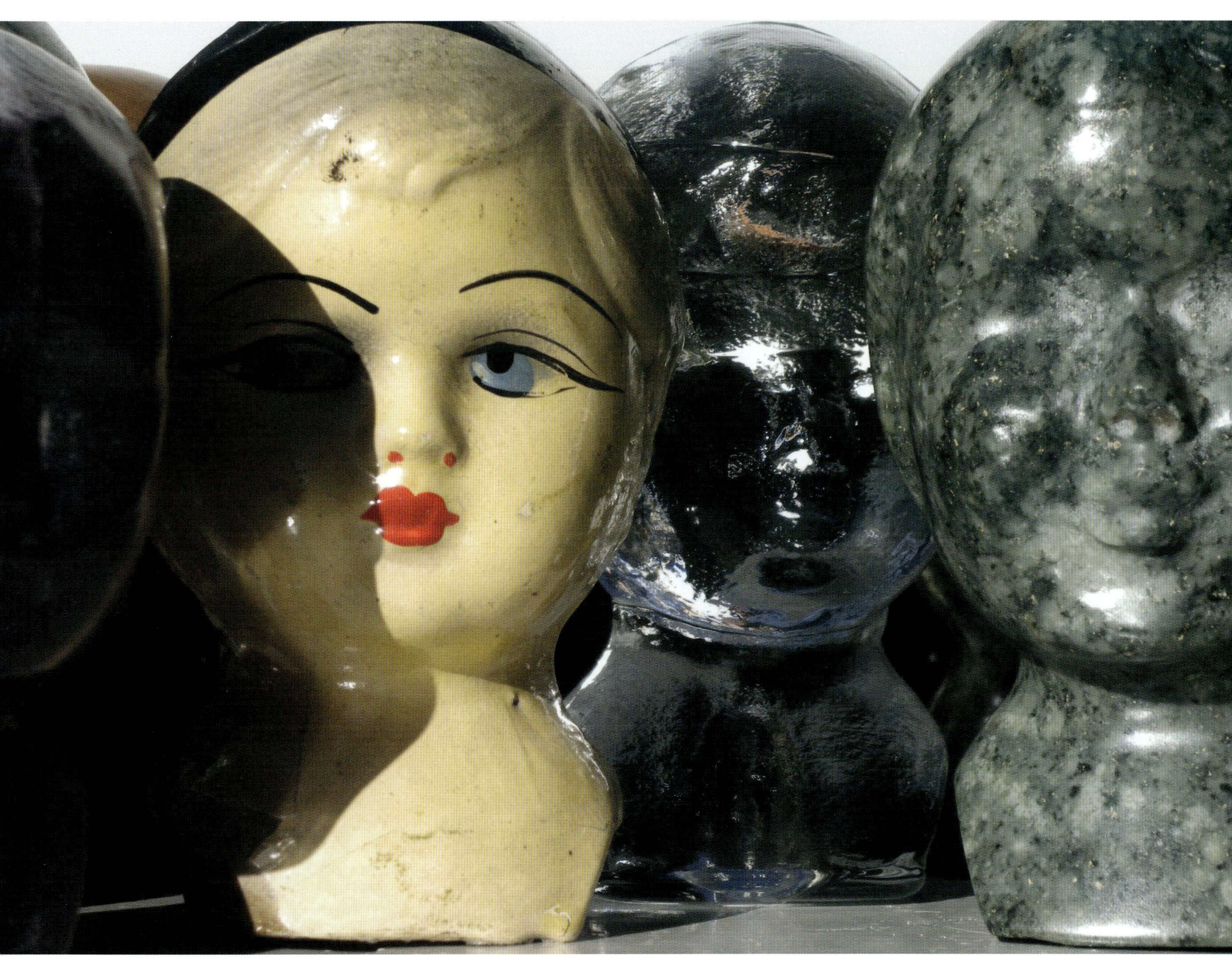

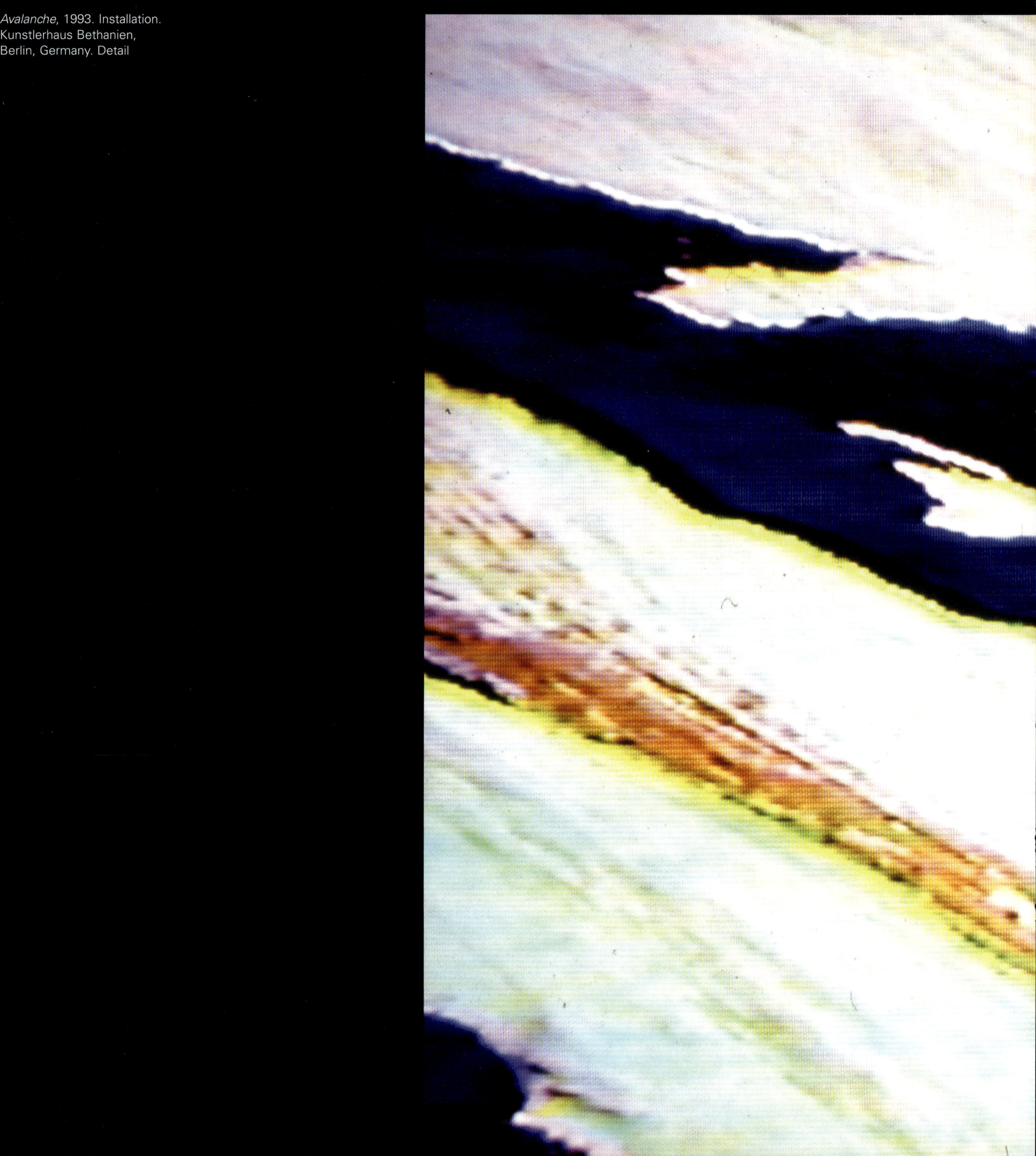

Avalanche, 1993. Installation.
Kunstlerhaus Bethanien,
Berlin, Germany. Detail

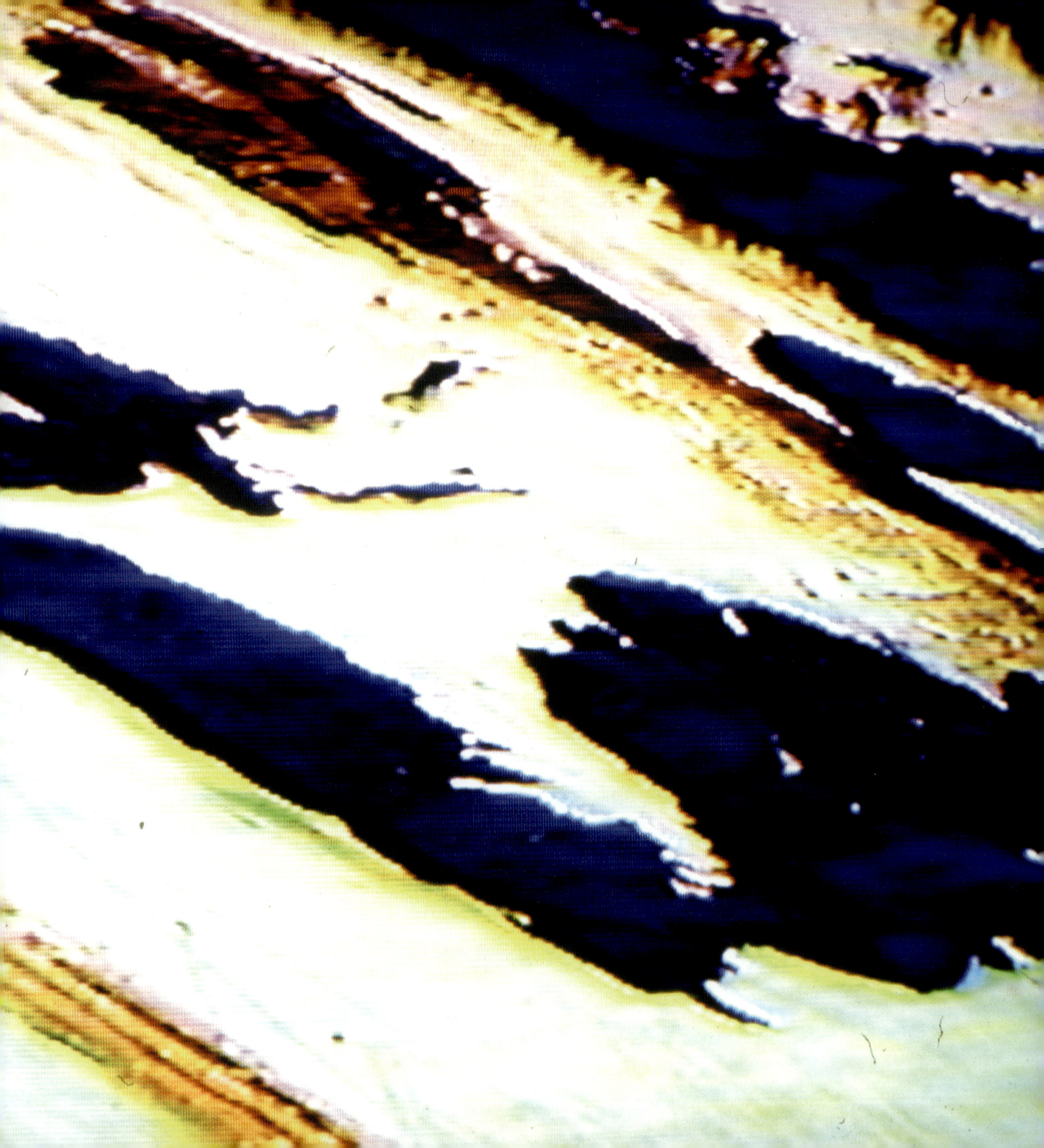

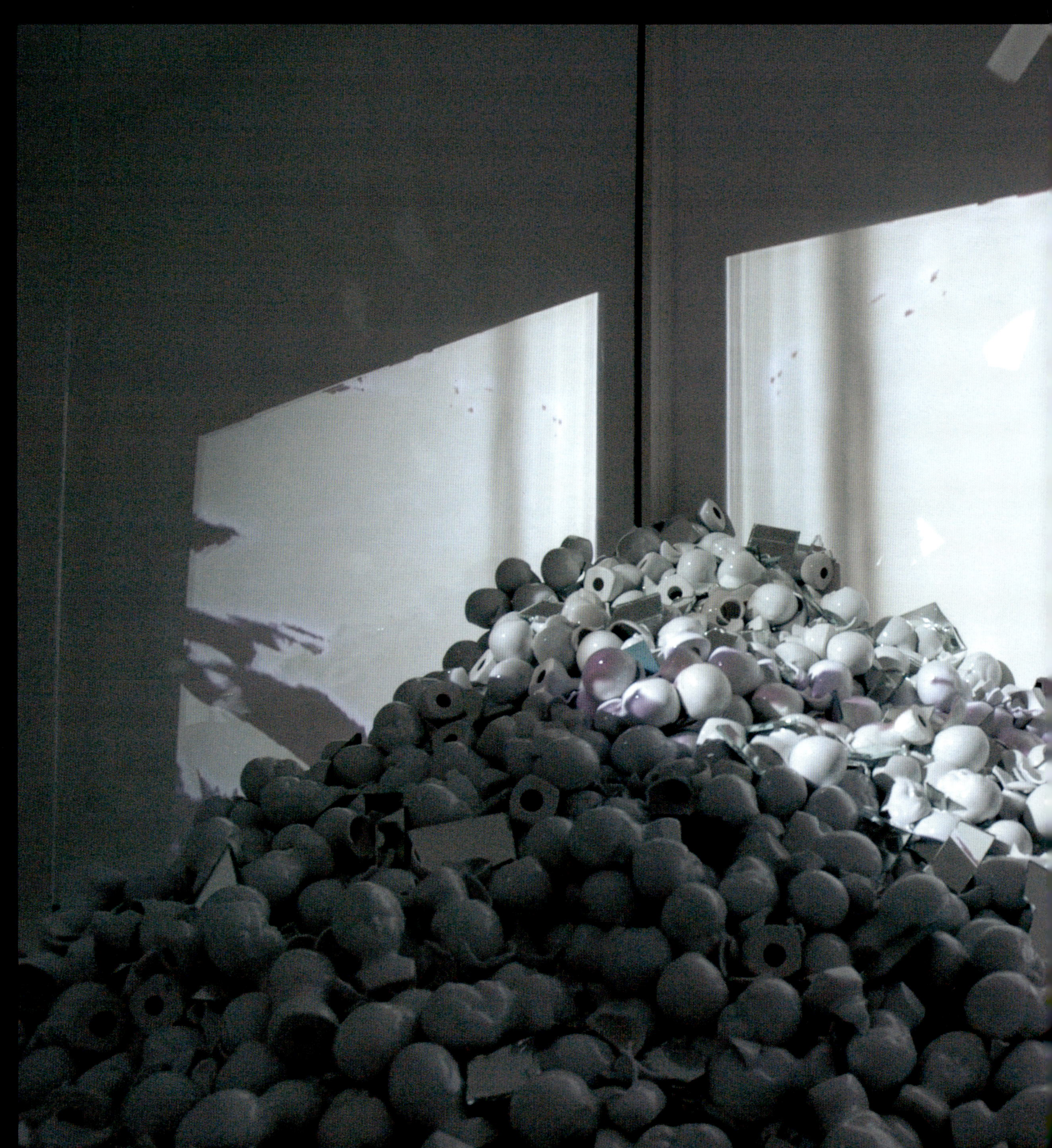

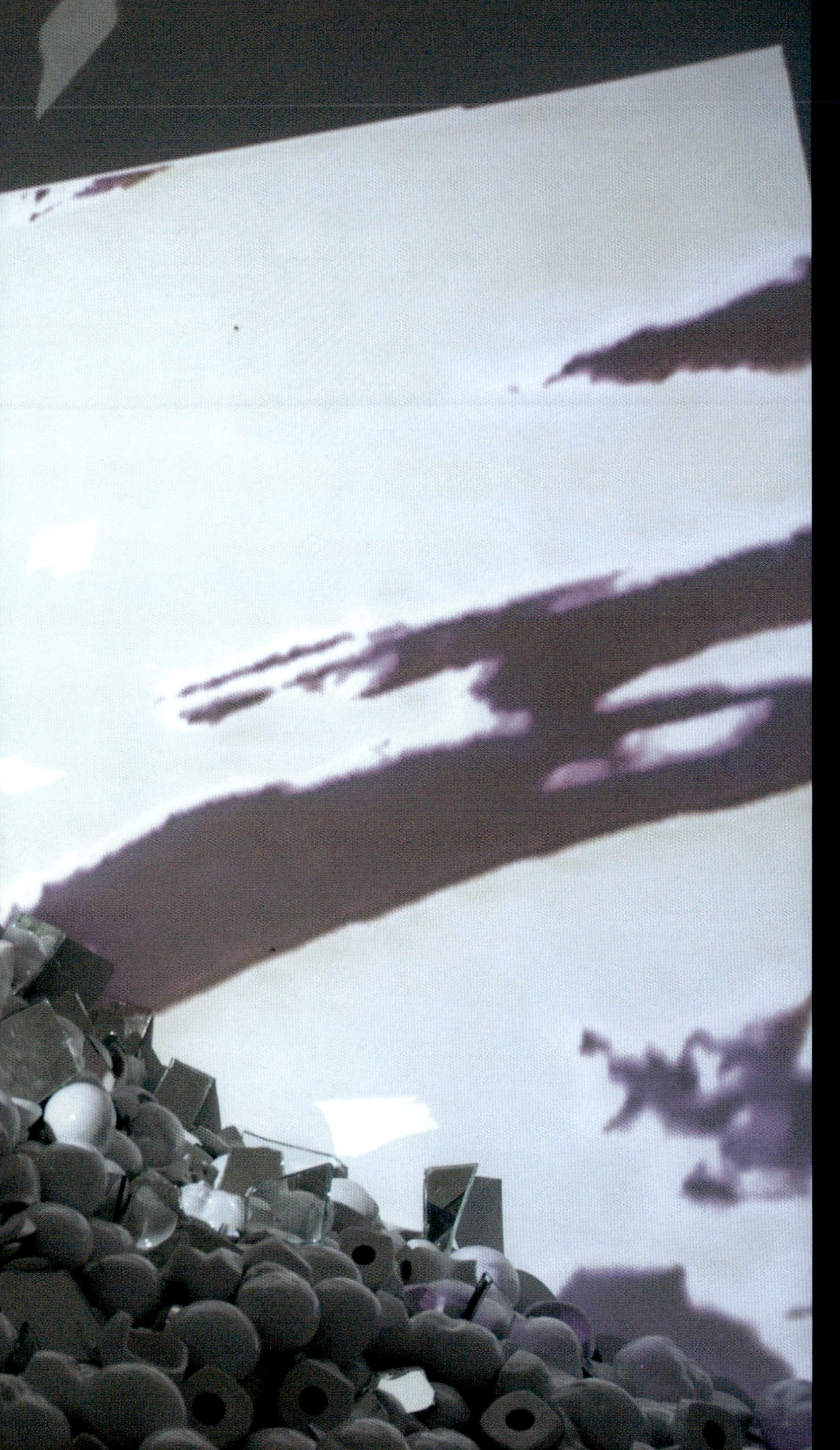

Avalanche, 2006. Installation.
The National Museum of Art,
Architecture and Design,
Oslo, Norway.

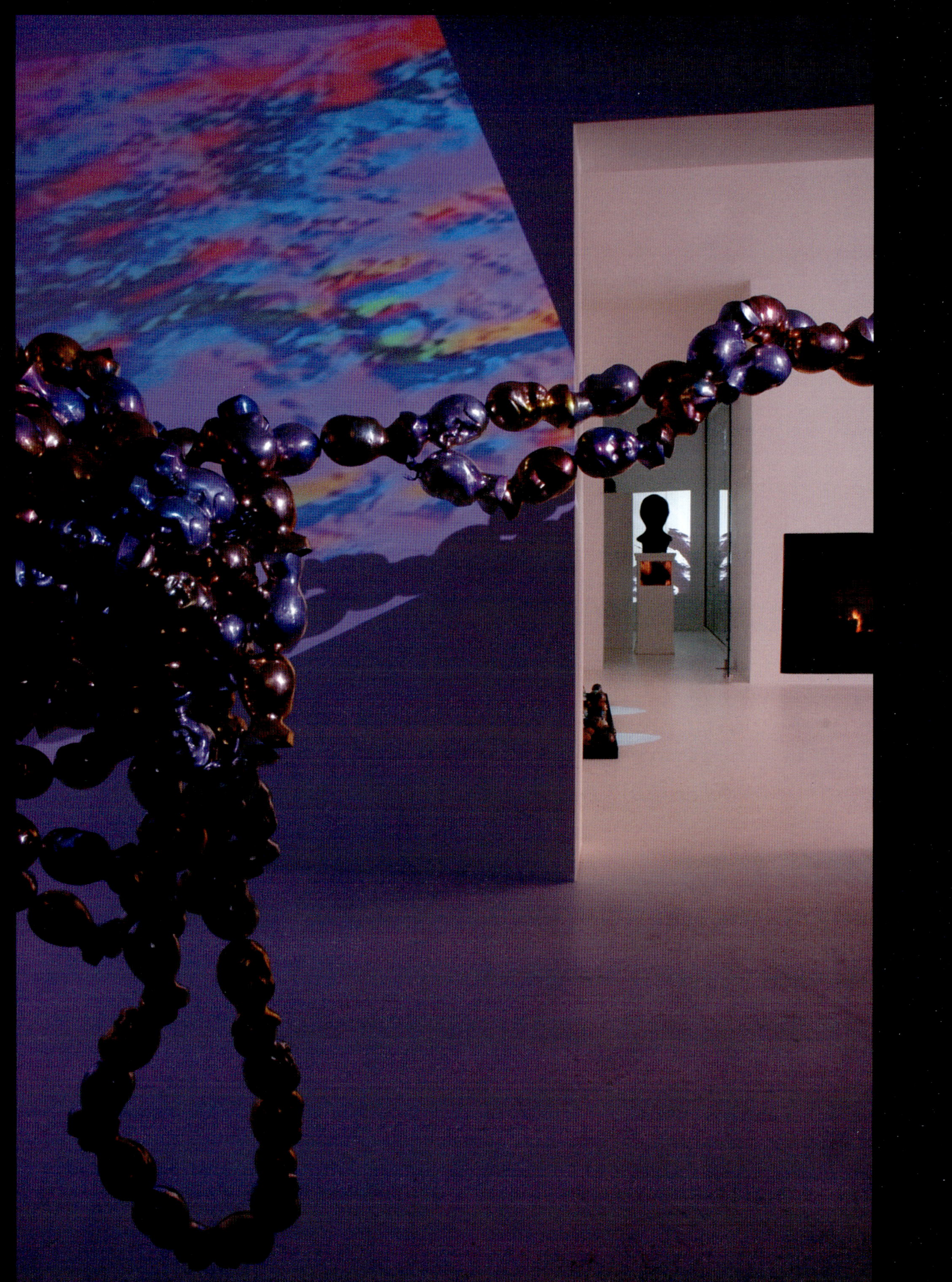

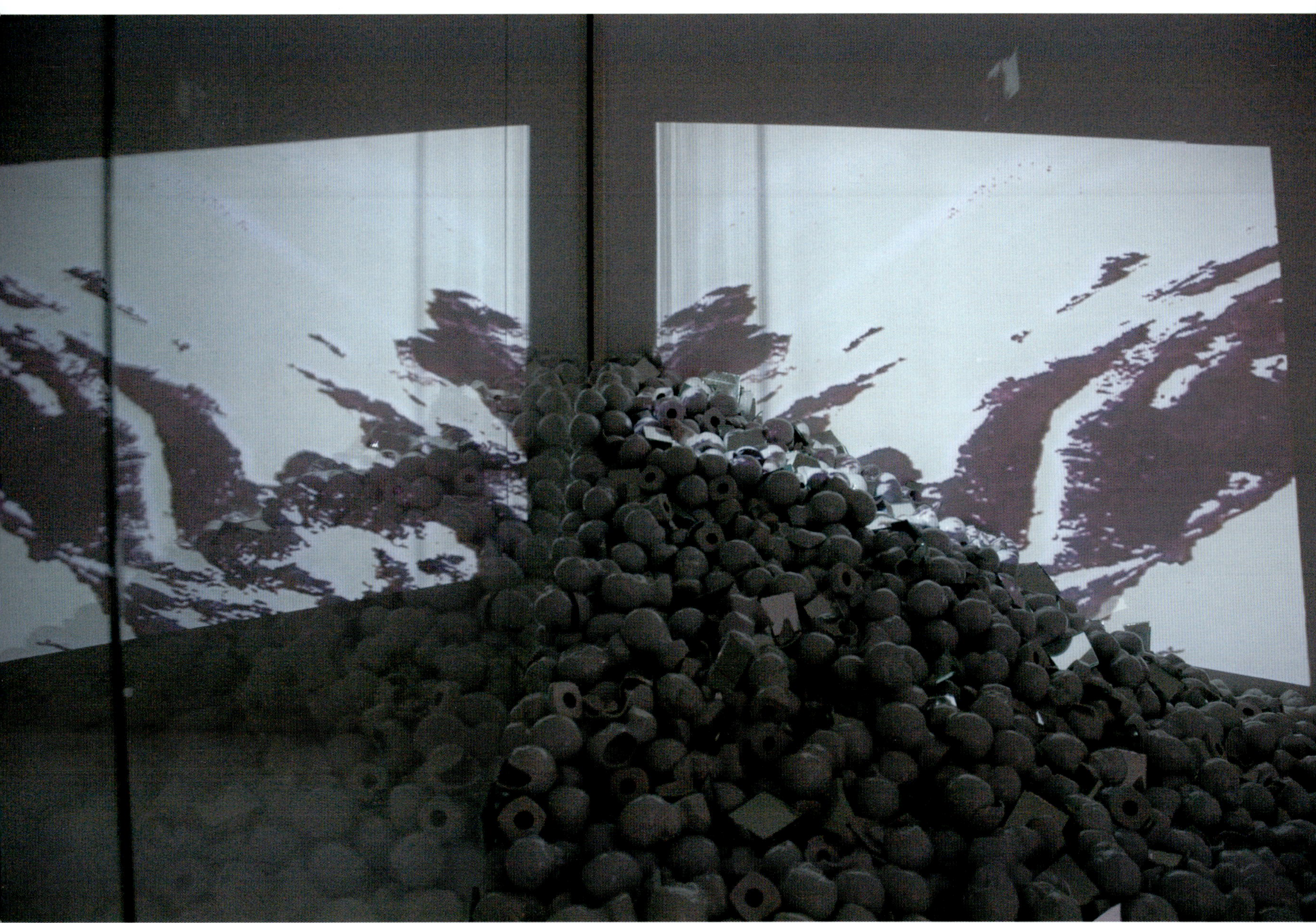

Gordian Knot, 2006.
Installation. The National
Museum of Art, Architecture
and Design, Oslo, Norway.

Avalanche, 2006. Installation.
The National Museum of Art,
Architecture and Design,
Oslo, Norway.

Blue, 2006. Installation. The
National Museum of Art,
Architecture and Design,
Oslo, Norway.

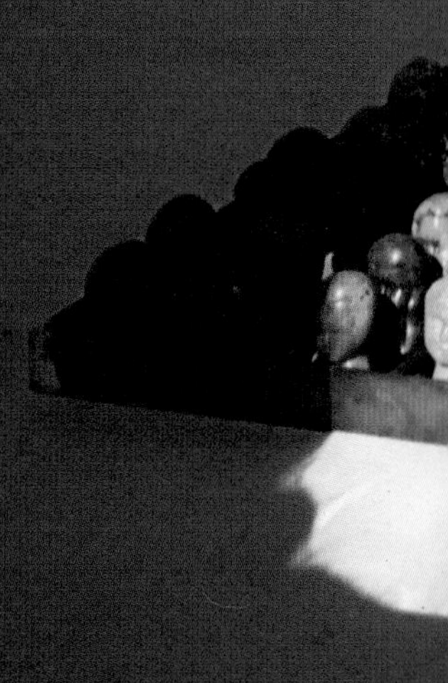

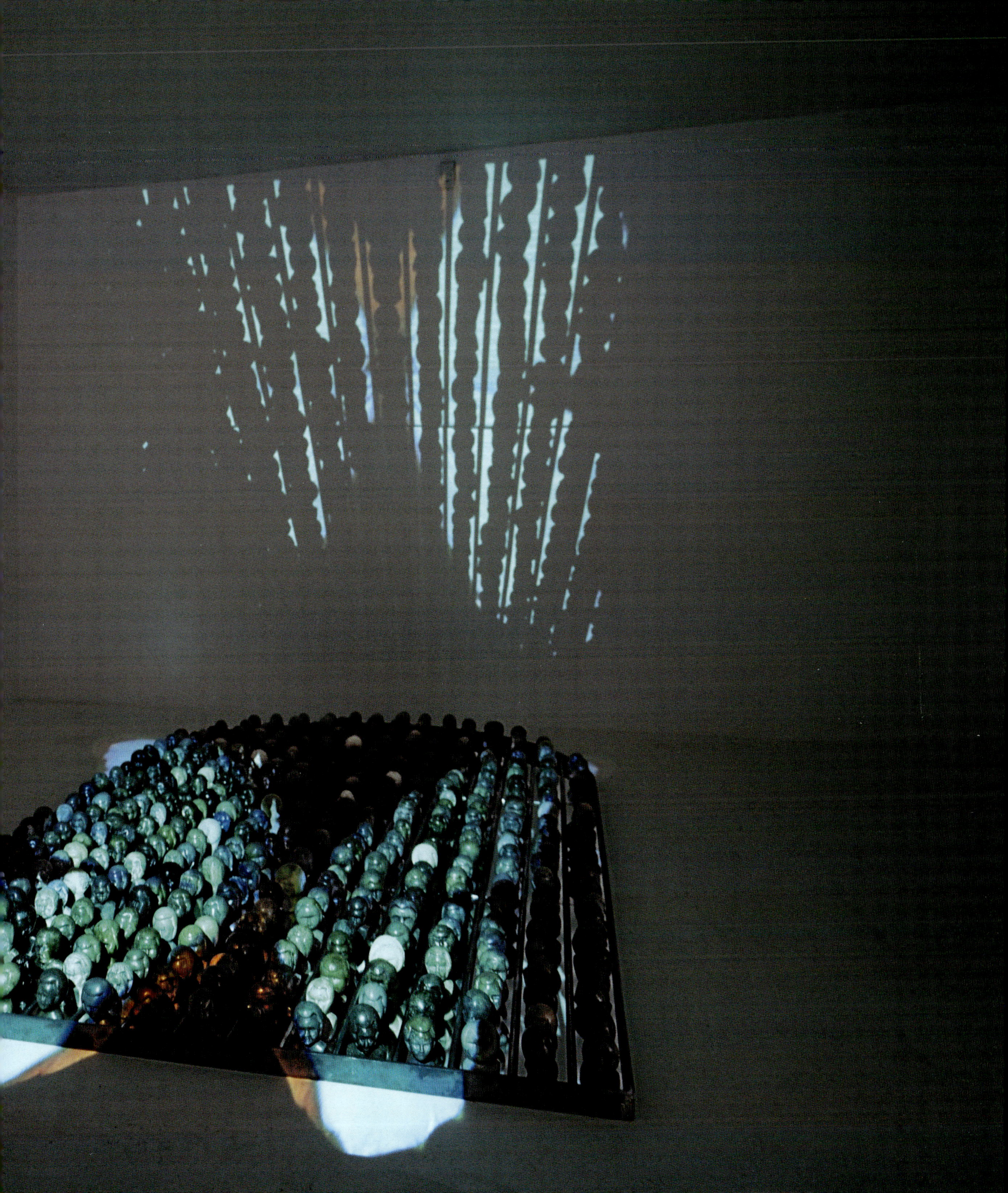

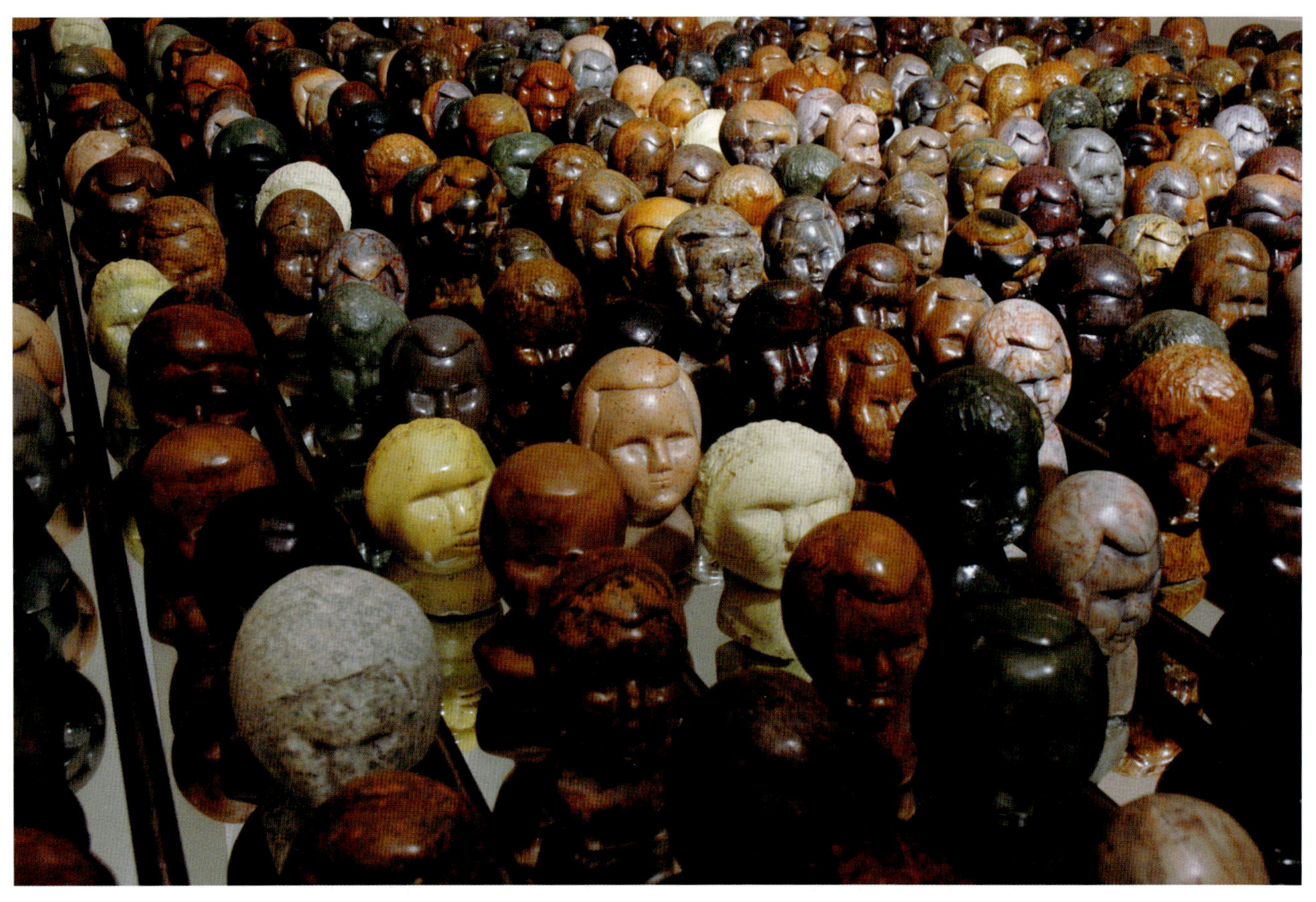

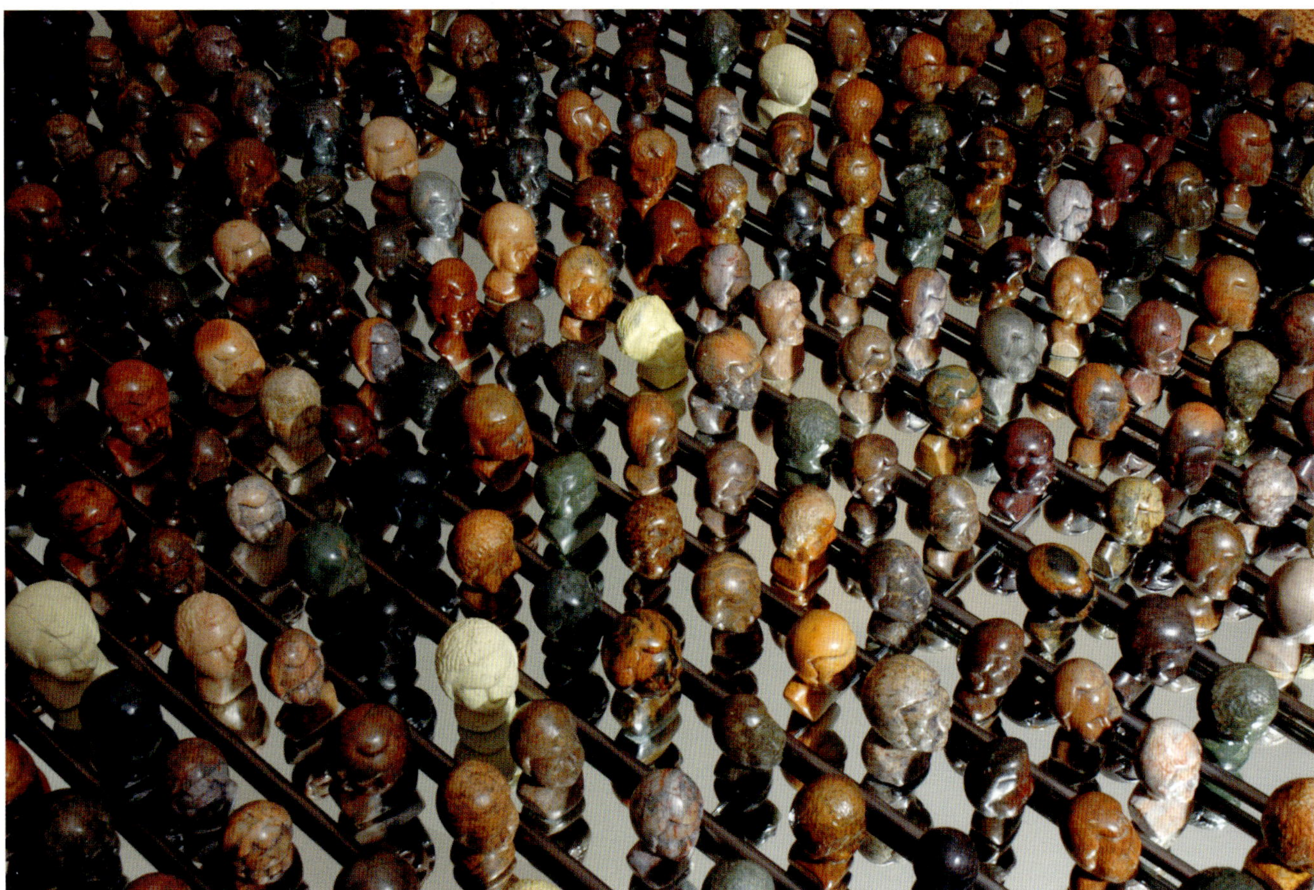

Global Groove, 2001.
Installation. The National
Museum, Harare, Zimbabwe.
Details.

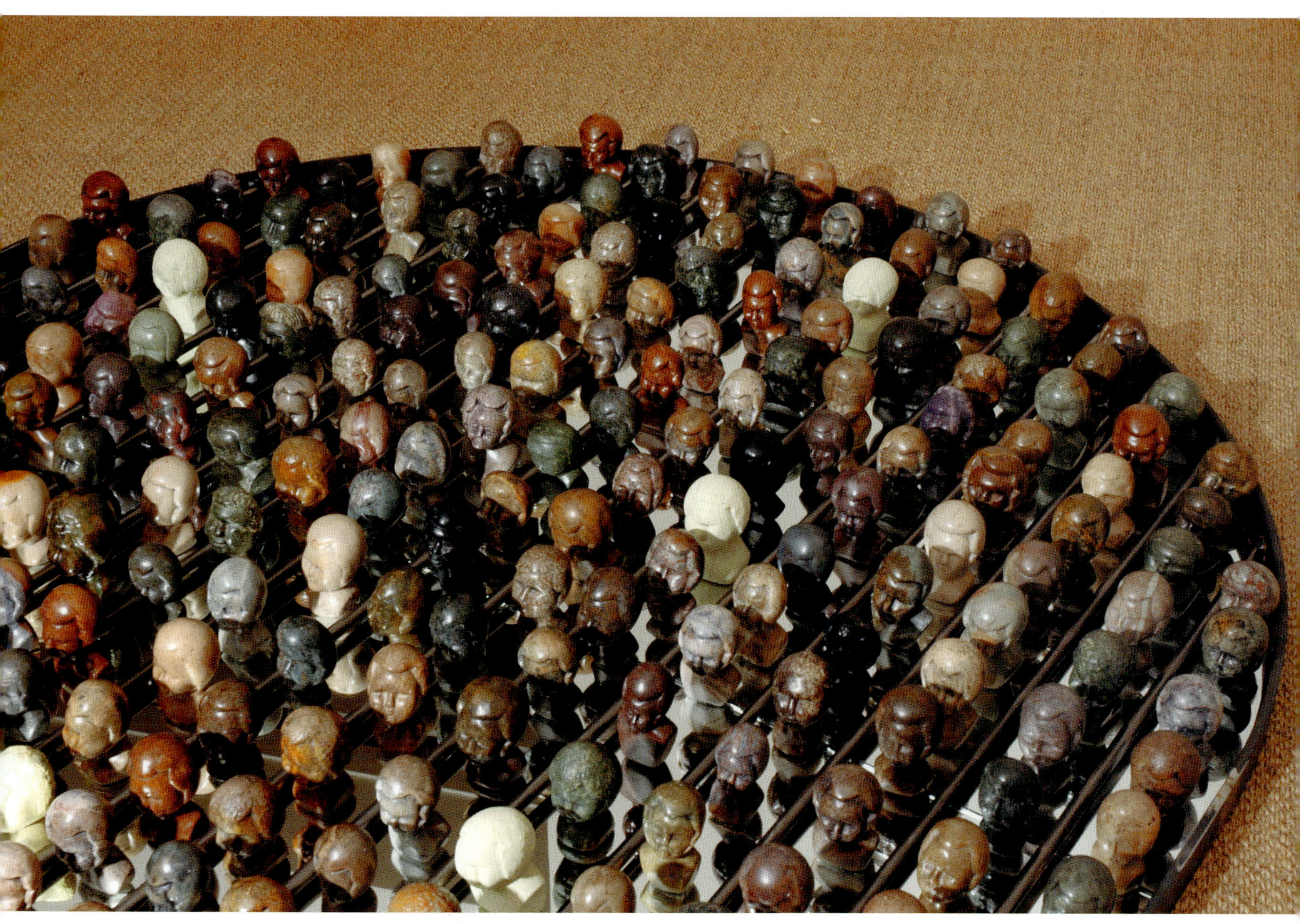

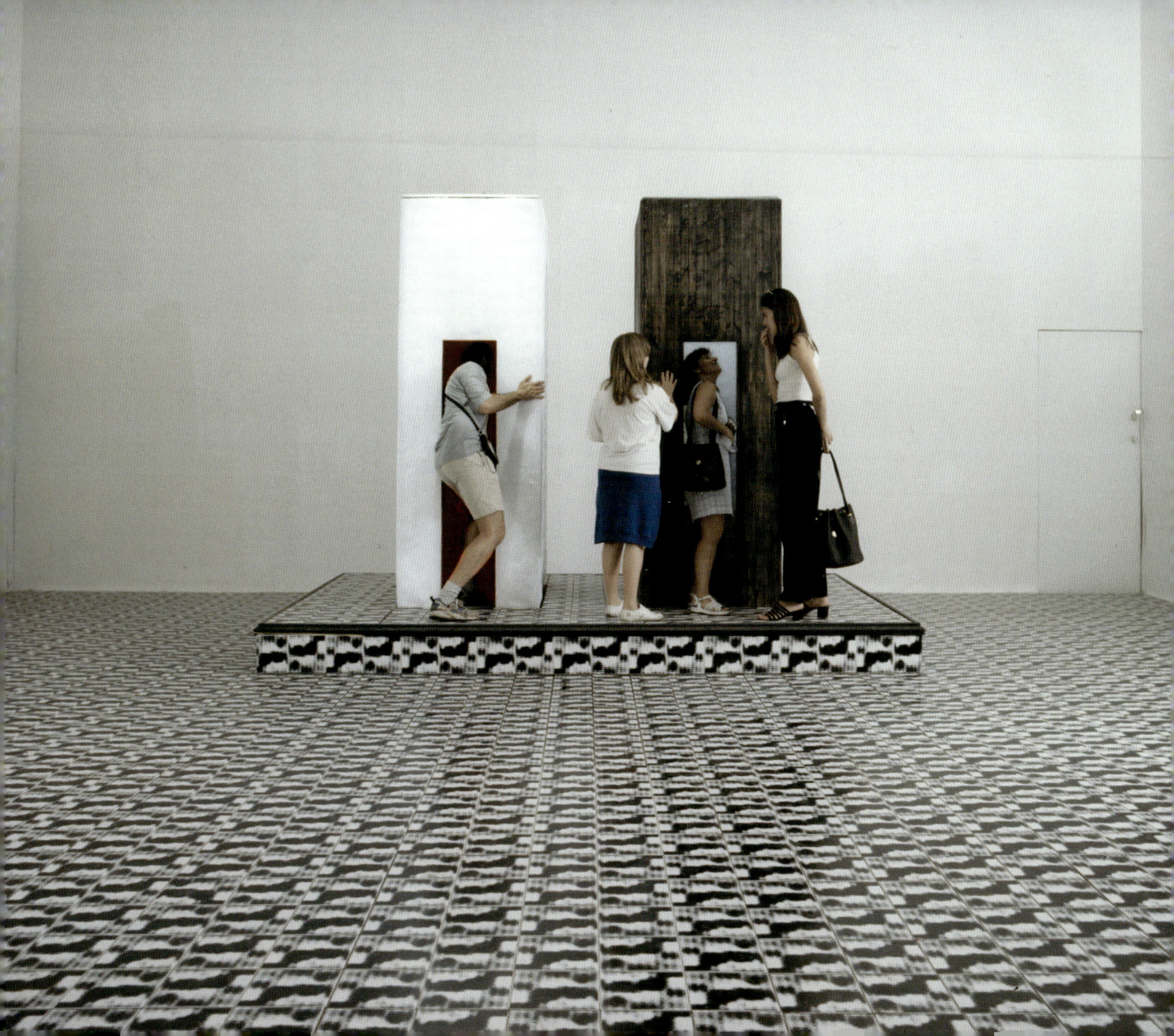

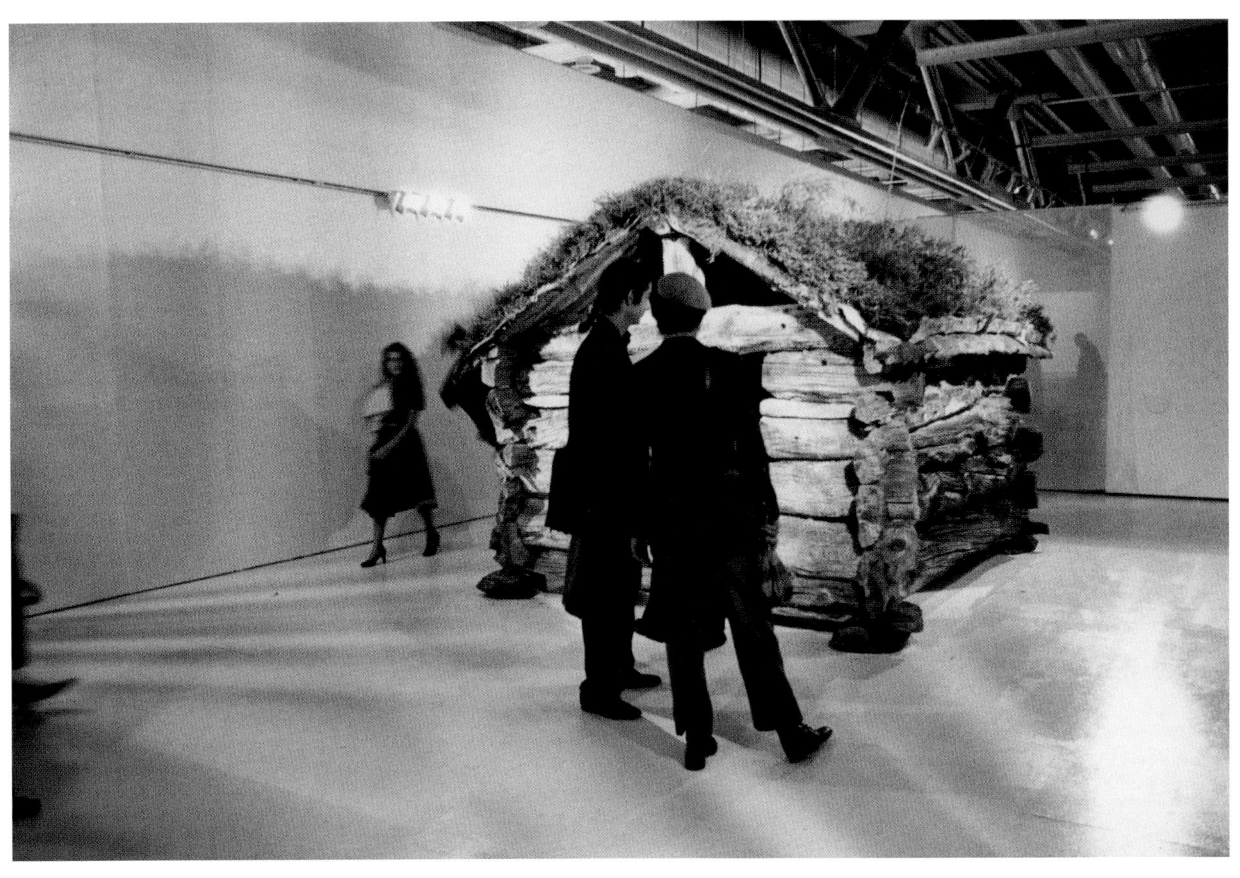

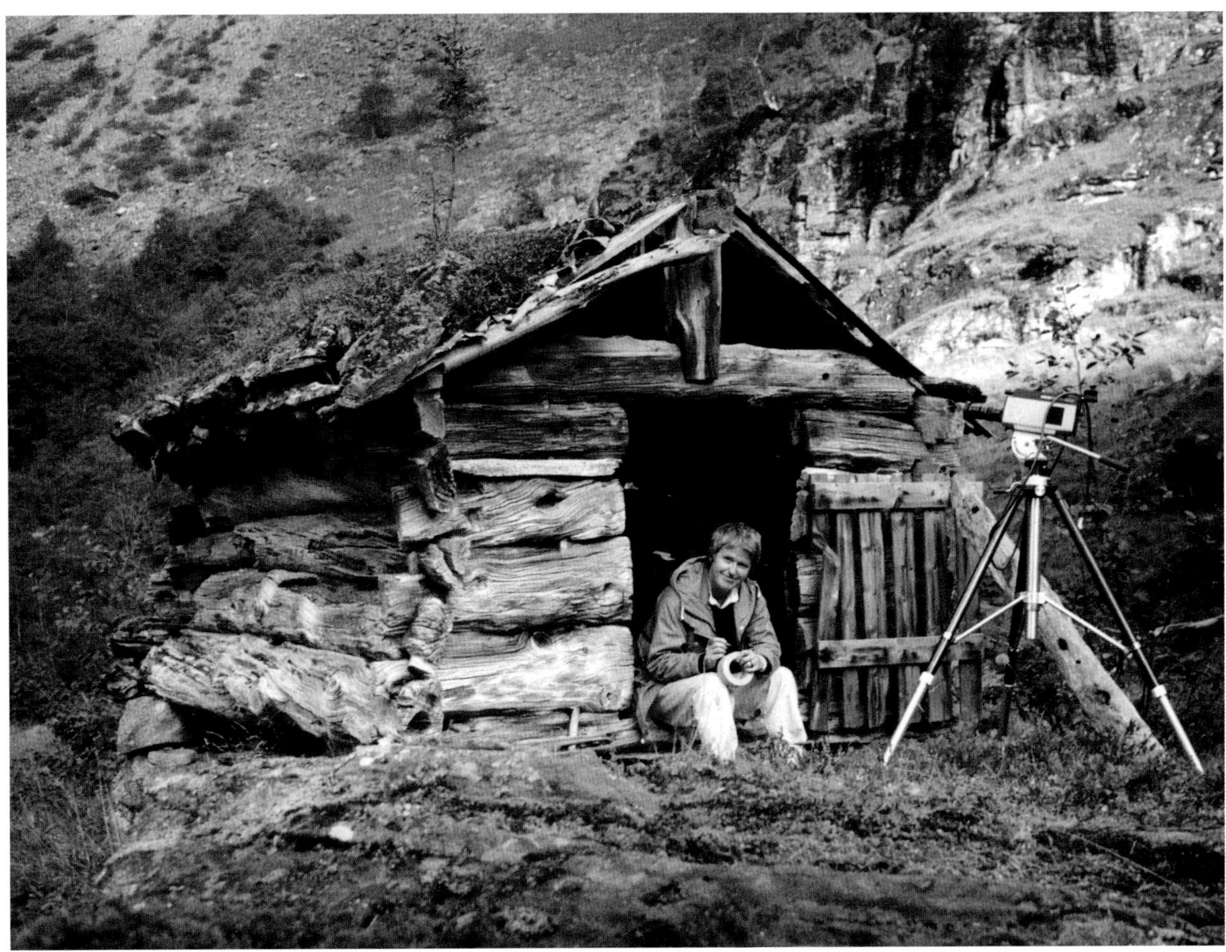

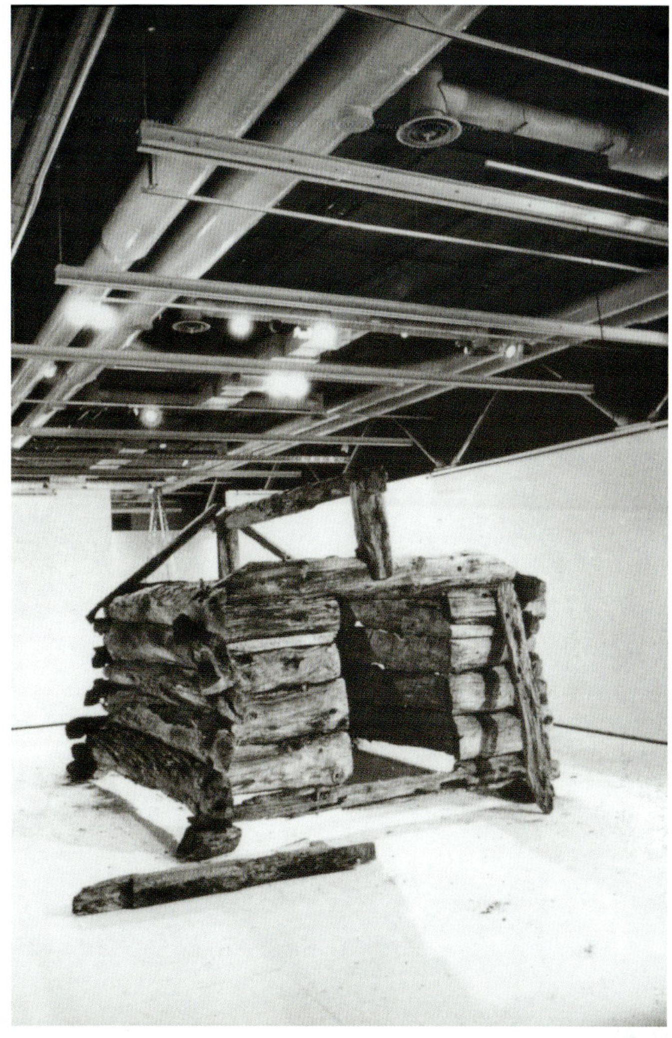

Project Gjerdeløa, 1980. Site-specific installation. Centre Georges Pompidou, Paris, France and Tafjord, Norway.

Mounting of *Project Gjerdeløa*, 1980. Centre Georges Pompidou, Paris, France.

Project Gjerdeløa, 1980. Centre Georges Pompidou, Paris, France. Detail

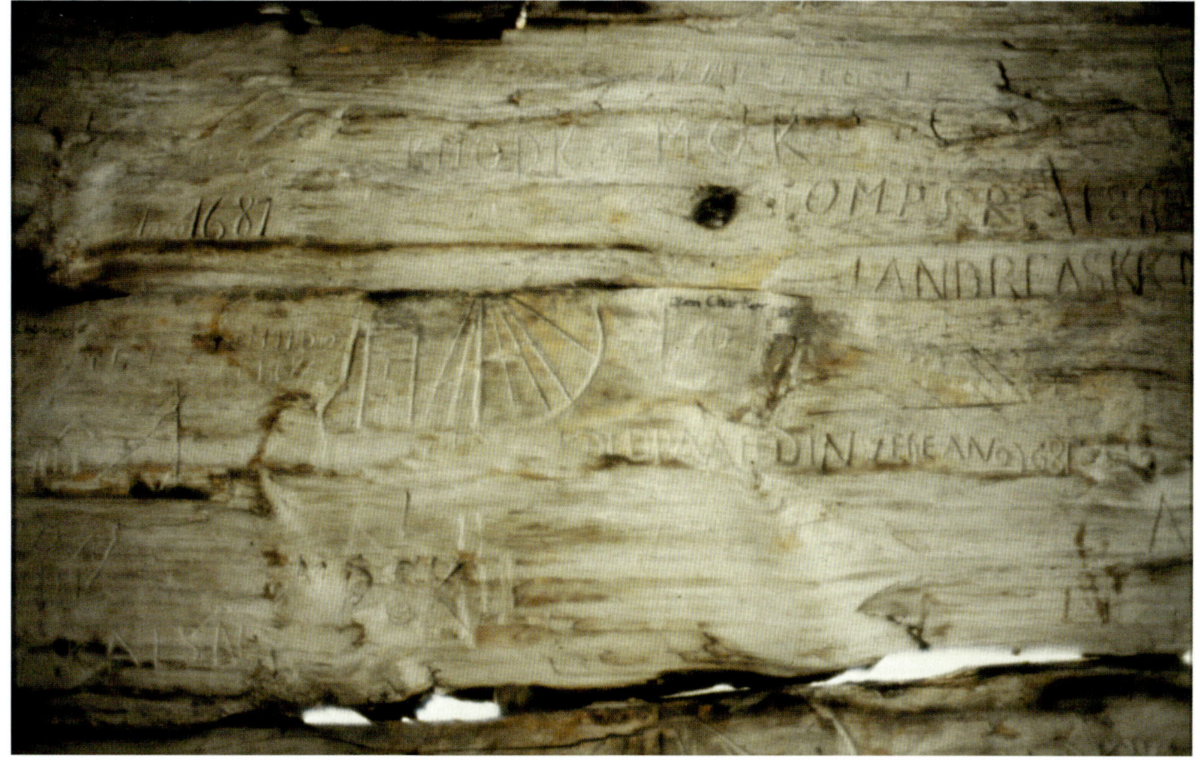

Project Gjerdeløa, 1980.
En route to Paris. Centre
Georges Pompidou, Paris,
France.

Marianne Heske's childhood
home in Tafjord, Norway.

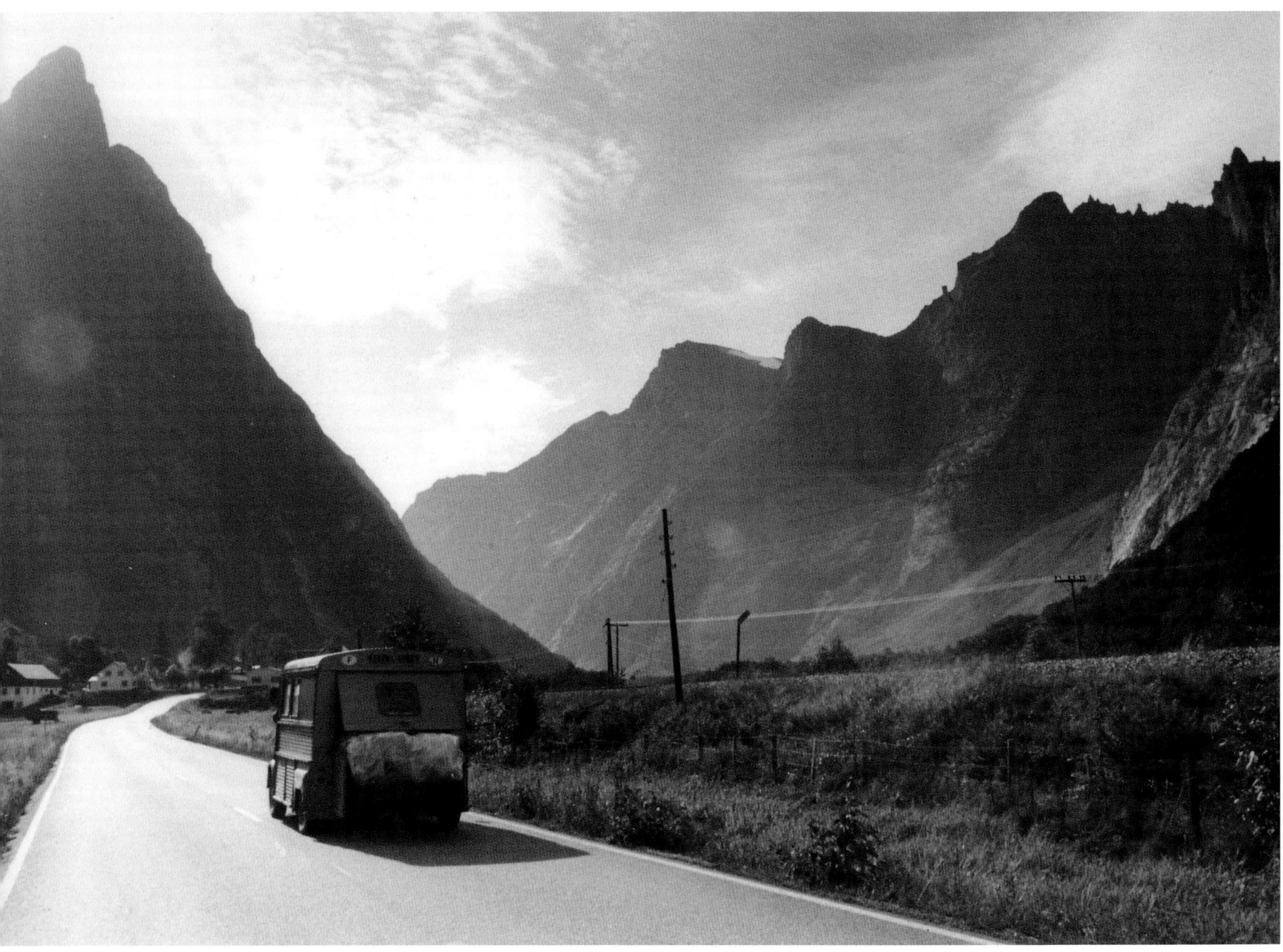

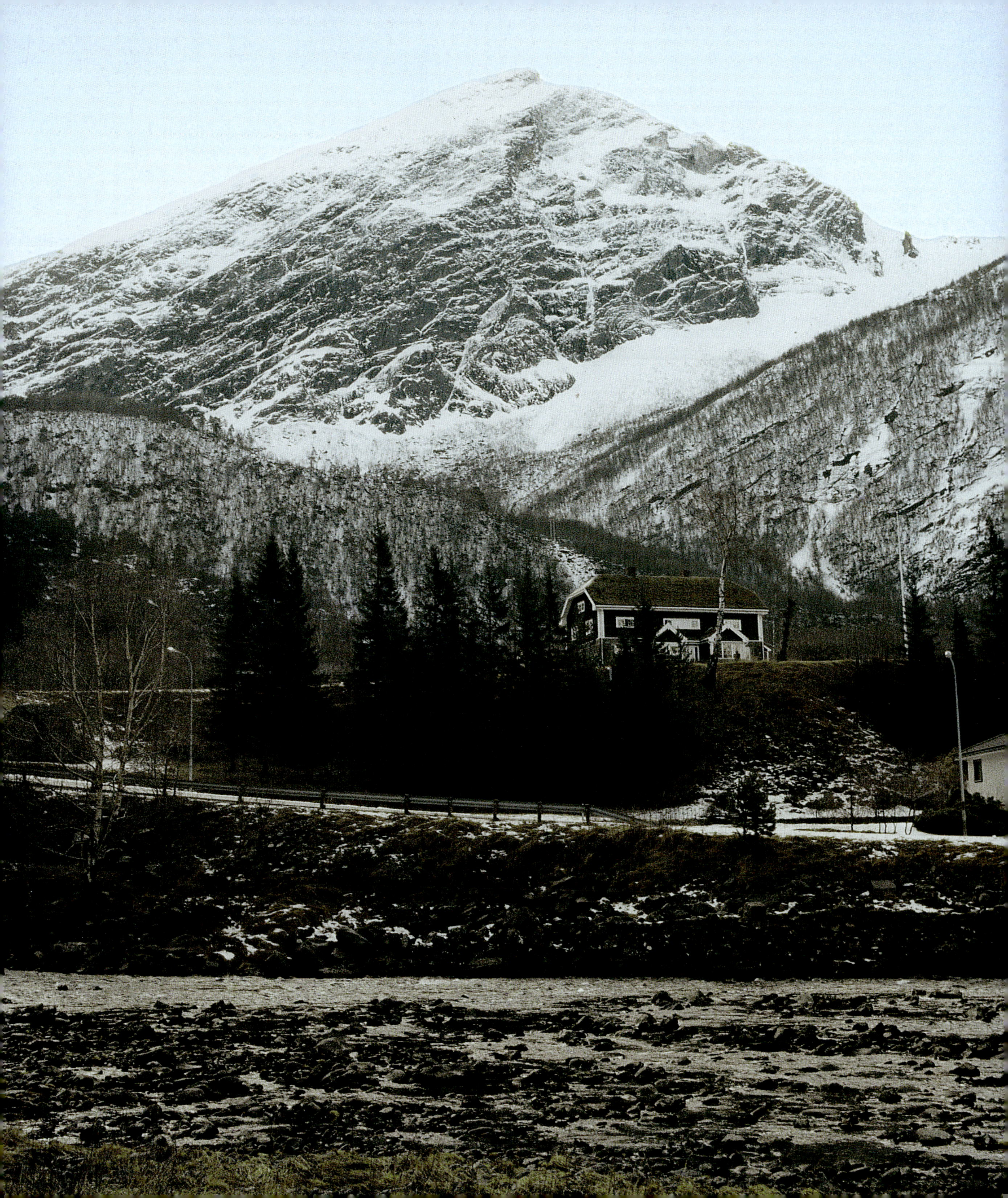

**Marianne Heske and Jon Fosse interviewed
by Hans Ulrich Obrist**

Hans Ulrich: First of all, thank you very much for making yourselves available to do this telephone conversation. I'm very interested in this dialogue between the two of you. I've been reading an account of your two works and it made me wonder how your dialogue started.
Marianne: I think our dialogue started because we share a similar background. We both come from fjords, from remote villages where we have experienced the isolated farms along the fjords. There is something very unique about the houses in the region where we both grew up. We have both made observations about the people living in the loneliness of these houses, their search for happiness, you know, and their sorrows and life and death and how life goes on generation after generation. I think we have something in common there.
Hans Ulrich: Jon could you maybe comment on that?
Jon: I agree with Marianne. I think it's very significant to grow up in such a landscape as the Norwegian fjords. The natural surroundings are quite impressive, and perhaps as a result, the way people act towards one another is somewhat strange. People from that region of Norway are not very talkative, and all over the western part of Norway they use a lot of irony. People never say what they really mean, only something close to it.
Marianne: I use words more metaphorically, and then I experience that people try to translate the metaphors. In our work we both use this "non-spoken fjord language" which is really difficult to translate.
Hans Ulrich: And how did you actually meet? When did you start talking? Can you tell me about that?
Marianne: Meeting is not necessarily about talking, but I called Jon because I had been thinking about it for years. We were supposed to have a project together about ten years ago—I don't know if you remember that, Jon—I *was* preparing for an exhibition but ended up not being able to do it. But also I was thinking about contacting him because I recognize myself in his work. So I contacted him, and that was only one week ago. We had a nice meeting and he generously proposed his piece called *Freedom* for this book. So, this book includes a kind of premiere of this piece.

Jon: Of course I have known Marianne's work for years, but I don't think we had met before we met a week ago. So I'm happy because of that, Marianne.
Marianne: Yes, I'm very happy as well. Hans Ulrich, do you know what we were discussing for a long time? We both have boats where we can observe what is happening on the land. I think we have something in common there too.
Jon: Oh yes, that might well be. I love to sail with my boat along the western coast of Norway.
Hans Ulrich: I think that's very interesting. The question I want to ask you is about the studio, because obviously ever since the sixties there has been a lot of talk about post-studio practice and artistic practice no longer being bound to a studio. It is interesting that you talk about both of you having boats. In the context of post-studio practice, I would like to know your thoughts on the boat as studio; because I met some years ago the late architect Ralph Erskine. You know, he was one of the key members of the Team 10 of architects. He came from England and had immigrated to Sweden very early in the twentieth century, and he had his architecture office on a boat. During the summer he would always work on the boat with all his assistants, and they drew buildings on that boat and they went wherever they were needed. So, talking about travel, about the house, about your boats, what is the importance of the studio and where is the place you most prefer to work?
Marianne: Well, speaking for myself first, I think I create all my works while on the move, while travelling. That of course is connected with my background, my childhood. We moved back and forth between two houses, one on the fjord and one out by the coast. So we travelled by boat and car. During this time I observed so many houses and made observations about the people who lived in them. Since then, I started to move houses myself. First I moved a very old log cabin from Tafjord, a small village on the fjord, to Centre Pompidou in Paris. The house is an empty container, but still a house made of

timber. The only traces of people in the house are the inscriptions on the timber walls that show the lives of people passing by. From that point on I continued to move houses. For example, the project *Voyage Pittoresque* was a video installation, a kind of tent-like house that was moved around in Scandinavia and in Europe. Basically it was a "travelling video installation" in a tent. After that I moved around two ice houses. The same thing goes for the houses I built on the Wilhelm Reich orgone theory, which were related to the idea of energy in containers in the form of houses. In my approach I sought to question concepts about inside-outside, internal-external, and vice-versa. Of course, the project was also about moving something non-concrete, like temperature. So, the project was not so much about the houses as such. I was interested in moving non-tactile things. In a sense, I was moving illusions. My interest in houses, or shelters, continues through my most recent house in Oslo, and Hans Ulrich, you were the person who really pushed me to take the initiative with the Norwegian building company Selvaag, who provided me with an actual house to embody the dolls and their mind-projections. I also included a human skull in the project, and a life-size bronze bust of the doll's head, which is the archetype for all the other dolls in my work. The metaphor of a doll or a marionette is the oldest symbol in mankind, mirroring the human being. Of course, the skull represents reality, and the bronze bust is inscribed with human faculties that are projected by scientists about the human mind. So basically it's all about illusions, projections and the force of mankind expressed in a playful way. So I think Jon is interested in some of the same ideas in his work. I saw his piece last week called *Svevn* in Norwegian, *Sommeil* in French and *Sleep* in English. The play is about a flat where people move in and out through different generations. It's about life and death.

Jon: For me writing in itself is a form of travel. When I'm writing I enter the unknown. So for me it's very important not to travel when I'm writing. I have tried it and it's impossible. Some years ago I was on the road a lot, over half the year, going to performances here and there. I tried to write during travelling but it just doesn't work. I don't get the concentration I need. It becomes too much for me. I have a cottage north of Bergen, an old fragile building, not what one would call a beautiful place, but I have an empty room with a sweeping view of the fjord, and I have done most of my writing in later years in this cottage. The state I enter when I am on my boat along the beautiful coastline is quite close to the state I enter also when I'm writing. So doing both at the same time would be too much for me. I get confused and nervous by it.

Hans Ulrich: I found it interesting that Marianne mentioned the presence of the house in your work. Could you tell me about the link between writing and architecture, and how writing and space are related?

Jon: For sure they are related. It is at least obvious when writing for the theatre. I've been living and writing in different houses over the years and I've experienced that in some houses I just cannot write. For instance, I had a house here in Bergen for several years and there were quite a few rooms in that house. I tried to write in each and every room but it was completely impossible to write in that house. I can't explain it but for me it is so. But now, in a tiny little cottage I manage to write very well and I think it has to do with a sense of security or shelter that is necessary for writing. A house can both give you shelter and inspire you to write, but one needs some kind of protection from the house to be able to write. My experience is that an old house can either be a perfect place for writing or it can be impossible to write there. I'm living in a new flat right now. It's an okay place for writing, quite good in fact. I don't know how to explain it but I just know it. So it is.

Marianne: It's funny because for me it's completely the opposite. I've had different ideas sometimes when I'm driving through landscapes or sitting on an airplane on the way to New York for instance. I like spacious, nonlimiting surroundings where I can observe what is going on around me. But I need to be alone.

Jon: I need to make my surroundings smaller. I prefer a small and empty room for writing if possible. More like a cave in a way.

Hans Ulrich: I wonder if there might be something relevant in terms of the importance of the house and the very basics of a form of shelter, the manner of living in both of your works. I wonder if this might have to do with a certain intensity of the experience as it relates to the here and now. There have been a lot of clichés out there about this idea, particularly related to Strindberg and all that. But still I think the anti-idea of the cliché is an interesting digression here, and one that relates to this very important notion of intensity of experience. Could you talk a little bit about this?

Marianne: I can definitely say something about that in relation to my experience of Jon's work. You cannot compare his work to the clichés about this Nordic image. I think that Jon and I each have our own personal way of approaching this issue. We share a very rare experience that is hard for non-Norwegians to understand. The unique experience Jon and I share from having lived by the fjord and having experienced the loneliness of those isolated houses has provided us with special insight. In our work, we reveal the small glowing points of life that you might see from the boat. Scattered inhabitation like this is so rare. I don't think Strindberg ever experienced anything like that. Not Munch either because, as far as I know, they were never there. Ibsen has written a little about this in his plays about the loneliness of people living in very isolated places and thinking that their little community is the whole world. So it's a very intimate and at the same time universal topic.

Jon: In my writing the house plays a very important part. The house as a motif and different scenes connected to the house—looking out the window for instance, looking at the fjords. It's a basic motif. In the play Marianne mentioned, *Sleep*, it's the flat that somehow talks. In a short novel that I wrote, *Das ist*

Alise, first published in Germany, there's an old house that may well be located in the western part of Norway which somehow tells the story not as a house but through its persons. It's very hard to understand why some motifs are so crucial in one's own writing. Of course it's very easy to imagine that it has to do with the bad weather around here and the importance of shelter. But of course it isn't that simple.

Hans Ulrich: In both of your works there is this moment of dialogue that happens, like in Jon's work there is this very intense dialogue. It might be someone like Claude Régy and there is obviously a big difference between that and the activity of writing because you're first of all a novelist and a writer. I always thought of writing as an authoritative activity. And the same question I would like to ask of Marianne is how you relate on the one hand, to it being an authoritative activity and it being a dialogue. What about the notion of collaboration in both of your practices?

Jon: Of course writing is a very lonely thing, and it ought to be. When I started to write for the theatre it was a really great experience for me to be taken out of this loneliness and to be able to share art with someone else. It wasn't at all painful to see my work done on the stage. It was a great relief. If it's a good production I don't feel at all that my writing is weakened or anything, on the contrary, it becomes stronger. For instance this production of Régy in Paris is strong in its interpretation, the director's voice is quite present. At the same time it is completely loyal to my writing. My plays can be done in many different ways of course, but if it's a great production it's a great common experience in art and of art. It becomes dialogue on each and every level. To me the best metaphor for writing is listening and I think a great director is also basically listening, to the text, to the actors, in order to make something that is not himself. Basically, writing for me is an act of listening and when you are listening you are naturally in a kind of dialogue.

Marianne: I feel the same as you more or less. I also feel like an observer and that is very lonely because I observe in silence, yet after a while I would like to share my observations and to be creative and contribute something to the world even though I know this sounds very naive. Most of my art is interactive, like walking in and out of the houses, like the ice houses in São Paulo and in Atlanta, the orgone houses in Düsseldorf and Berlin, and walking in and out of the house at Centre Pompidou and touching the walls. It feels very lonely to have these ideas and to express them publicly, but it's all about sharing and observing.

Hans Ulrich: Earlier you mentioned this notion of direct engagement with the work. How much do you think the viewer does? Is it half? Is it more? And Jon, you have talked about these intense "Olympian" moments. Even if they are inexplicable there are moments of *entente,* moments of responding between the public and the author, and as you write beautifully in your text there are moments when the author and the public experience something together that makes them both understand something they did not understand before.

Jon: Of course if you are working with theatre you will soon learn that the performance can change a lot from one night to another and to a large degree this has to do with the audience. Different audiences somehow change the spirit of everything. How important this is depends on the production. If there is a very strict production, as for instance the productions of Régy, the audience doesn't influence it that much I would say. But if you have a less strictly structured production the audience can change the meaning of it, they can turn a very tragic moment into a comical moment. That's a very strange thing. My writing is a kind of tragicomical writing. One night a moment can be a very funny moment, another night a very sad moment. This has to do with the audience and the interaction between the performers and the audience.

Marianne: What you are saying now is really the essence of my art. Because it's about how it's interpreted. How it's perceived. It's incredible how people can interpret things also as you say in a completely opposite way. We all project so many different things onto the work. My little doll's head for instance is all about projections and illusions. So I leave it open for people to project their own illusions onto it. In the same way, the houses I move around are also about people being free to interpret them, which they invariably do. I don't want to put any limits on it. And maybe that is why my works are timeless. It's about perceptions. My last house, *A Doll's House*, was also about projections and how people perceive these projections. It's a never-ending circle.

Hans Ulrich: Can you tell me about projects that have yet to be realized, projects you haven't had the time to do, and projects that might never be realized?

Jon: I want to go back and write more prose, and perhaps write one more really long novel. Right now I'm writing so much for the theatre that I haven't had time for it for years and I don't know when I will find time for it. But a long period with slow concentration for writing prose—that's a hope and a wish.

Hans Ulrich: Is there any kind of unwritten novel—a novel you have thought of and haven't written yet?

Jon: I don't write like that. I have to have an empty mind when I sit down and then the writing just happens. I don't plan in advance.

Marianne: Neither do I, I let it happen by itself and the house that stands in Oslo is a typical example of this. It just happened after our discussion, Hans Ulrich. Suddenly the house is there. It's filled not only with dolls—there aren't as many dolls as I thought there should be. Instead I've filled it with projections that symbolize all kinds of human emotions like desire, hope, fear and happiness—all these constantly changing mental states that are found in the walls of every house. As you say Jon, some houses you can write in and other houses you can't write in, so I think you would have difficulties writing in this house in Oslo with all the projections. It would be very disturbing. At the same time the skull is there and the bronze bust, which represents eternity. It's very important to have the bronze bust. But the skull is there next to it so it's about the projections and the mental states. I think I would like to continue to work with projections and the ever-changing mental states of human beings and maybe also to express and symbolize that with the dolls. I'm really into mental states but also like Jon I don't plan too much what I would like to do ahead of time, it just happens. I always focus on being in the moment.

Hans Ulrich: There are just a few more questions I would like to ask. One question relates to the houses and about life and death, because obviously this idea of a house is always related to life but also death. Also, I wonder if you could both comment a little bit about the importance of memory. It's interesting to consider that our conversation this morning would not have happened without Pierre Restany, who, shortly before he died, suggested that Marianne and I should have this conversation. You could say we are having this conversation this morning in memory of Pierre Restany.

Marianne: I would say that we exist in a dance between life and death, desperately searching for the "truth", and this is a masked drama because we don't know what it's about. But we are dancing and it's behind the mask.

Jon: I think the house as a motif in my writing has a lot to do with death. For instance, in a play like *Someone Is Going To Come*, when someone enters the house they are entering a place of shelter and love but they are also somehow entering death. It's hard to explain. In a good production like Régy's this becomes obvious. But to explain it and say too much about it is difficult. It is just so.

Hans Ulrich: Now one last question about minimalism. Quoting from an interview in *Abend*, which I read in 2003, Claude Régy said: "I always react to the term minimalist. Few authors have been able to infuse so much complexity in so few words as Jon Fosse has been able to do. In fact he is not at all minimalist. His work is completely full. What is actually minimalist is the number of syllables, the fact that there are short lines often interrupted, indicated by the duration of the silence, the rhythm, the writing." So this whole idea of your work being minimalist and yet being full seems to relate to the houses in some way. Could you both comment on full minimalism?

Jon: It's an interesting concept. It's the first time I've heard this way of looking at it and at least for my writing it's a good description. It is a kind of full minimalism.

Marianne: It's also a good description of my work because I have few words. That is only the wrapping. And what Hans Ulrich is saying that even though the wrapping is very minimalistic it's so full and to me, similar to a small project like the installation of the dolls, it looks so simple because all the dolls look the same. But still it's so full that it demands a lot for the public to understand it fully and also these houses that I move around look more like tents, like houses, but still they are full even if they're empty.

Hans Ulrich: Jon, Claude Régy says that you use very few elements but at the same time create something very rich with them. Would you say then that it's about repetition?

Jon: Of course it has to do with that. But it is also about using the silence; it has to do with making the silence talk. If you compare let's say Racine to Shakespeare, you will see that Racine uses quite a few words in comparison to Shakespeare. But, at least to me, in his play *Phèdre* he is saying as much as Shakespeare is saying. So it's basically just two attitudes to writing, and both have to do with making silence speak. It's about using words but letting the silence say the rest.

Marianne: Shakespeare has famously written: "All the world's a stage and all the men and women merely players."

Jon: Basically I think there are two different attitudes to writing: for instance, the maximalism of Joyce and the minimalism of Beckett.

Hans Ulrich: Well I think that's a great conclusion so I thank you both very much for taking the time for this conversation.

Marianne: Thank you.

Jon: Thank you.

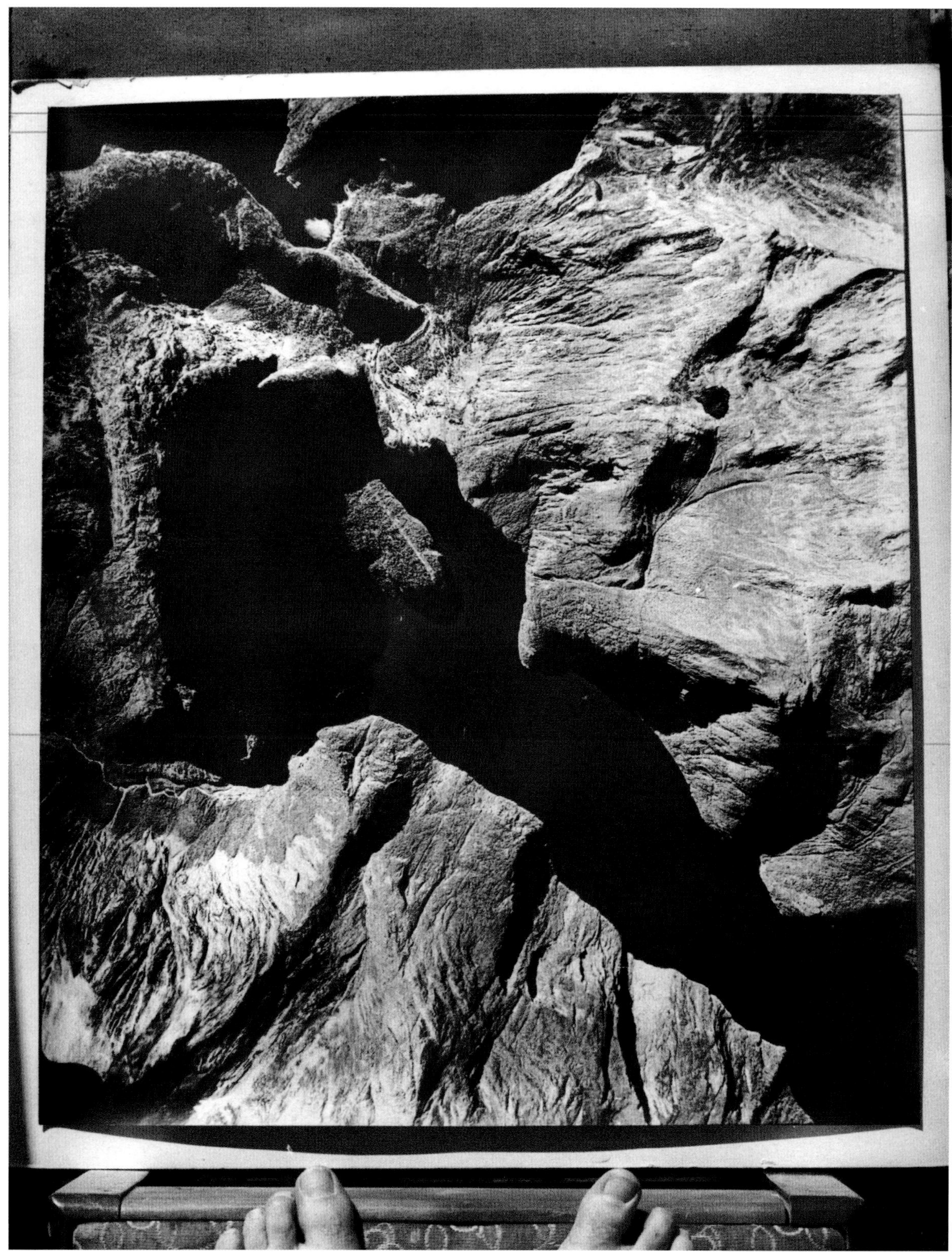

Photograph of air photo of
Tafjord with the artist's toes.

Mountain of the Mind, 1990.
Installation. Clocktower
Gallery, New York, USA.

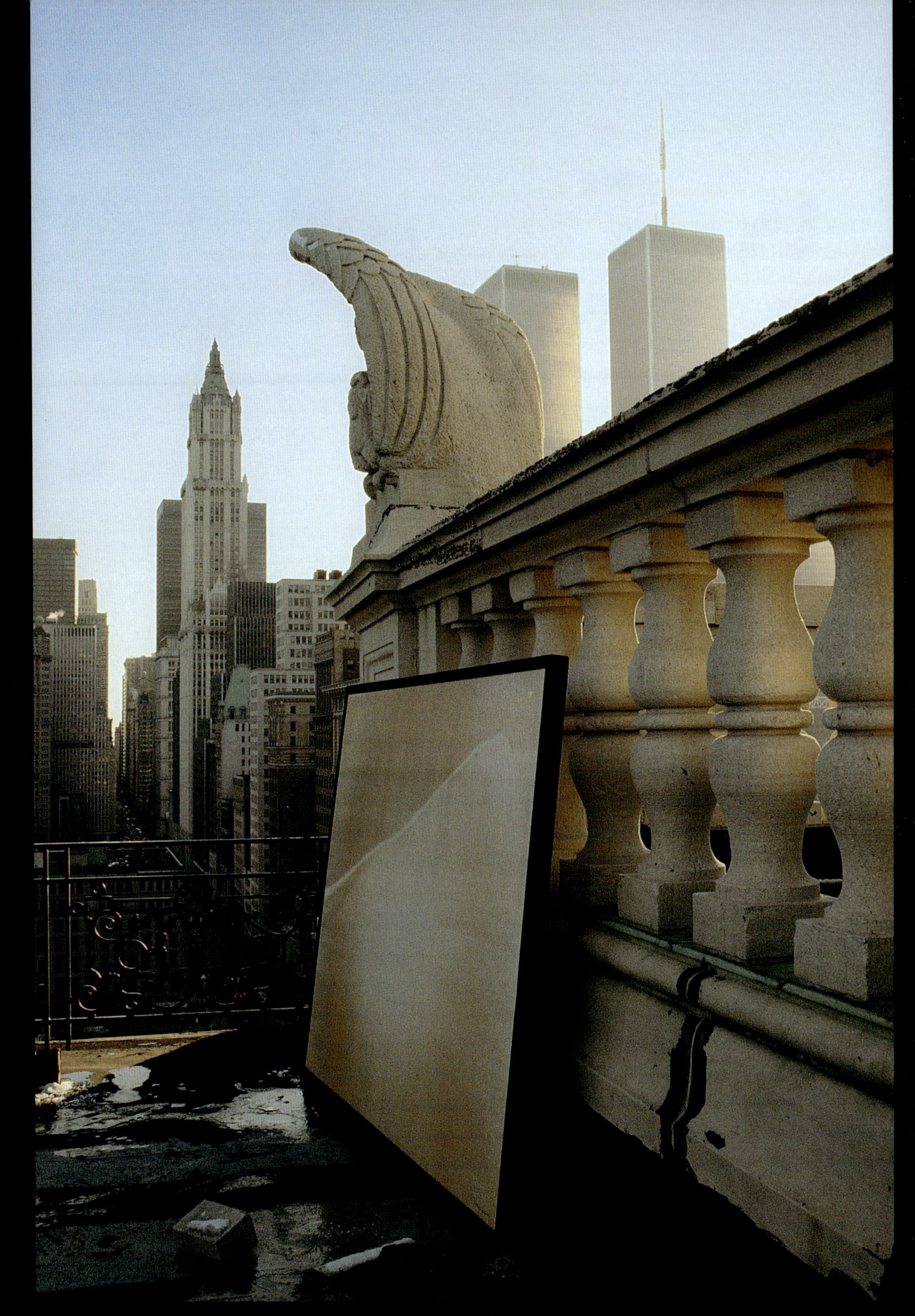

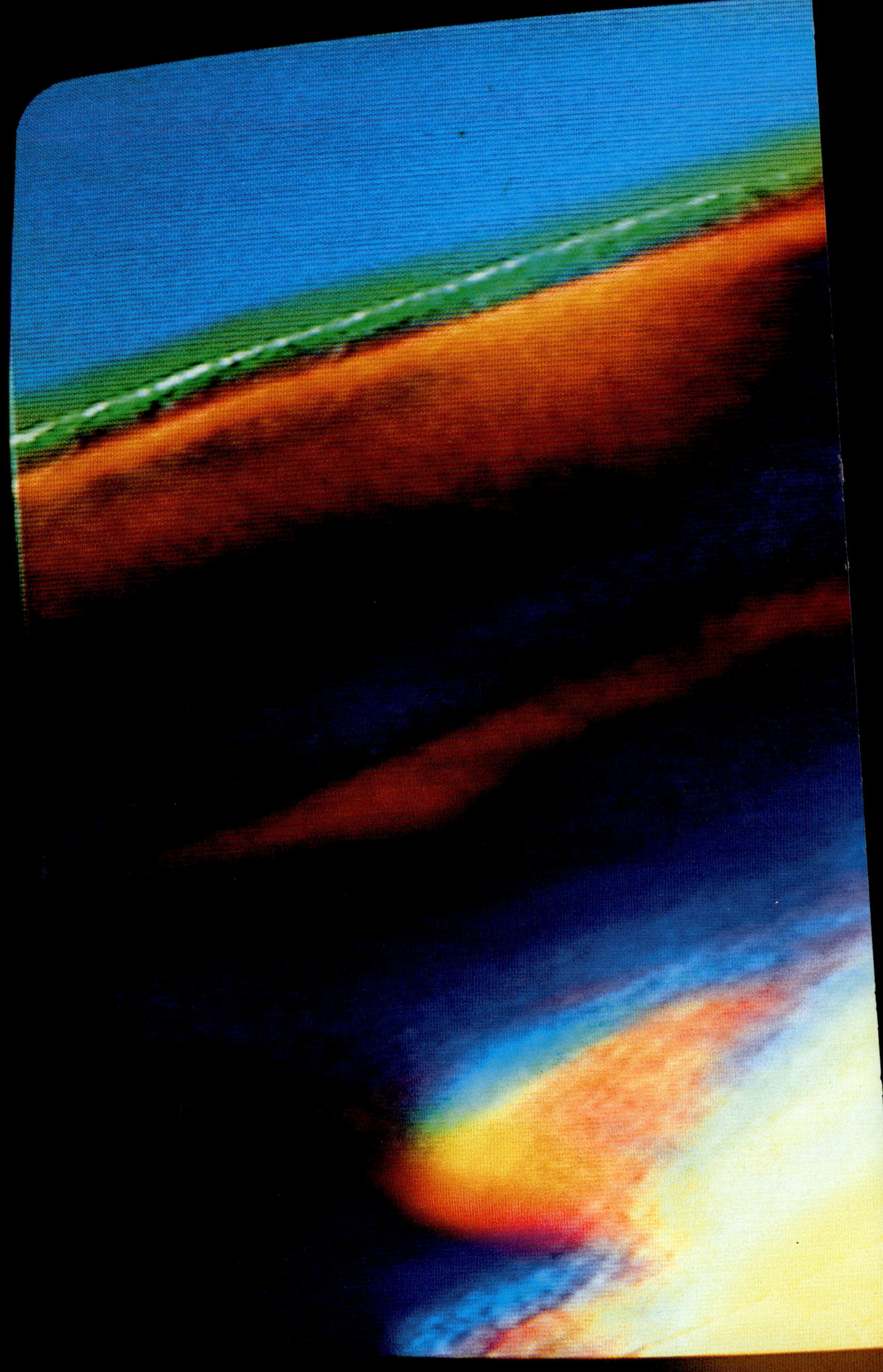

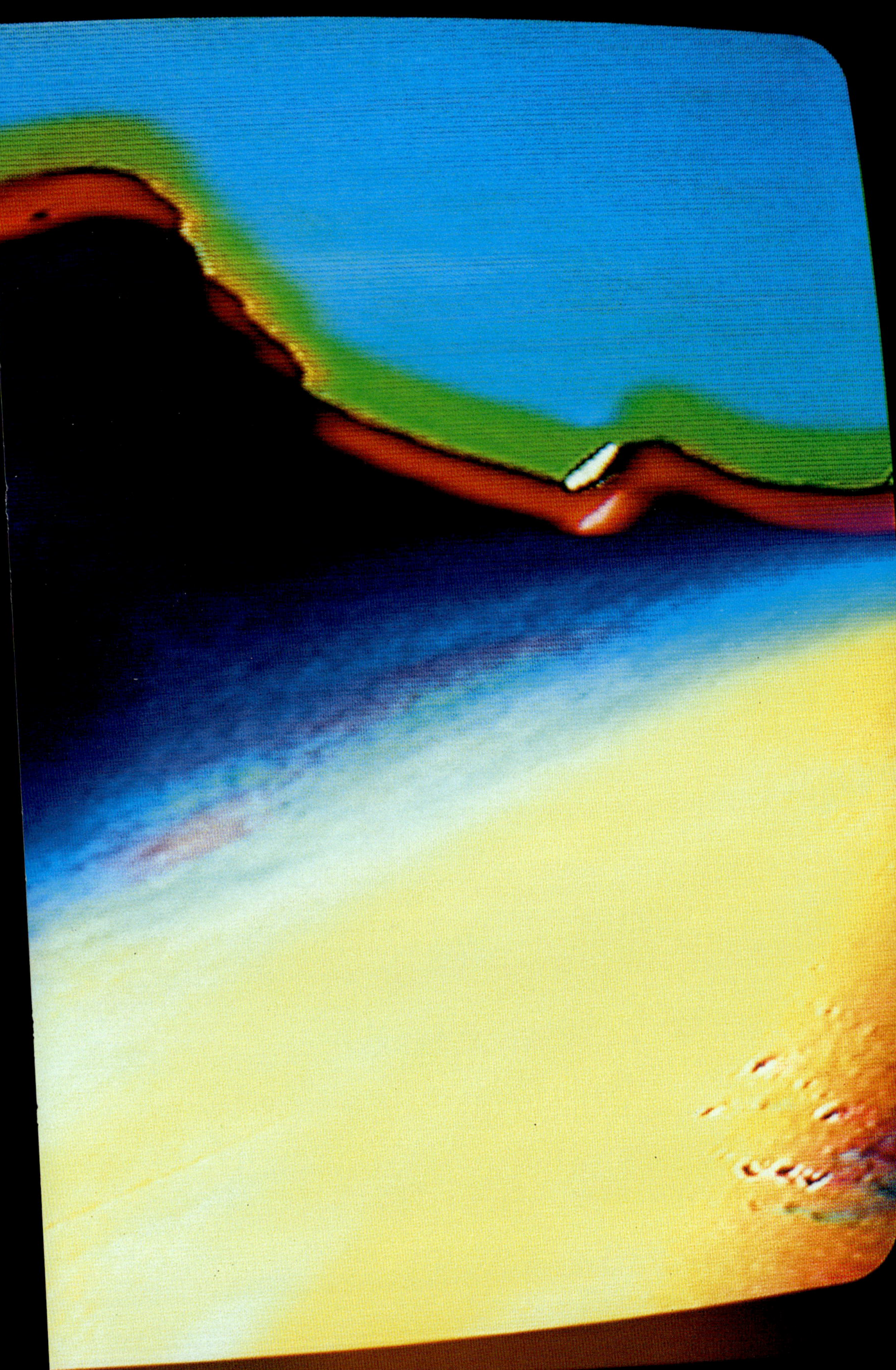

Mountain of the Mind,
undated. Video painting,
acrylic print on canvas.

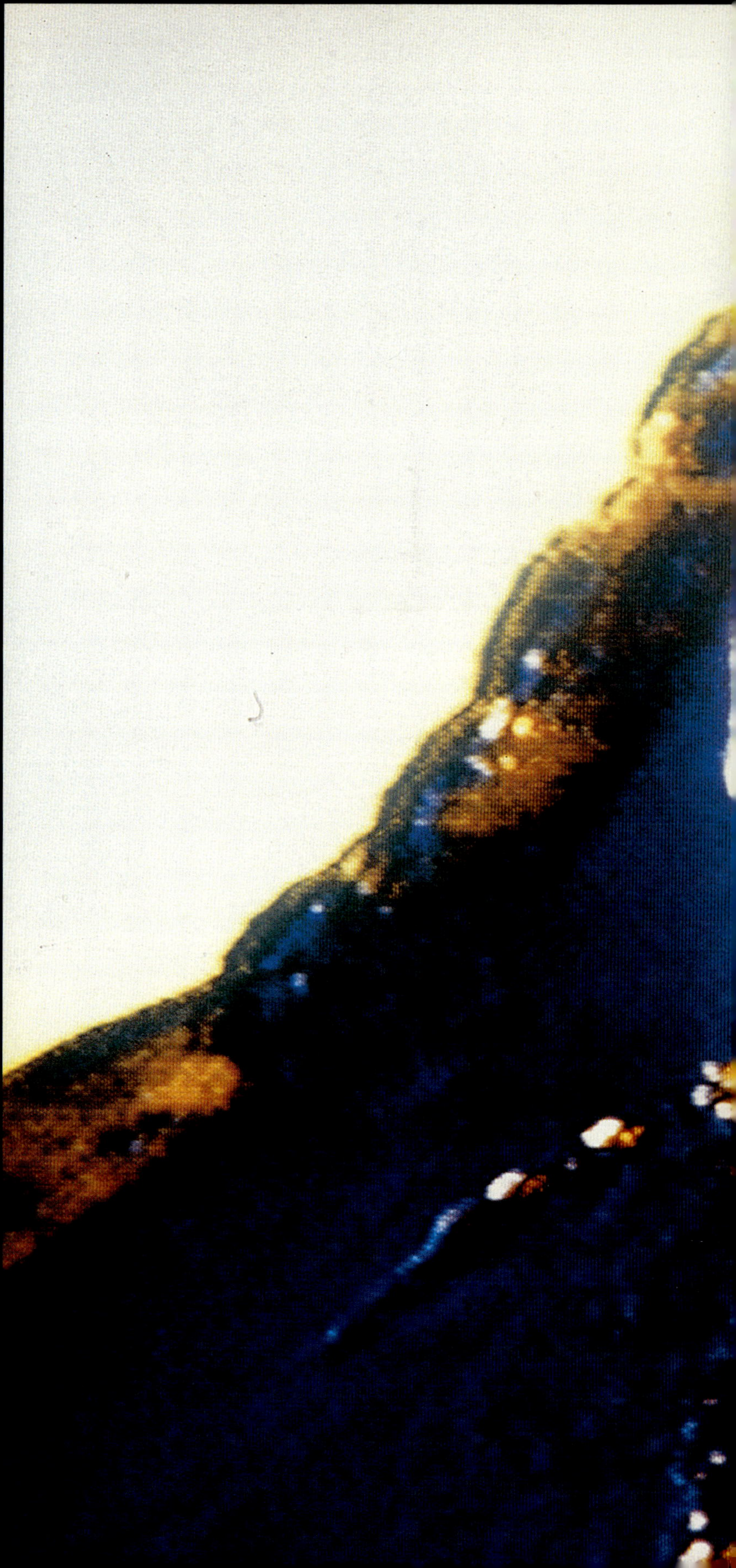

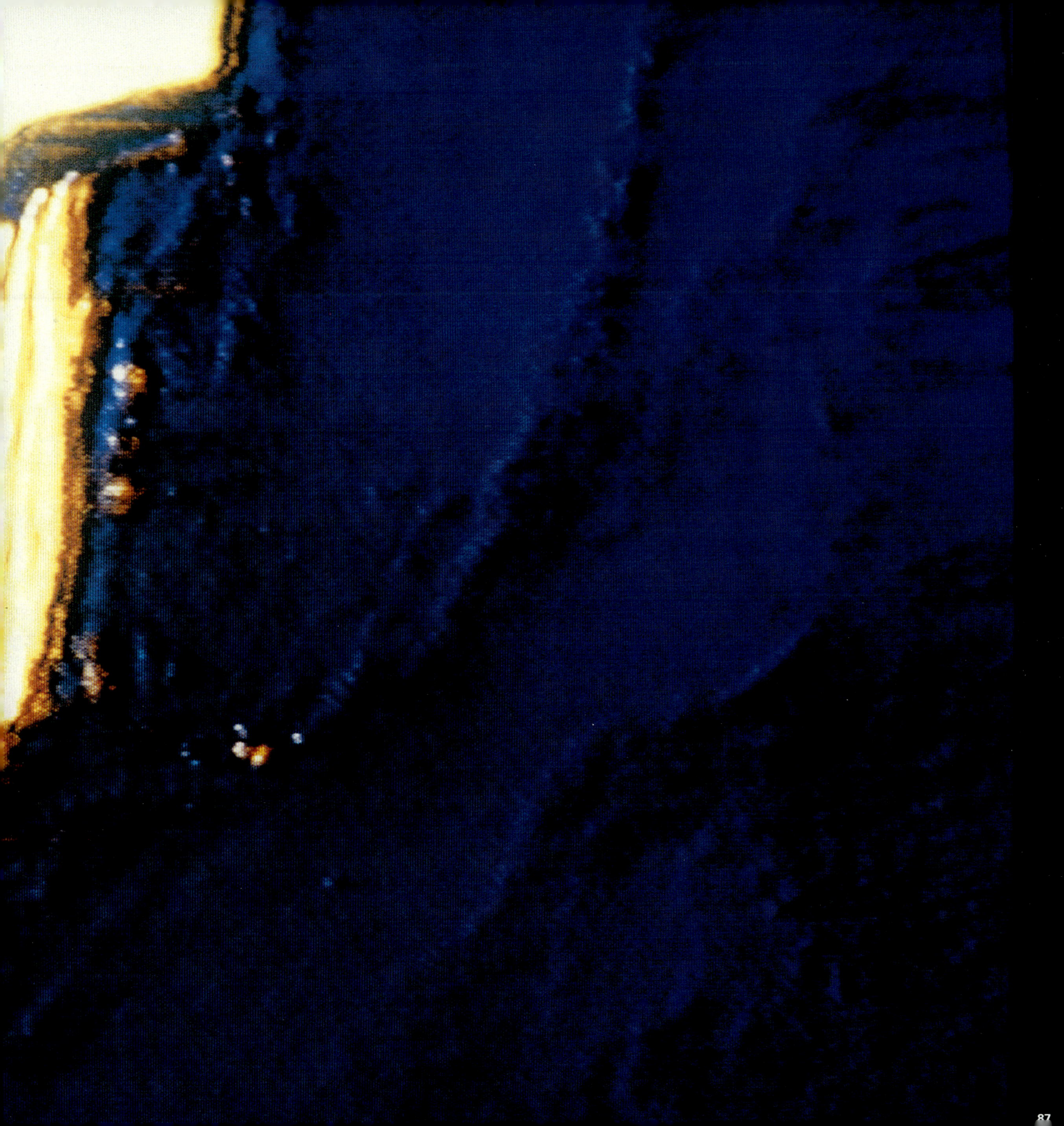

Full Moon Mountain, 2002.
Video painting, acrylic print on
canvas. Details.

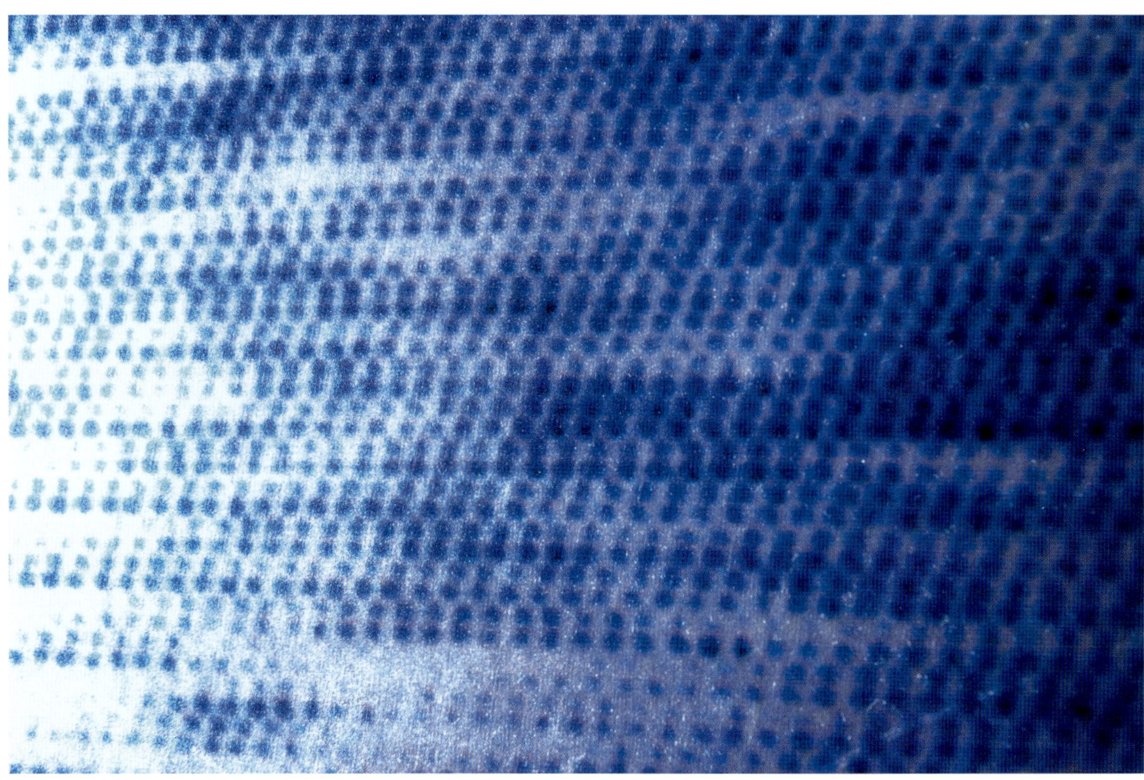

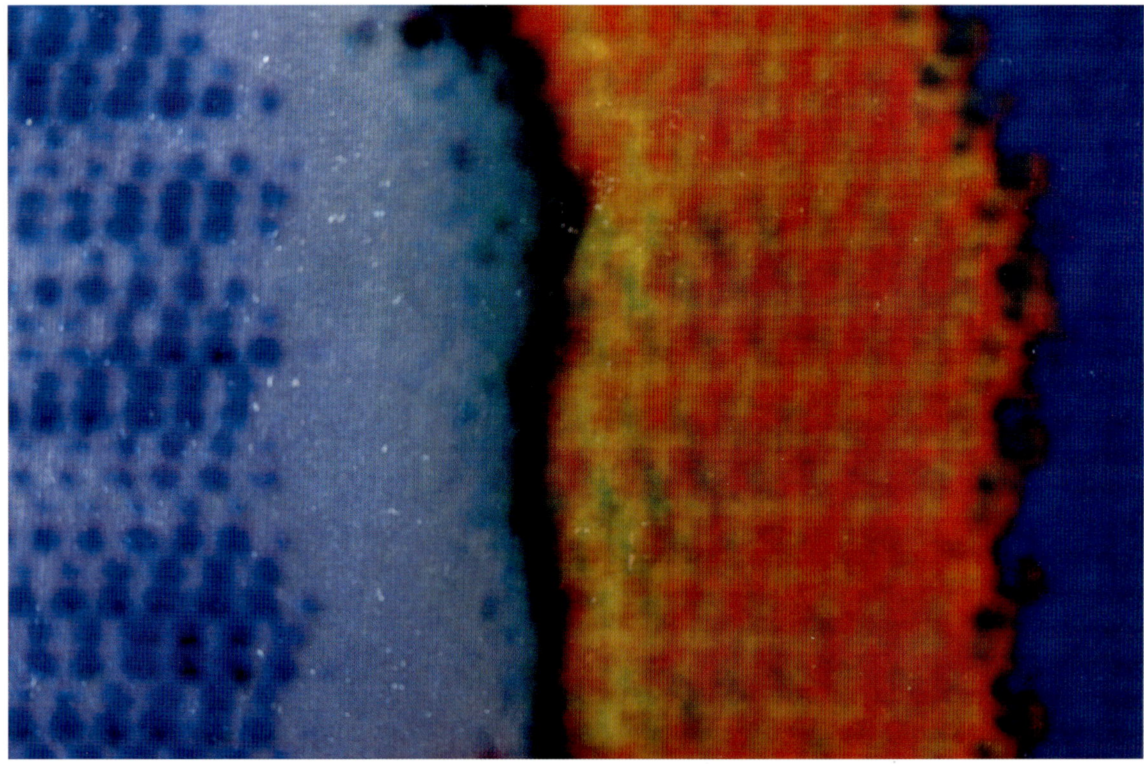

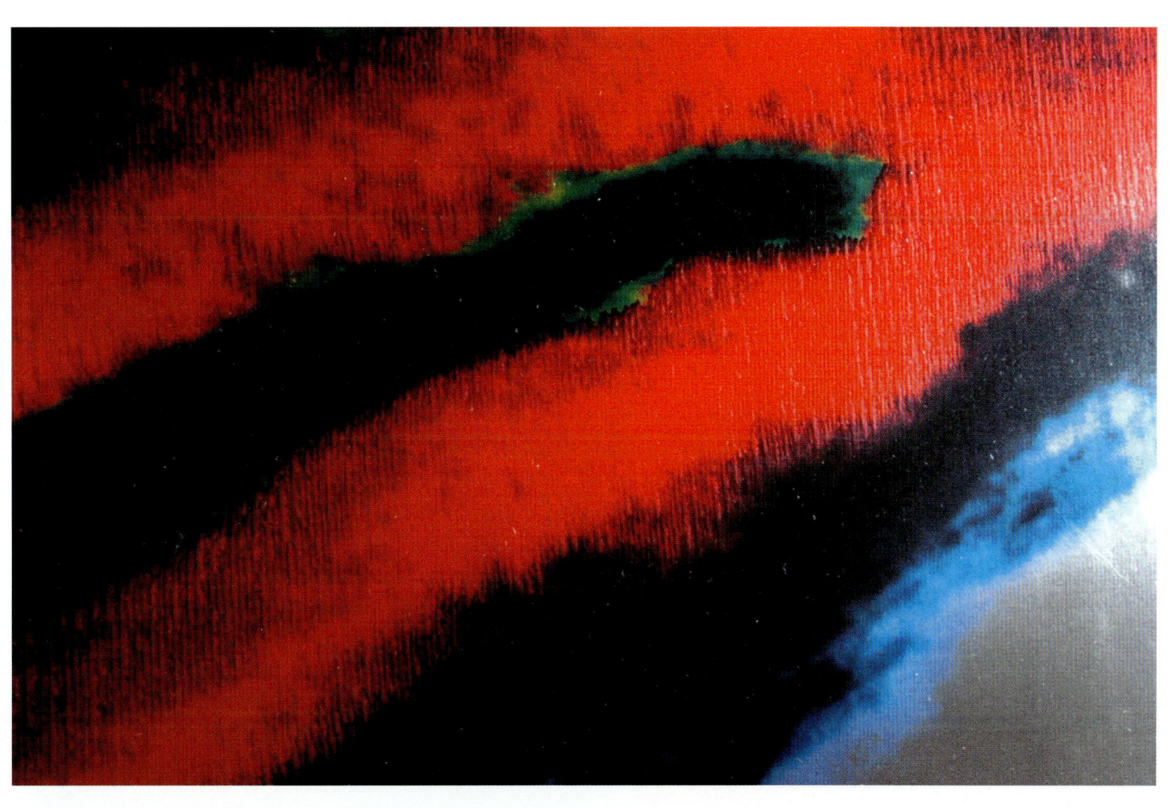

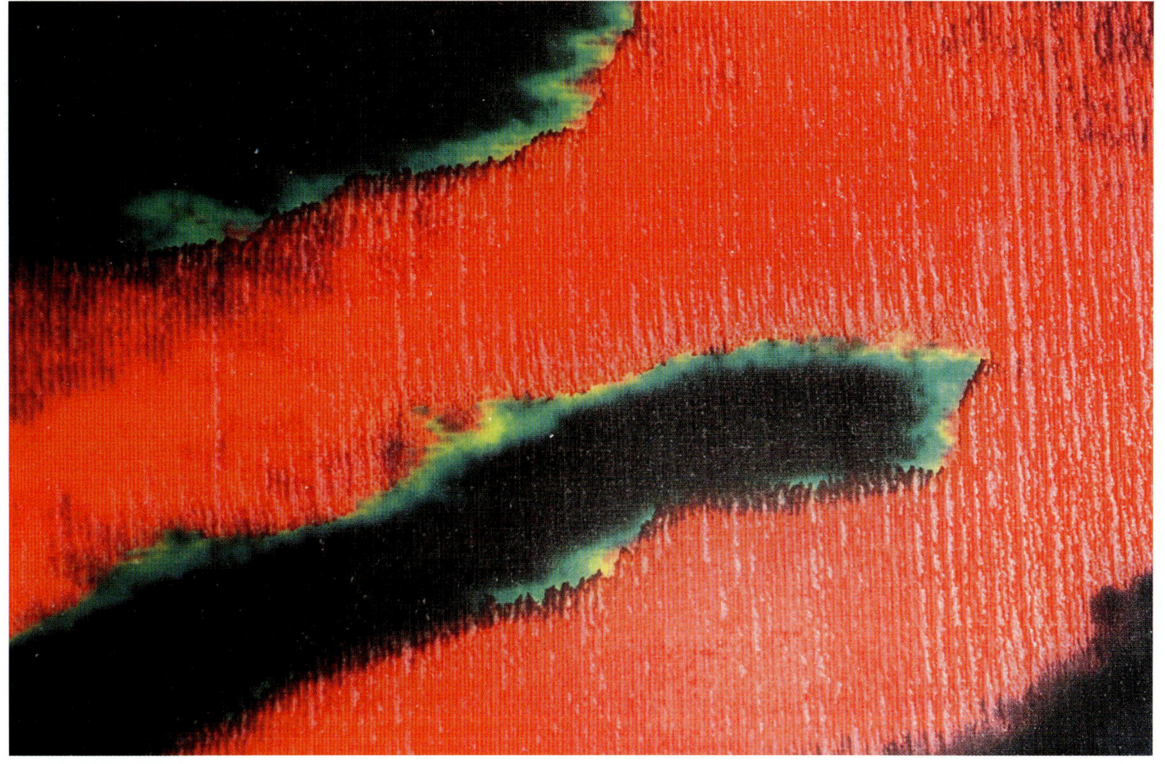

Full Moon Mountain, 2004.
Video painting, acrylic print on
canvas. Details.

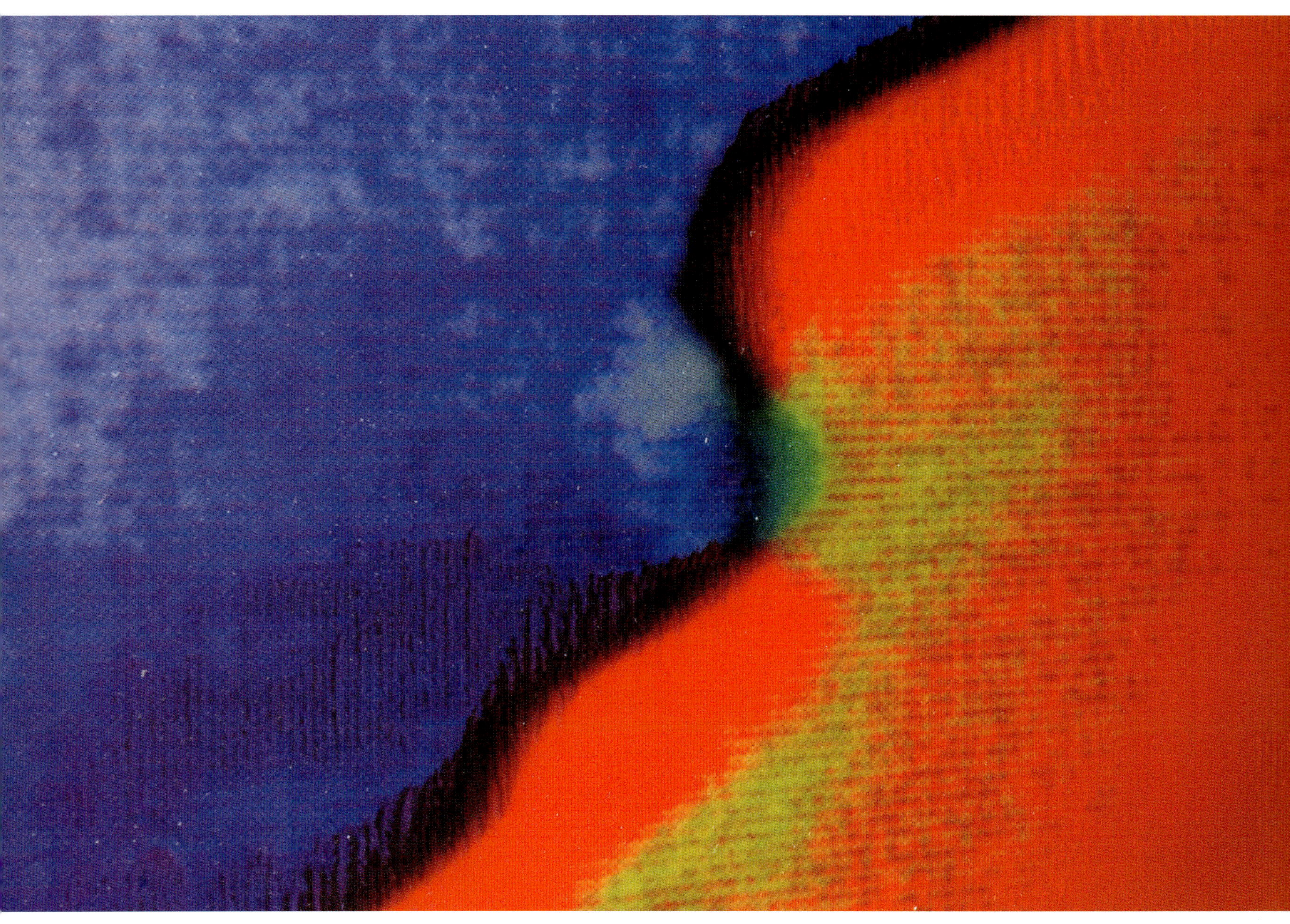

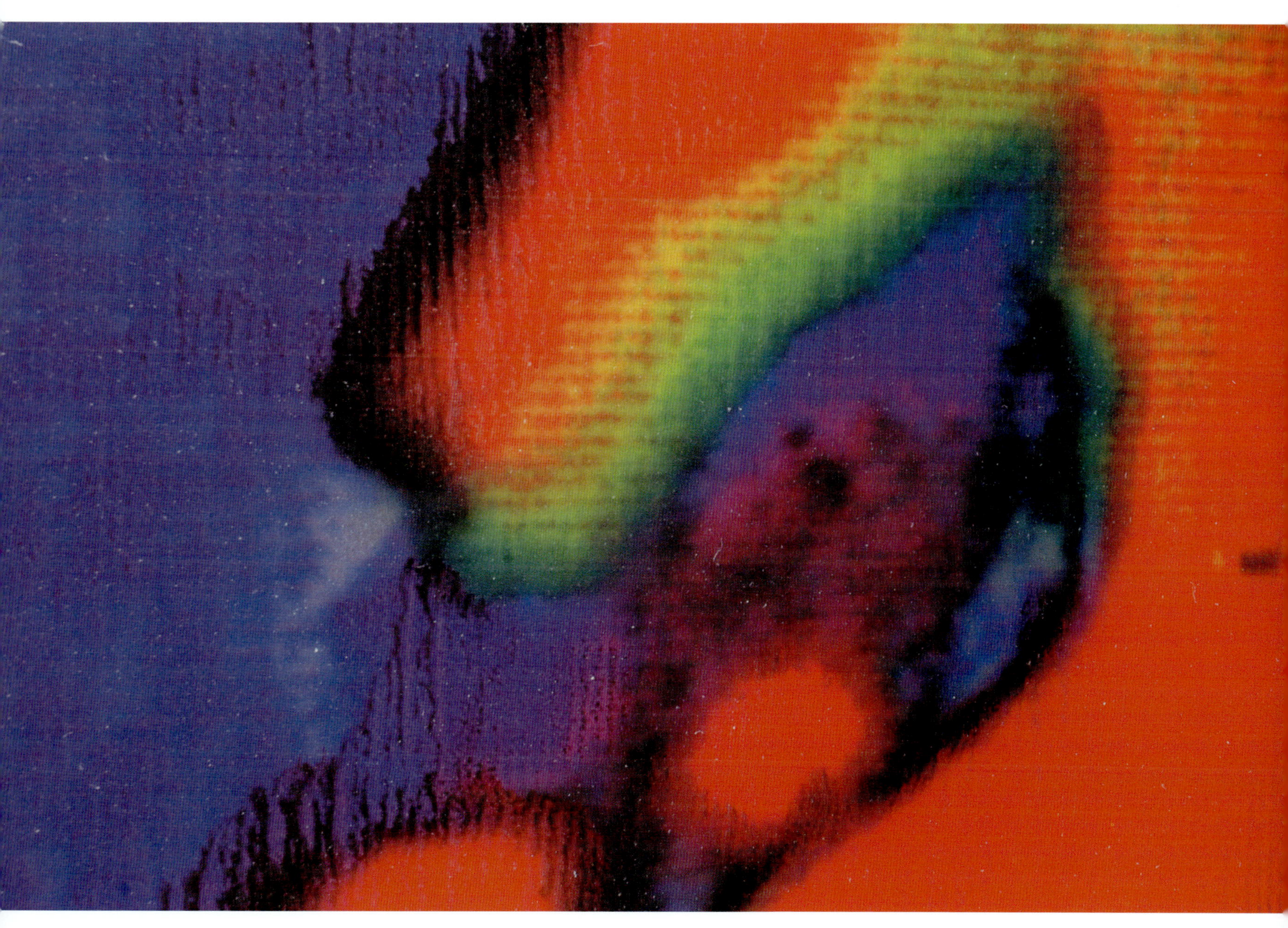

Full Moon Mountain, 2003.
Video painting, acrylic print on
canvas. Details.

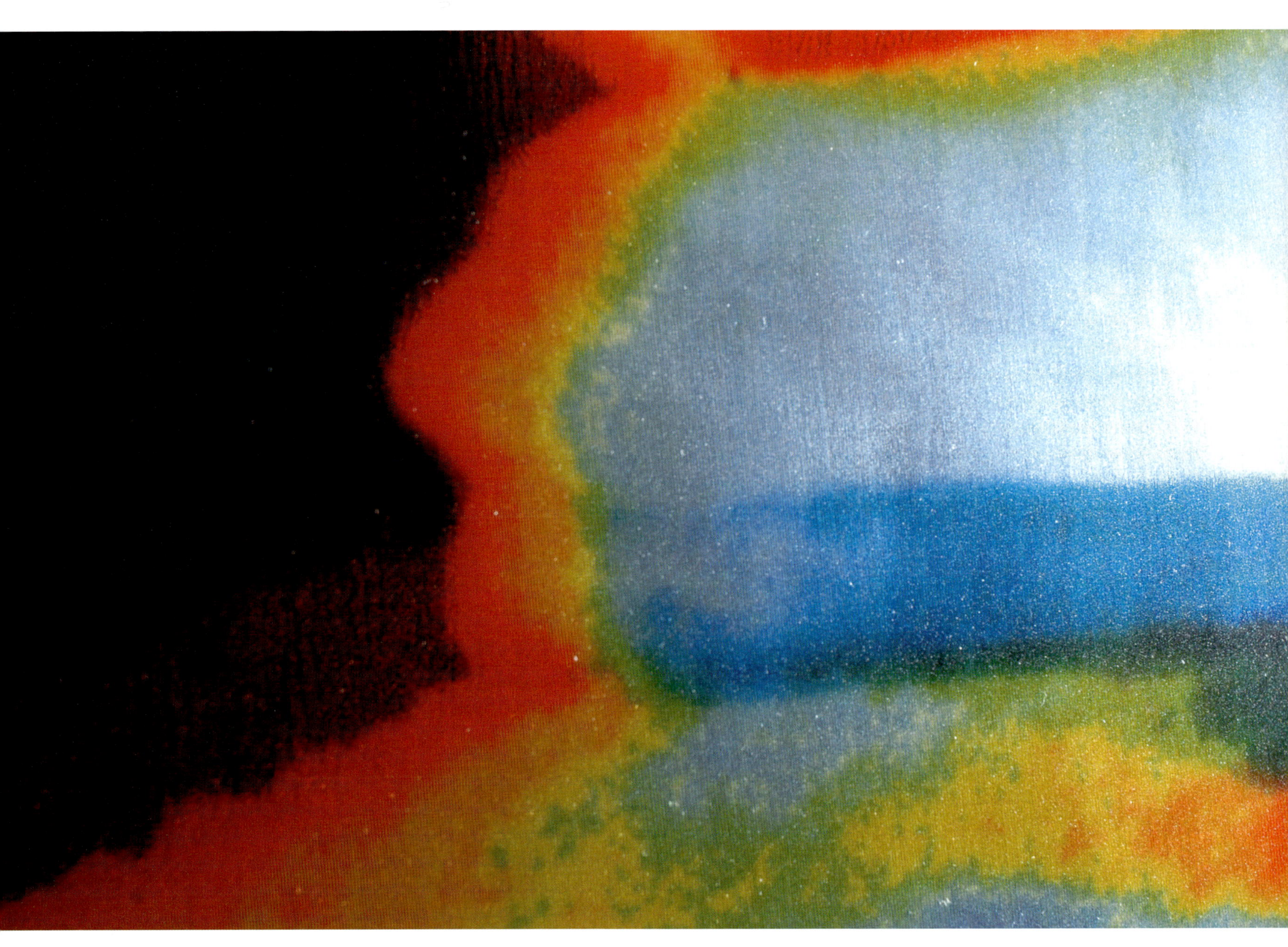

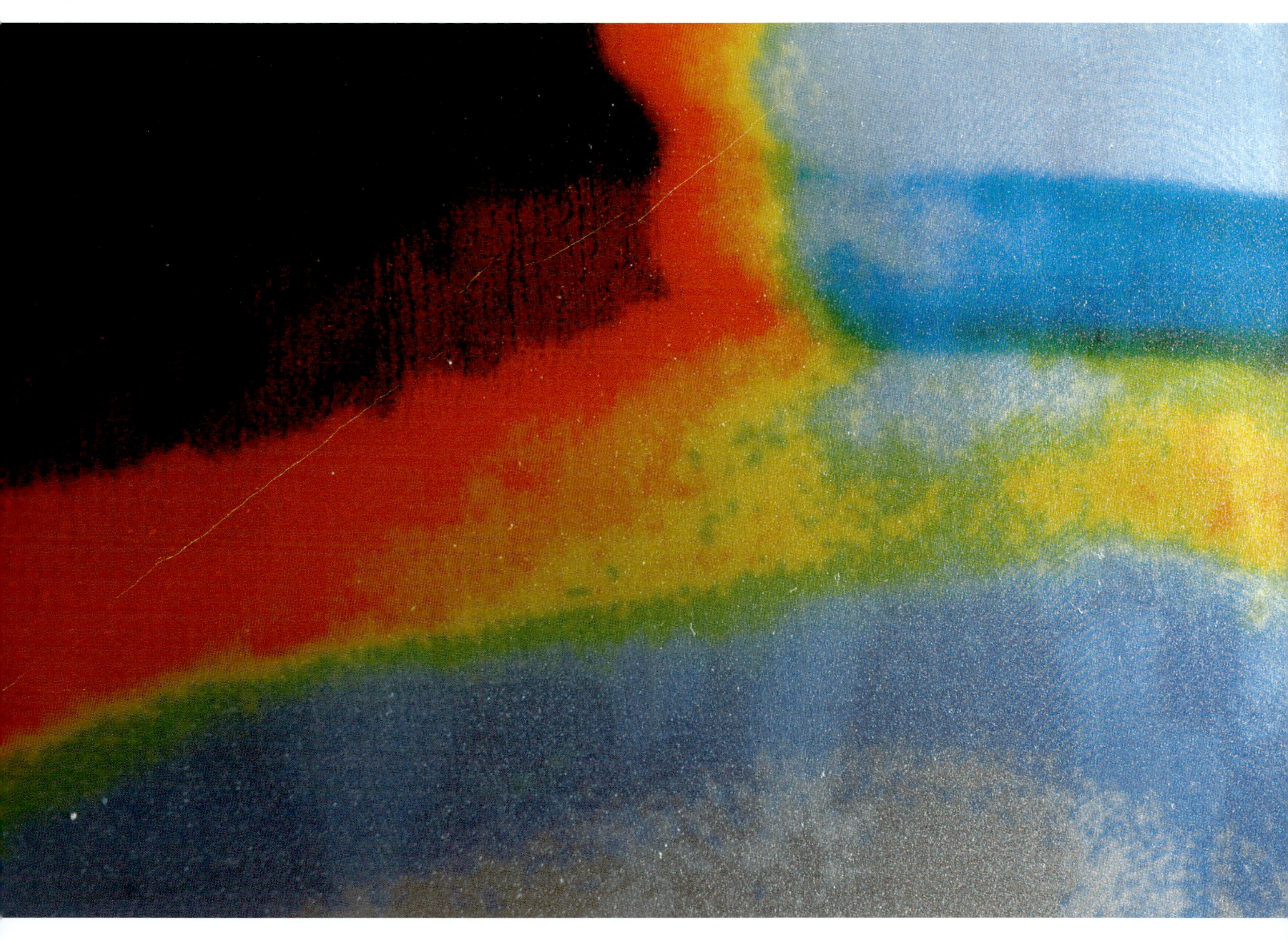

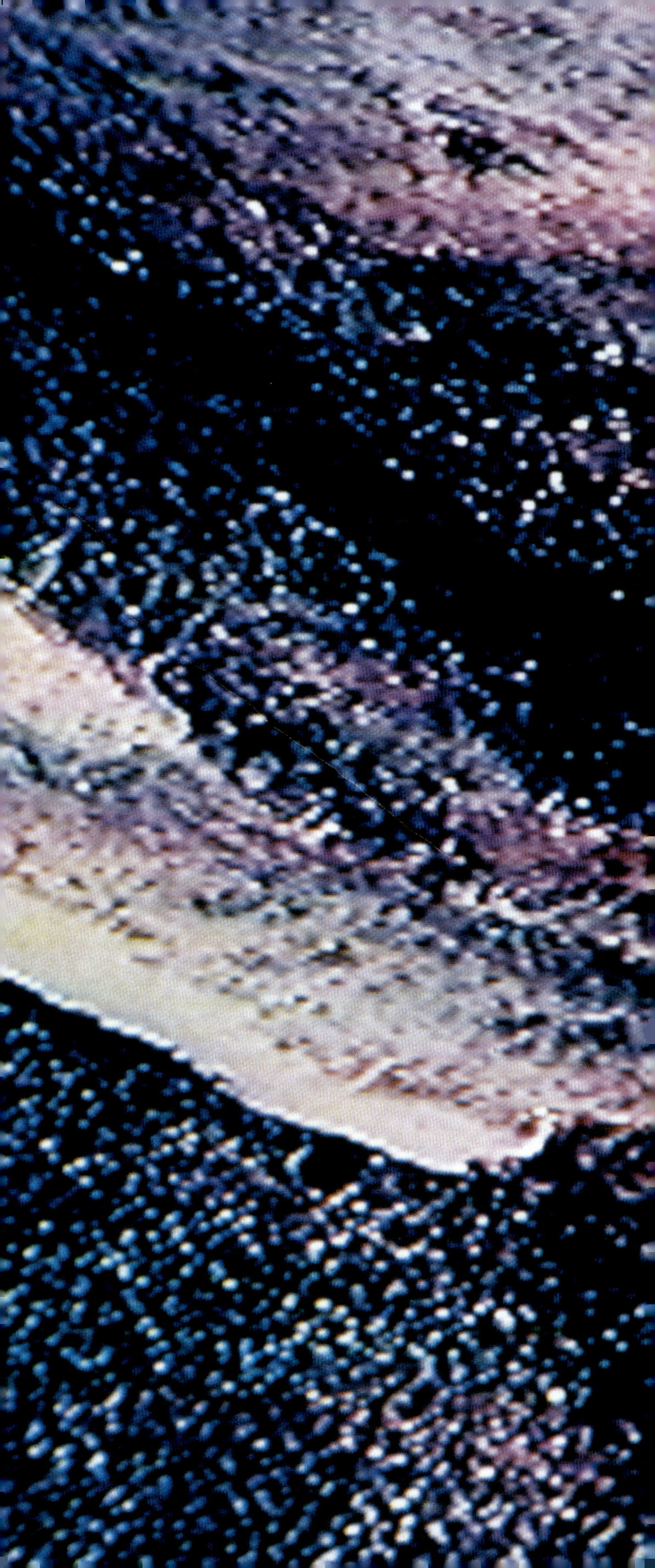

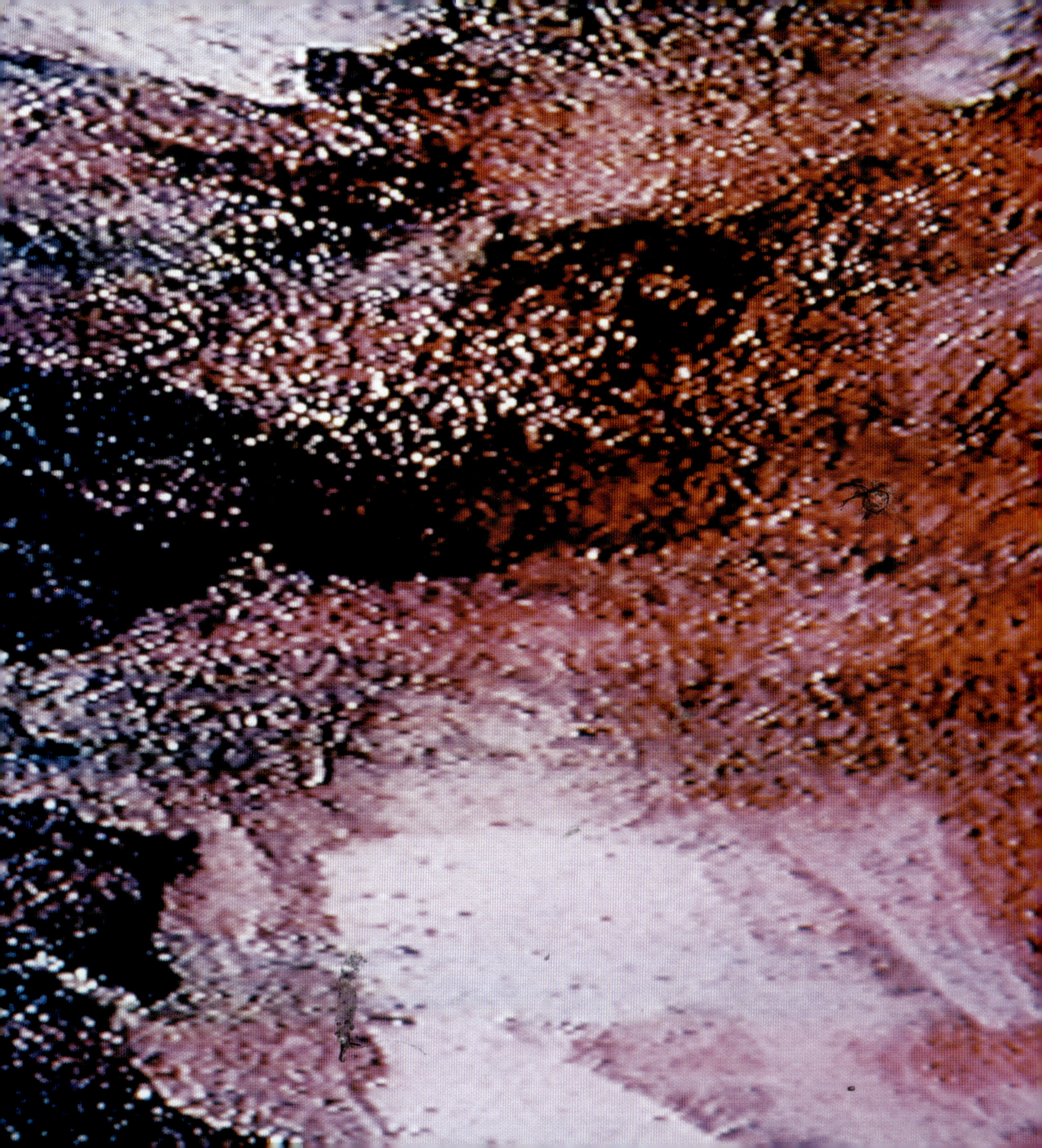

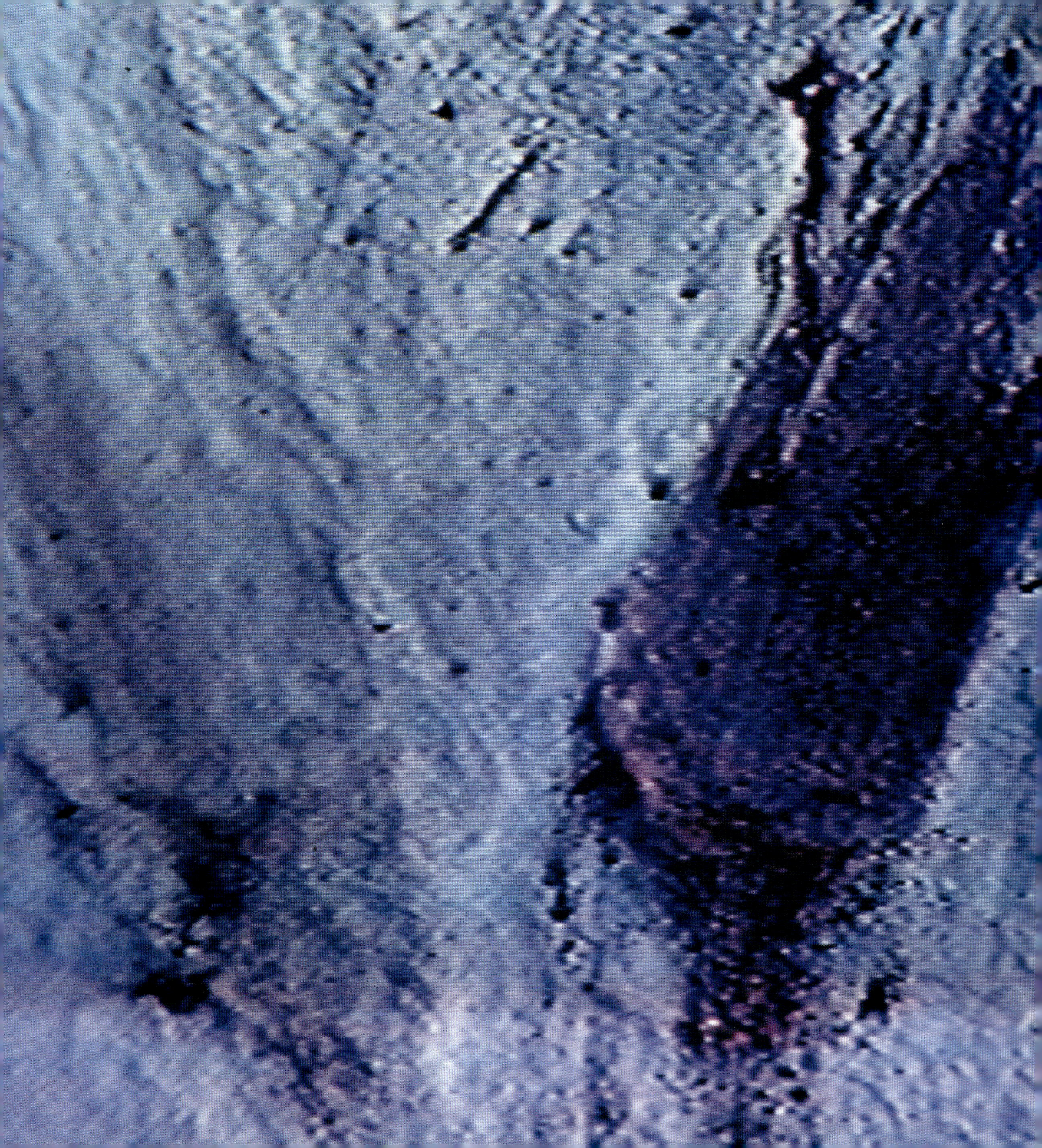

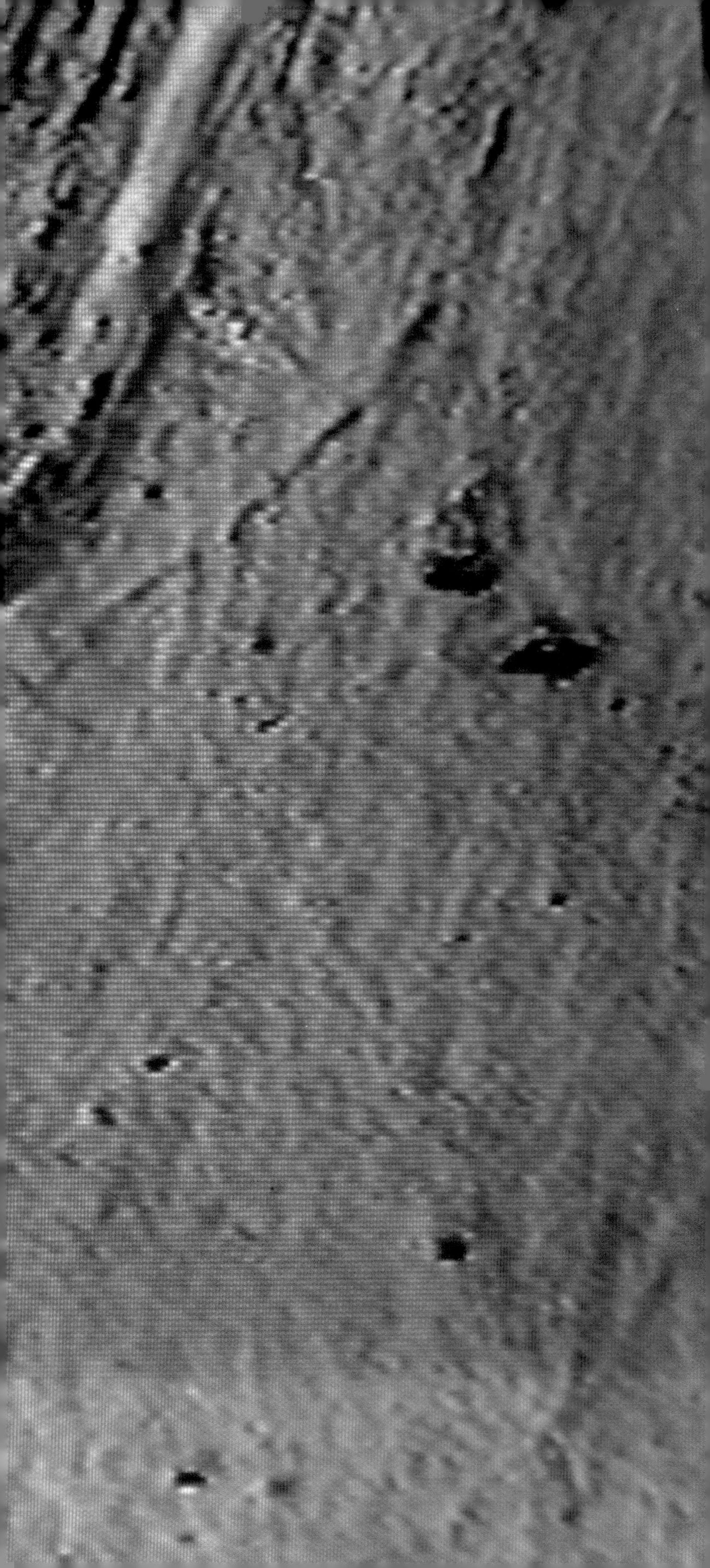

Avalanche, 1993. Installation.
Kunstlerhaus Bethanien,
Berlin, Germany. Detail

Following pages
Petrified Video, 1993. Video
installation in stone avalanche
in Tafjord, Norway.

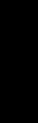

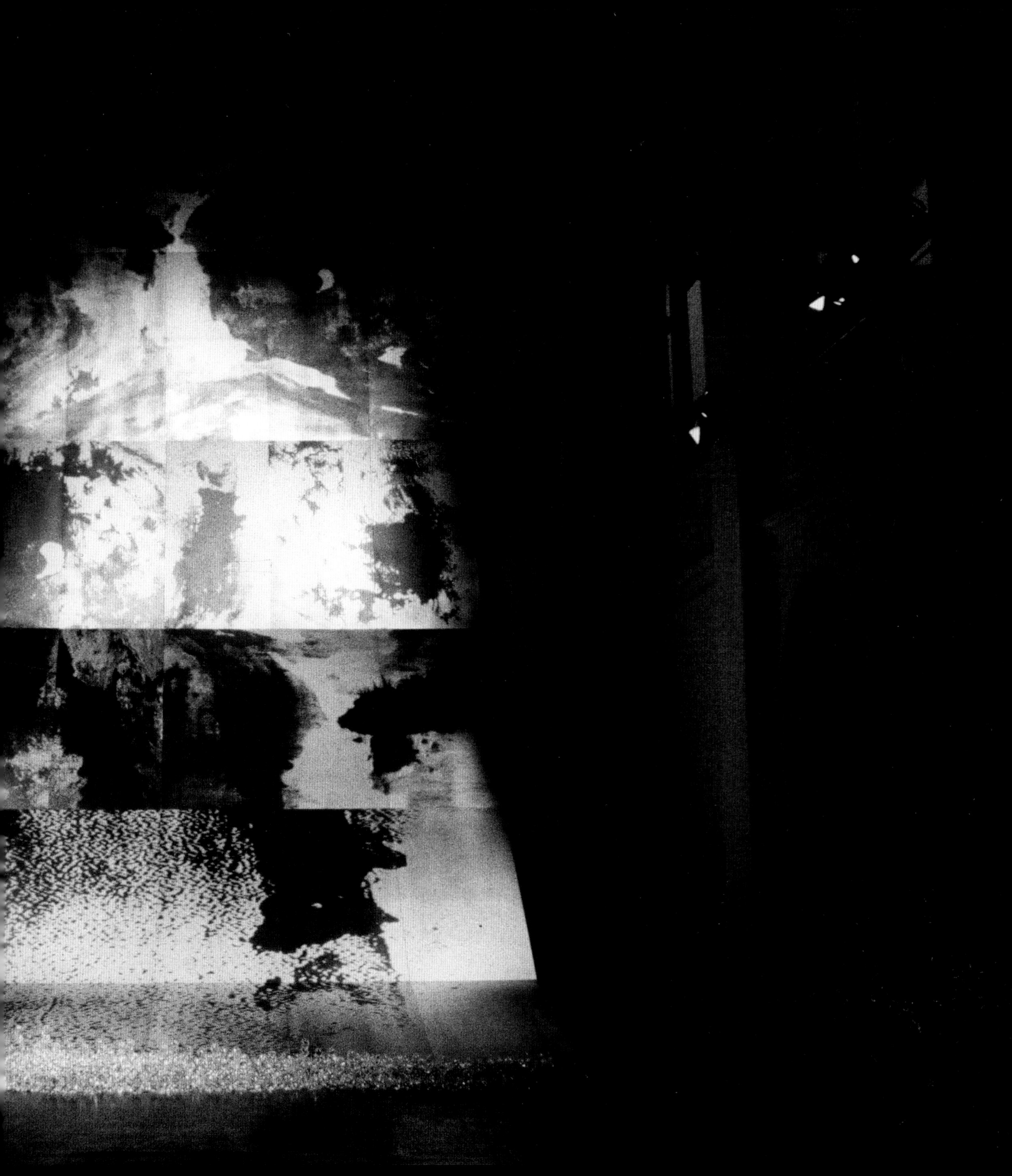

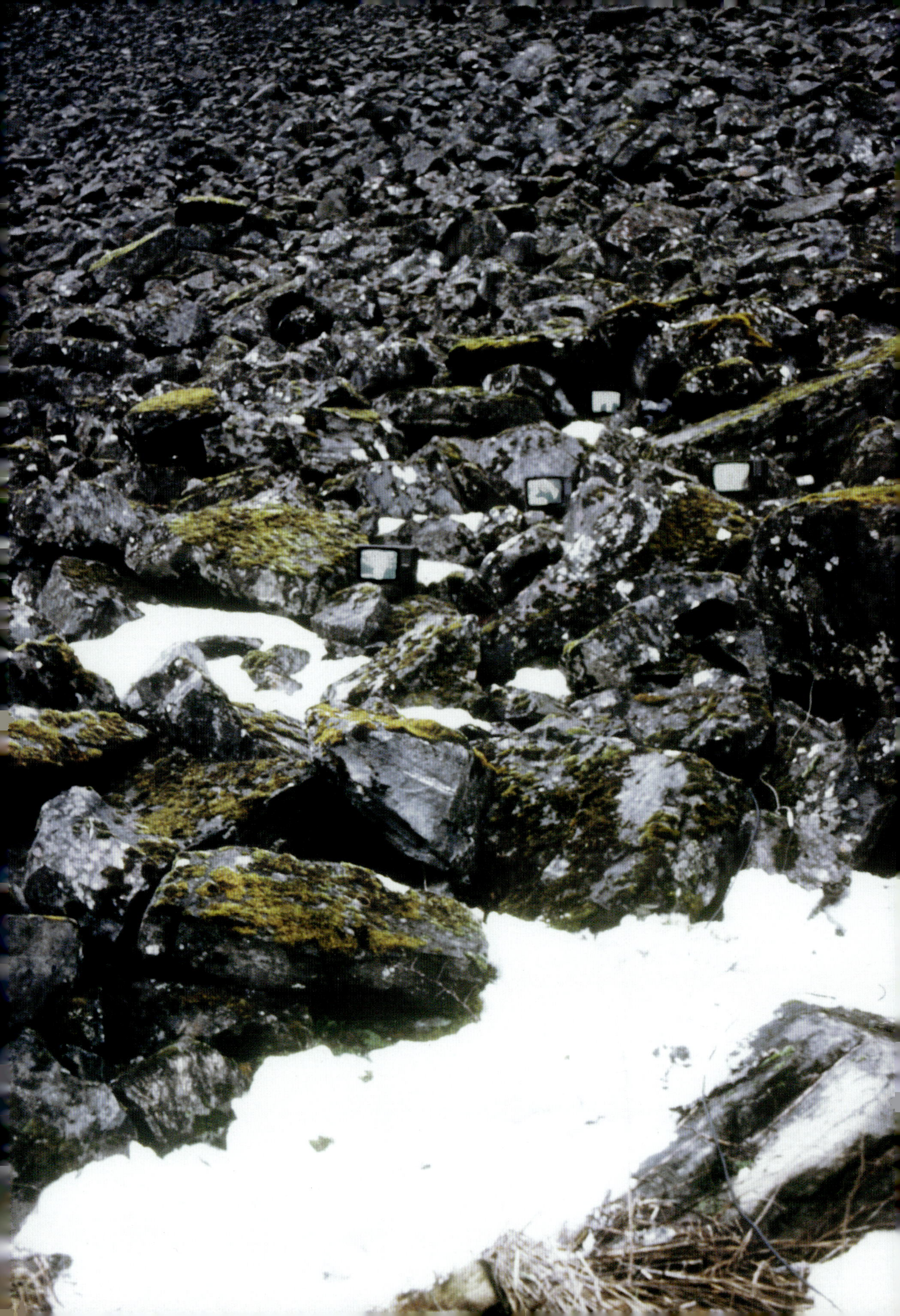

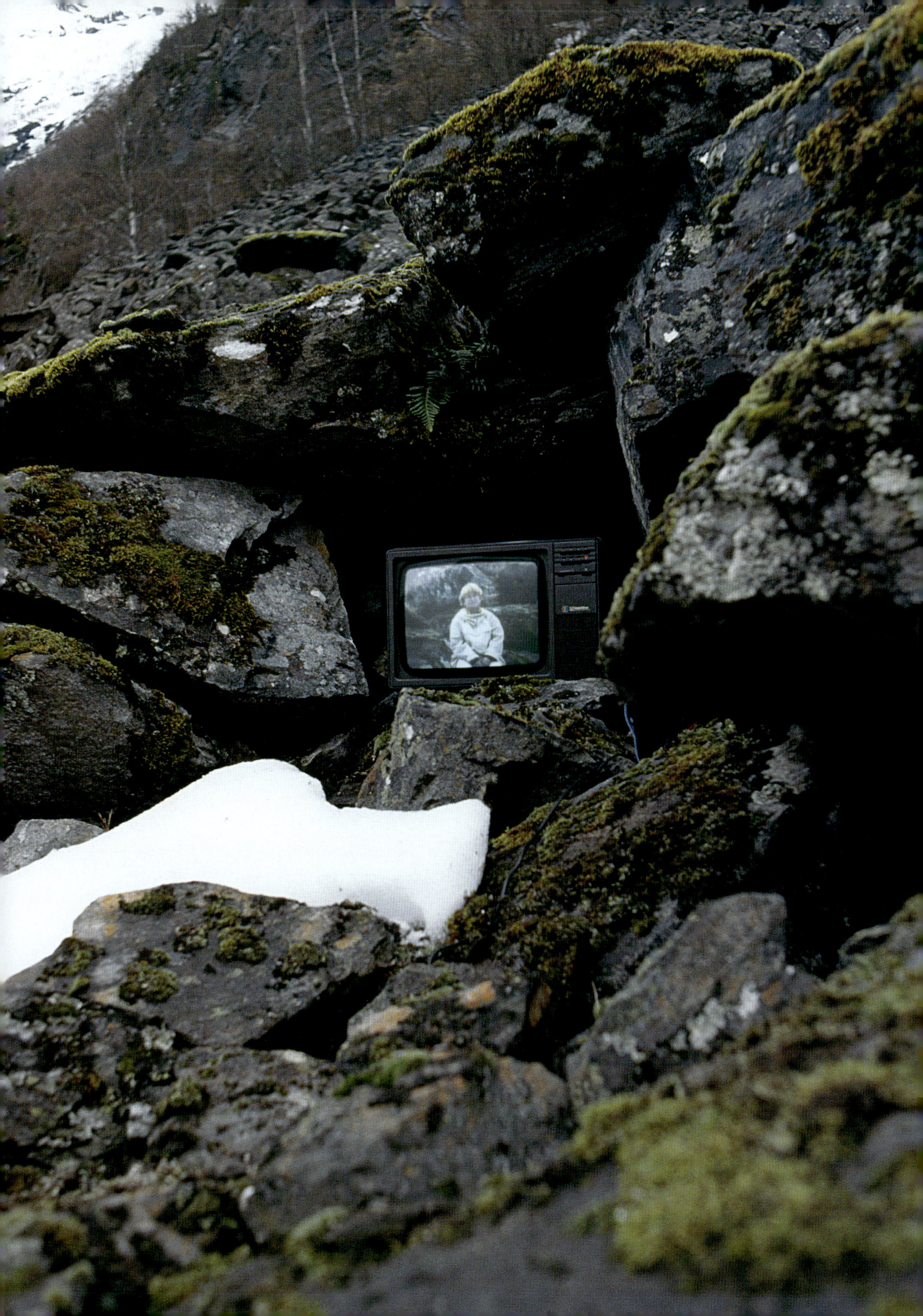

Photograph from video shoot
in Sogn, Norway, 1982.

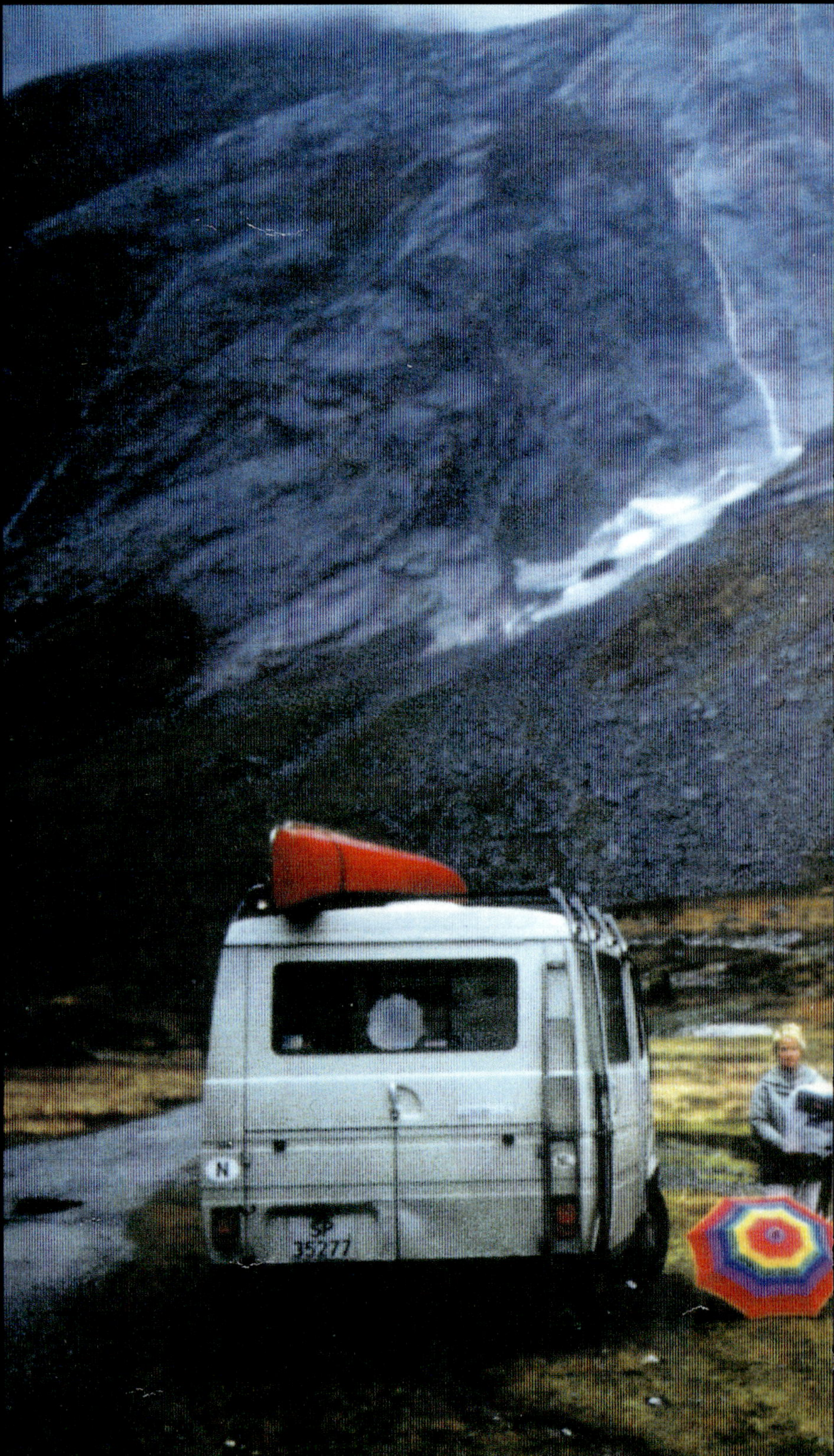

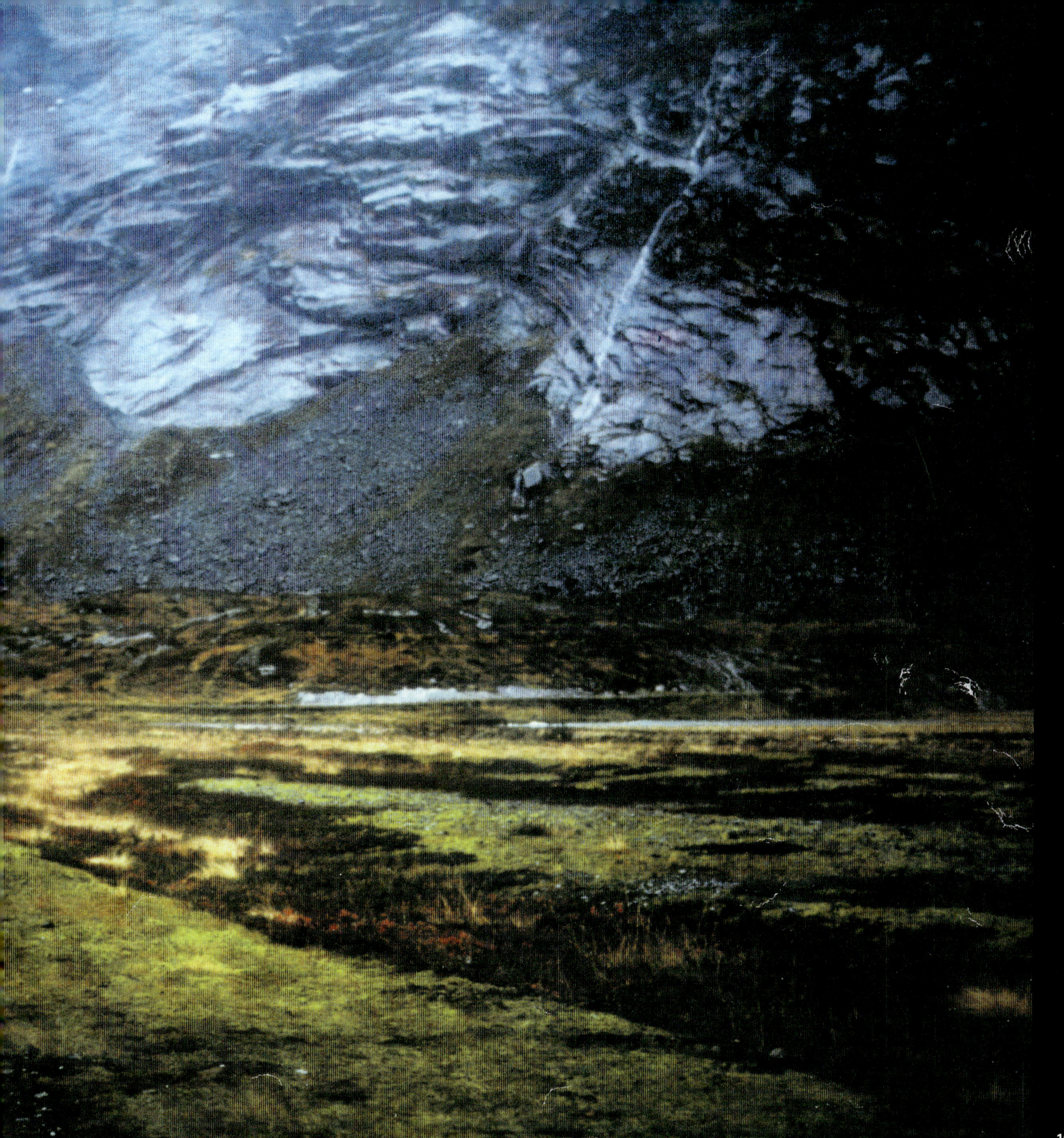

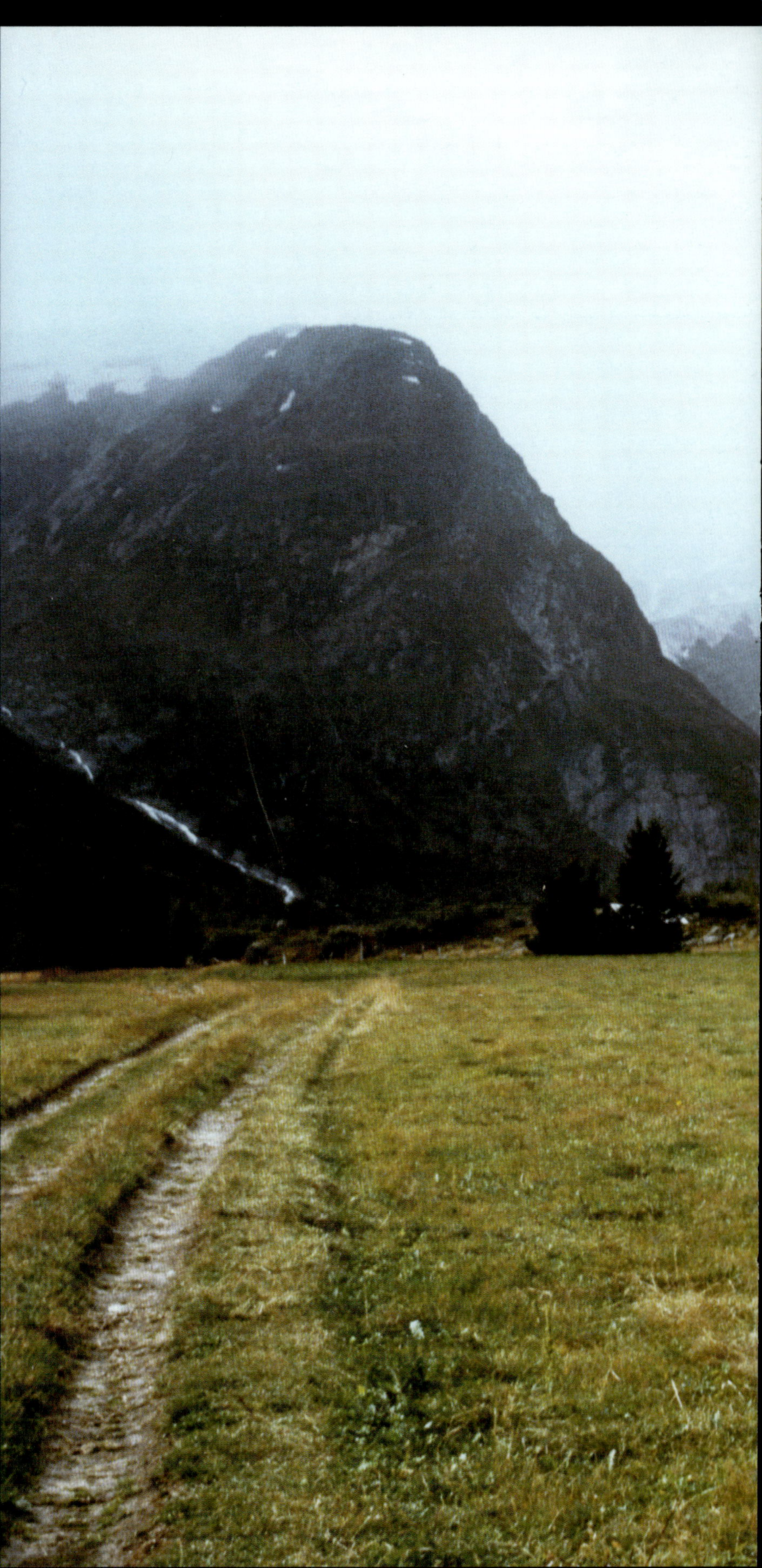

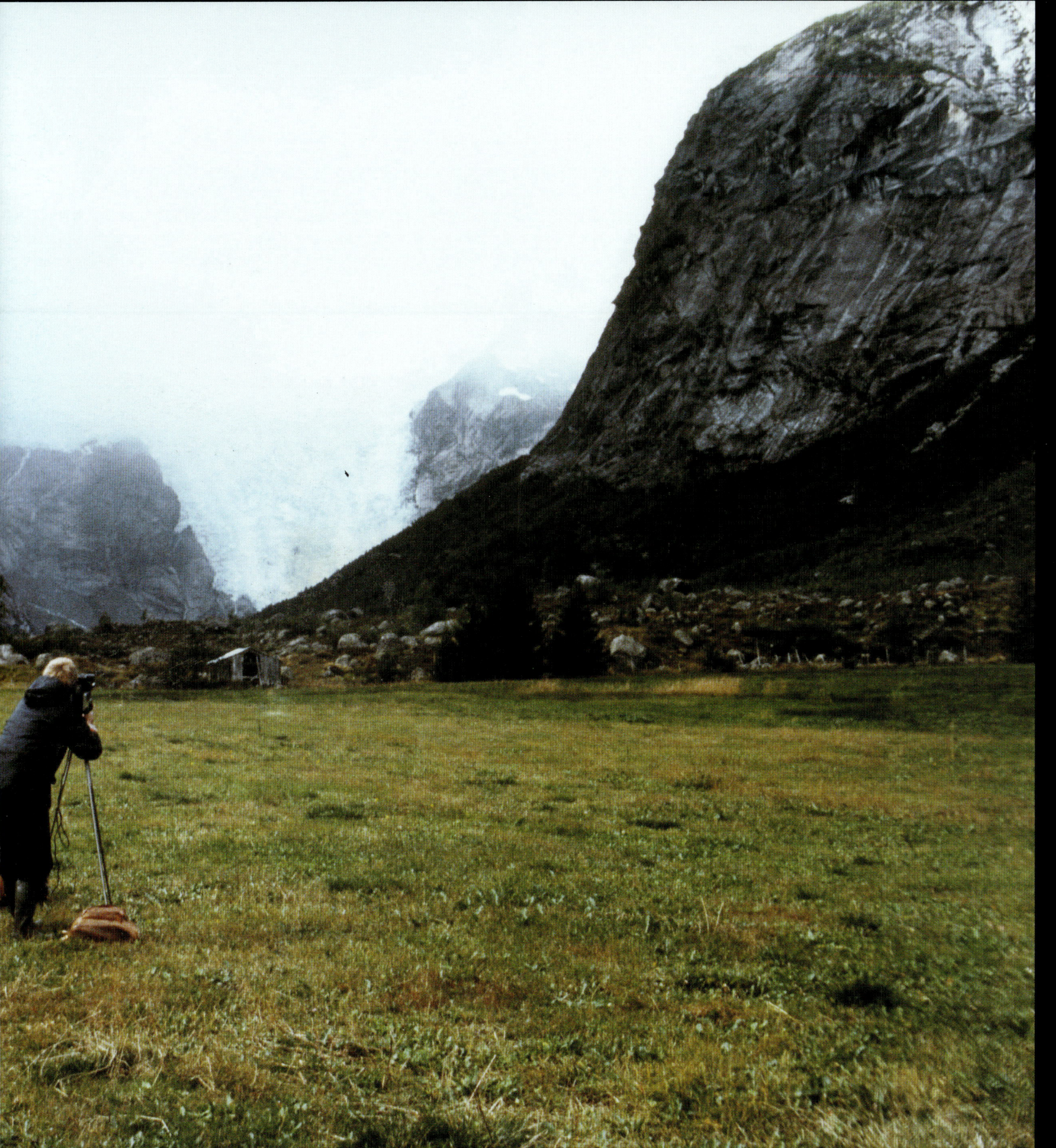

Petrified Video, 1993. Video installation in stone avalanche in Tafjord, Norway, detail featuring Nam June Paik.

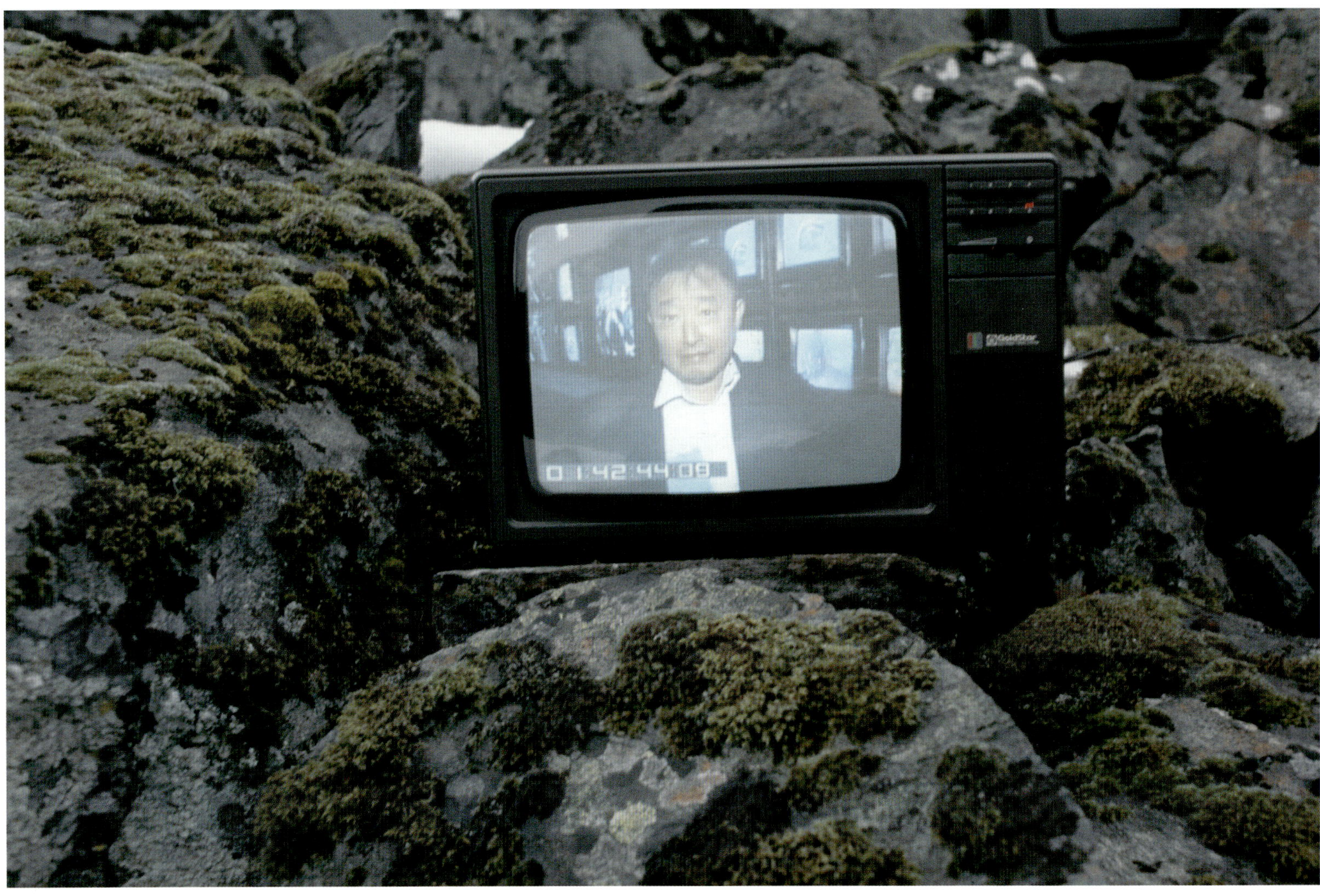

Mountain of the Mind, 1990.
Installation. Clocktower
Gallery, New York, USA.

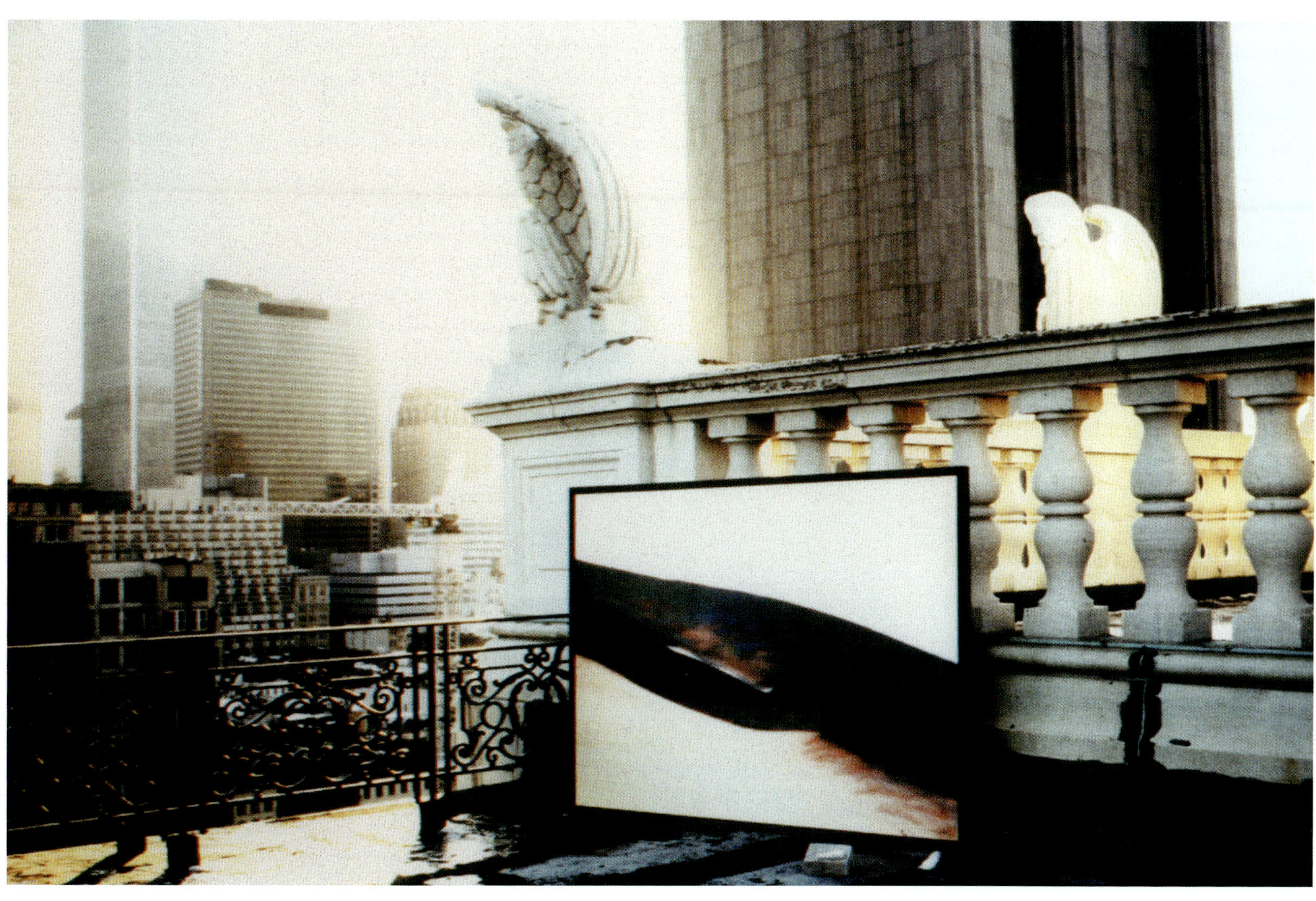

Jon Fosse

Translated
by Neil Howard

Freedom

Freedom is part of Det Åpne
Teater's Ibsen International
short text challenge 2006

Characters THE WOMAN
THE MAN
THE SECOND WOMAN

Black. Lights up. THE WOMAN *stands, looking down.*
Long pause.
THE WOMAN *looks up, towards* THE MAN

THE WOMAN But you see
well
you do understand that
yes
yes that
Yes that I
quite short pause
Wanted to be free
quite short pause
I didn't want to go round
with all those ties
that I had entered into
quite short pause
and of course I was
yes so young
yes when I became tied
yes when I entered into
quite short pause
yes the ties
quite short pause
yes the ties
you know so well

THE MAN Yes

THE WOMAN And I wanted to create
Yes my own ties
quite short pause
I wanted
stops

THE MAN But now you are free

THE WOMAN Yes I suppose so

THE MAN And now you don't want to be free

THE WOMAN No I don't want to be free

THE MAN Why don't you want to be free

THE WOMAN Because one
when one is free
one is not free
at all

THE MAN Why not

THE WOMAN Because then one
is tied
tied and tied
by just one's self

THE MAN Yes

THE WOMAN And the one who is tied
by and to her self
is
stops, short pause

THE MAN Lonely

THE WOMAN No
Yes
Pause

THE MAN But the others they are there
yes they are everywhere
it is impossible to be alone
because the others
they are there

THE WOMAN   Yes
yes exactly
quite short pause
but in relation to the others
one doesn't become free
short pause
and then there's my children

THE MAN   Your children
quite short pause
yes your children
of course
yes
yes a child is a tie isn't it
yes of course

THE WOMAN   Yes

THE MAN   And you want to be free
quite short pause
Not be tied
yes
yes to
stops

THE WOMAN   Yes
Pause

THE MAN   And now you are free

THE WOMAN   Yes
Pause

THE MAN   And now you don't want to be free

THE WOMAN   No
Pause
Or yes

THE MAN   Yes you can be
quite short pause
yes lover
yes
yes
yes with whoever you want

THE WOMAN   Yes

THE MAN   With one or the other

THE WOMAN   Yes

THE MAN   Go to bed with whoever you want

THE WOMAN   Yes

THE MAN   You are free

THE WOMAN   Yes
Pause
But I
stops

THE MAN   Don't you want to be free?

THE WOMAN   Yes

THE MAN   Wasn't it as you imagined?
To be free

THE WOMAN   No
Pause

THE MAN   Freedom is not a good thing

THE WOMAN   No
quite short pause
But it is a condition

THE MAN   It is a condition
Short pause
Yes like death
quite short pause
like loneliness

THE WOMAN   Yes

THE MAN   But it isn't good
quite short pause
yes doesn't one try
all one can
laughs briefly
yes almost
to get away from freedom
permanent relationships
laughs briefly
having dogs
a permanent residence
regular income
a permanent job
quite short pause
yes children

THE WOMAN   Freedom is a good thing too
quite short pause
If you are shut in
quite short pause
yes then you want to go where you
                                                               want to go
there is nothing else you want

THE MAN   But there is something else

THE WOMAN   No

THE MAN   Another person
other people
are not a room one is
shut up in

THE WOMAN   Aren't they?

THE MAN   No

THE WOMAN   Never

THE MAN   Never
Pause

THE WOMAN   But
quite short pause
now
yes now I have tried being free
and now
yes now I would like to tie myself
quite short pause
yes that is what it is called
to tie oneself

THE MAN   Yes

THE WOMAN   To you
To the children

THE MAN   So that's what you want

THE WOMAN   Yes
quite short pause
yes I regret
or
quite short pause
yes I regret it
I should not have gone
it was wrong of me
I shouldn't have done it

THE MAN   And now you want to go back

THE WOMAN   Yes
             Pause

THE MAN   But it's not possible

THE WOMAN   Not possible

THE MAN   No it's not possible

THE WOMAN   Why not

THE MAN   No

THE WOMAN   But can you not forgive?

THE MAN   Yes
             quite short pause
             Yes I have no difficulties
             forgiving
             quite short pause
             it's just that
             yes to see the other
             like oneself
             and to see that the other

THE WOMAN   *interrupts*
             Yes

THE MAN   *continues*
             yes is like oneself
             yes that the other
             quite short pause
             Yes also has freedom
             As their damned condition

THE WOMAN   Damned condition

THE MAN   Yes

THE WOMAN   What would a person be
             without freedom

THE MAN   What would a person be
             without death

THE WOMAN   What would a person be
             without loneliness

THE MAN   Yes
             Pause

THE WOMAN   A person without freedom
             is
             quite short pause
             yes a stone
             a tree
             quite short pause
             no that was badly put
             quite short pause
             but a person
             without freedom
             is not a person

THE MAN   Yes
             Pause
             Yes that is the condition of the soul
             quite long pause

THE WOMAN   But I miss
             stops

THE MAN   You miss

THE WOMAN   Yes

THE MAN   What do you miss?

THE WOMAN   You

THE MAN   You miss me
                 quite short pause
                 but it was me
                 you couldn't stand
                 that I was close
                 quite short pause
                 that I was there
                 yes like a tie
                 quite short pause
                 yes like a constraint
                 quite short pause
                 as if I was a room
                 that shut you in

THE WOMAN   No
                 quite short pause
                 no it wasn't like that

THE MAN   You wanted to travel
                 meet others
                 get close to others
                 quite short pause
                 that was what you
                 called freedom

THE WOMAN   Yes
                 yes maybe

THE MAN   But if you got too close
                 quite short pause
                 yes what then?

THE WOMAN   Did I come too close to you?

THE MAN   How could I know

THE WOMAN   And the journey

THE MAN   *continues*
                 became the journey's constraint
                 the journey's tie
                 to travel
                 is the greatest constraint
                 of all

THE WOMAN   Yes
                 Pause
                 But
                 quite short pause
                 can't I come back
                 to you
                 to the children
                 THE MAN shakes his head
                 But why not?

THE MAN   Because you are free

THE WOMAN   But I don't want to be free

THE MAN   But you are free

THE WOMAN   Aren't you?

THE MAN   No
                 Long pause. Footsteps are heard.
                 THE SECOND WOMAN comes in

THE MAN   *To THE SECOND WOMAN*
                 Yes
                 Yes you must say hello to
                 Yes my first wife
                 THE WOMAN and THE SECOND WOMAN go
                 over and take each other's hands
                 I don't suppose you've met each other
                 before

THE WOMAN   No

THE SECOND WOMAN   No never
                   Pause

THE WOMAN   *To THE SECOND WOMAN*
                   Yes I just wanted
                   Yes to pop in
                   I
                   quite short pause
                   say hello
                   yes

THE SECOND WOMAN   Yes
                   Pause
                   You're in your old parts
                   yes

THE WOMAN   Yes
                   laughs briefly
                   yes you might say so
                   Pause

THE SECOND WOMAN   Yes
                   Pause

THE WOMAN   *to THE MAN*
                   Yes it was nice
                   talking to you again

THE MAN   Yes
                   yes it was

THE WOMAN   But I suppose I'd better go
                   Pause

THE SECOND WOMAN   Nice to meet you
                   Pause. THE WOMAN goes. Long pause
                   What did she want

THE MAN   Just to say hello

THE SECOND WOMAN   She just came

THE MAN   Yes
                   quite short pause
                   yes there was a ring at the door
                   and there she stood
                   she just stood there

THE SECOND WOMAN   Yes
                   Short pause
                   And she didn't want
                   yes anything in particular

THE MAN   No
                   Pause

THE SECOND WOMAN   Sure

THE MAN   Yes
                   Long pause. Lights down. Black

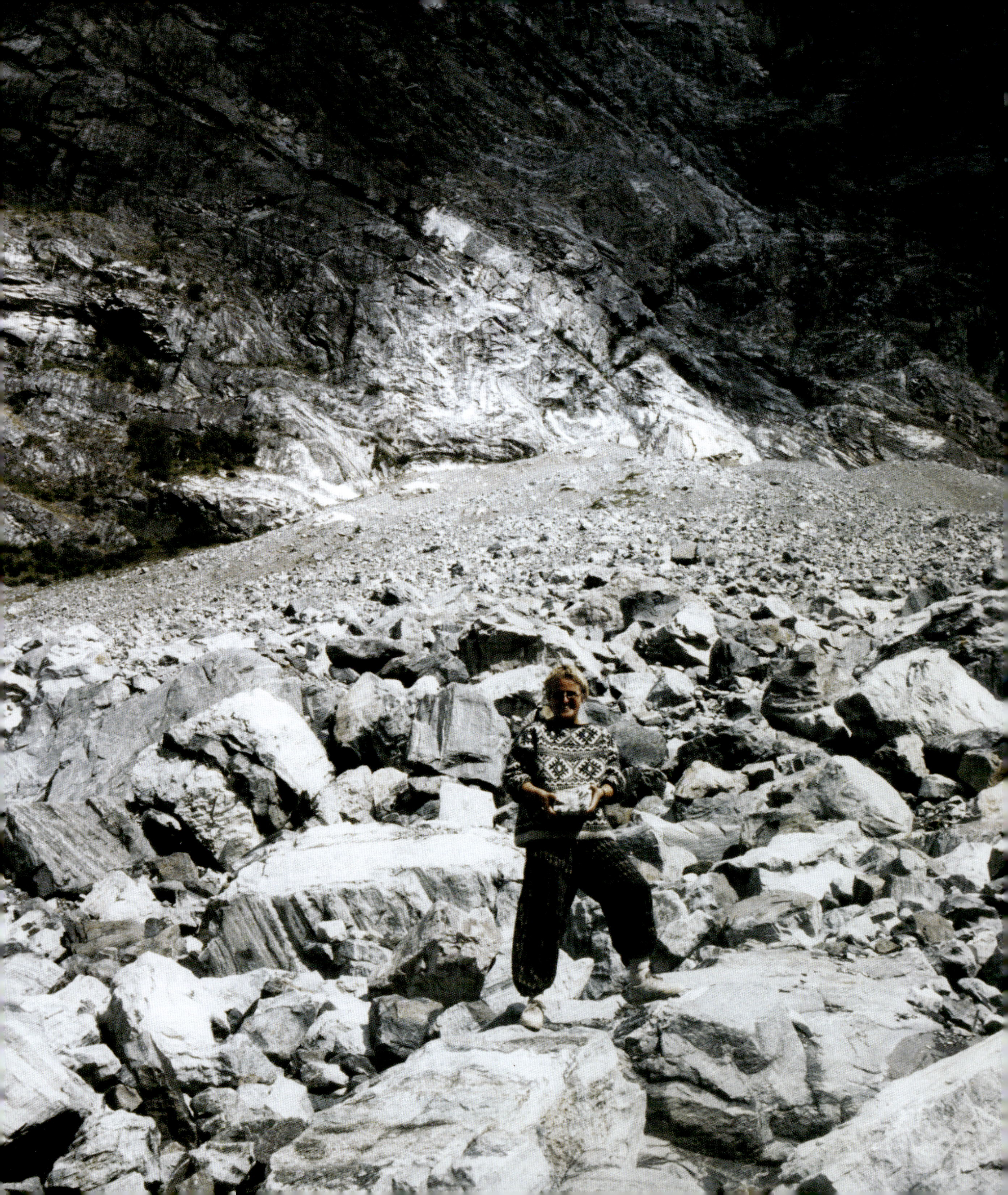

Biography

Born 1946, Ålesund, Norway.

Education
1967–71
The National College of Art and Design, Bergen, Norway.
1971–75
Ecole Nationale Supérieure des Beaux-Arts, Paris, France.
1975–76
Royal College of Art, London, England.
1976–79
Jan van Eyck Academie, Maastricht, The Netherlands.

Selected Solo Exhibitions
1973
Cité Internationale des Arts, Paris, France.
1978
Galleri F15, Moss, Norway.
Bonnefantenmuseum, Maastricht, The Netherlands.
1981
Henie-Onstad Art Center, Høvikodden, Norway.
1982
Galleri St. Agnes, Roskilde, Denmark.
1984
Galerie Art Contemporain J&J Donguy, Paris, France.
1985
Galleri Doktor Glas, Stockholm, Sweden.
1986
Henie-Onstad Art Center, Høvikodden, Norway.
1987
Galleri Ojens, Gothenburg, Sweden.
1989
Galleri J.M.S., Oslo, Norway.
Le Lieu, Québec, Canada

1990
Nahem Contemporary, New York, USA.
P.S.1, The Clocktower Gallery, New York, USA.
1991
Galerie J&J Donguy, Paris, France.
1992
Porin Art Museum, Pori, Finland.
1993
Künstlerhaus Bethanien, Berlin, Germany.
Art Museum of Düsseldorf in Ehrenhof, Düsseldorf, Germany.
Bergen International Art Festival, Norway.
1994
Galleri Wang, Oslo, Norway.
1995
Gallerie J&J Donguy, Paris, France.
1998
Galerie Benden & Klimczak, Cologne, Germany.
2000
Werkstatt Europa 2000 with the installation *Trollvideo*, Forum Kunst, Rottweil, Germany.
2002
To Whom it May Concern, The Museum of Contemporary Art, Oslo, Norway.
Plus Minus Zero, Henie Onstad Art Center, Høvikodden, Norway.
Trollene på Finnskogen, Finnskogen, Norway.
2004
Molde International Jazz Festival, Molde, Norway.
2005
Illuminations, National Library of Norway, Oslo, Norway.

2006
A Doll's House, Gallery Kaare Berntsen, Oslo, Norway / The National Museum of Art, Architecture and Design, Oslo, Norway.
Leo the Lion, Bollywood Film Festival, Mumbai, India.
2008
Hå Gamle Prestegård, Stavanger, Norway.
Peer Gynt-festival, Vinstra, Norway.
2010
Global Groove, Fort Jesus, The National Museums of Kenya, Mombasa, Kenya.
Petrification of STONE STORY, Tafjord, Norway.
Heaven & Earth, The Stenersen Museum, Oslo, Norway.

Selected Group Exhibitions
1975
Femmes Peintres et Sculpteurs, Musée d'Art Moderne de la Ville de Paris, France.
1976
Video International, Aarhus Art Museum, Denmark.
Life Styles, Institute of Contemporary Art, London, England.
1977
Video and Film Manifestatie, Bonnefantenmuseum, Maastricht, The Netherlands.
1978
Landscape, Henie-Onstad Art Center Høvikodden, Norway.
1980
International Impact Art Festival, Kyoto Municipal Museum of Art, Kyoto, Japan.

Biennale de Paris, Centre Georges Pompidou, Paris, France, Project *Gjerdeløa*.
London Video Arts, ACME Gallery, London, England.
Experimental Environment, Reykjavik, Iceland.
1985
Dialogue on Contemporary Art in Europe, Gulbenkian Foundation, Lisbon, Portugal.
1986
Biennale di Venezia, Nordic Pavillion, Venice, Italy.
Norealis, DAAD Galerie, Berlin, Germany.
1988
Olympiad of Art, Museum of Modern Art, Seoul, South Korea.
1989
International Impact Art Festival, Kyoto Municipal Museum of Art, Kyoto, Japan.
1991
7 Cities, 7 Countries, Leuwarden, The Netherlands.
1992
Il paesaggio culturale, Palazzo delle Esposizioni, Rome, Italy.
1994
Winterland, Munich, Germany, Barcelona, Spain, Tokyo, Japan, and Atlanta, USA.
Project for Europe, Copenhagen, Denmark.
1995
At the Century's End, National Museum of Women in the Arts, Washington D.C., USA.
West of the Moon, Astrup Fearnley Museum of Modern Art, Oslo, Norway.
Seoul International Art Festival, Seoul, South-Korea.

Photograph from the project *Jimdalen - Chaun*, 1992. Rock from Tafjord, Norway, transported to Siberia, Russia.

Aquilo, Sammlung Ludwig, Museum Moderner Kunst, Vienna, Austria.
1996
Aquilo, Museo d'Arte Moderna, Bologna, Italy.
23rd International Biennal of Sâo Paulo, Brazil.
1997
Electra, Henie-Onstad Art Center, Høvikodden, Norway.
1999
Open 999, International Sculpture Festival, Lido, Venice, Italy.
2000
Sub Rosa, Charlottenborg, Copenhagen, Denmark.
Norwegian Pavilion, World Exhibition EXPO 2000, Hannover, Germany.
2002
A Doll's House, Henie Onstad Art Center, Høvikodden, Norway.
Mirage, Suzhou Art Museum, Suzhou, China.
2003
Kaohsiung International Container ArtsFestival, Kaohsiung, Taiwan.
2004
Is it Art?, Xian, China.
Open Asia, International Sculpture Festival, Lido, Venice, Italy.
New Creative Vanguard, Advance Art Center, Shanghai Duolun Museum of Modern Art, Shanghai, China.
2005
Norge, Contemporary Landscapes from the Collection of Her Majesty Queen Sonja of Norway, Scandinavia House, New York, USA.

The Basic Exhibition, The National Museum of Art, Design and Architecture, Oslo, Norway.
Two Asias, Two Europes, Shanghai Duolun Museum of Modern Art, Shanghai, China.
2006
Icebreaker, Galleri GAD, Oslo, Norway.
Post Nora, Ibsen Year 2006, Bejing, China.
2006–08
Nicht nur Lachs und Würstchen, Norwegian Technological Museum, Oslo, Bergen, Trondheim, Berlin, Leipzig.
2007
To Live With Contemporary Art, Galleri F 15, Moss, Norway.
Talking About Painting, The National Museum of Art, Design and Architecture, Oslo, Norway.
Art 4, The National Museum of Art, Design and Architecture, Oslo, Norway.
The 5th Uiwang International Placard Art Festival, Korea.
Only Colours, Château La Roche-Vernaise, France.
2008
The Mountain in Norwegian Art, Henie Onstad Art Centre, Høvikodden, Norway.
Lofoten International Art Festival, LIAF, Svolvær, Norway.
Festspillene I Nord-Norge, Harstad Art Center, Harstad, Norway.
Biennale des Couvets, Galerie Le Lieu, Québec, Canada.
The Norwegian Short Film Festival in Grimstad, Norway.

2008–09
Whatever Happened to Sex in Scandinavia?, Office for Contemporary Art (OCA), Oslo, Norway.
2009
Kunsten å falle, Preus Museum, Horten, Norway.
Statens Høstutstilling, Oslo, Norway.
2010
Blodig alvor, Bergen Kunstmuseum, Bergen, Norway.
"God natt da du…" Surrealisme i norsk kunst 1930–2010, The Stenersen Museum, Oslo, Norway.
Norse Soul, Katzen Art Center, American University Museum, Washington D.C., USA.

Selected Collections
Shanghai City Art Collection, China.
Bonnefantenmuseum, Maastricht, The Netherlands.
Her Majesty Queen Sonja's Art Collection, Norway.
The National Museum of Contemporary Art, Oslo, Norway.
Henie-Onstad Art Center, Høvikodden, Norway.
The National Gallery of Oslo, Norway.
Ville de Paris, France.
Bibliothèque nationale de France, Paris, France.
The Museum of Modern Art, Novi Sad, Yugoslavia.
The Nordic Graphical Union.
Nordisk konstsentrum, Helsinki, Finland.
Norwegian Council for Cultural Affairs.

Bergen Art Gallery, Norway.
City of Oslo Art Collections, Norway.
Malmo Museum of Modern Art, Sweden.
Shanghai Duolun Museum of Modern Art, China.
Parc de la Villette, Paris, France.
University of Oslo, Oslo, Norway.
The Kistefos Museum, Norway.
Preus Photo Museum, Horten, Norway.
Astrup Fearnley Museum of Modern Art, Oslo, Norway.
Tor Juul Collection, Norway.

Commissions
1993
School of Health and Social studies, Stavanger, Norway.
1994
Amoco, Stavanger, Norway.
1995
Mannheller tunnel, Sogn og Fjordande, Norway.
1997
Rikshospitalet, Oslo, Norway.
2000
Radiance of the Seas, Royal Caribbean Cruise Line, Norway.
2001
Tønsberg Cultural Center, Tønsberg, Norway.
2003
Sogn og Fjordane County council, Norway.
Ullevål University Hospital, Oslo, Norway.
2005
Shell/Hydro, Ormen Lange Gas Terminal, Aukra, Møre og Romsdal, Norway.

2007
Kirkelund primary school, Skiptvet, Østfold, Norway.
Rauma Cultural Center, Åndalsnes, Norway.
2008
Luster Savings Bank, Norway.

Awards
1997
"Vakre Vegers Pris" 1997 for Mannheller tunnel, Sogn og Fjordane, Norway.
2005
Nominated for ZKM (Zentrum fur Kunst und Medientechnologie) Media Prize, Germany, for the video *A Phrenological Self-Portrait*.
2006
Axel Waldemar Johannessens Pris.
Ingerid Fegerstens stiftelse, Billedkunstprisen 2006.

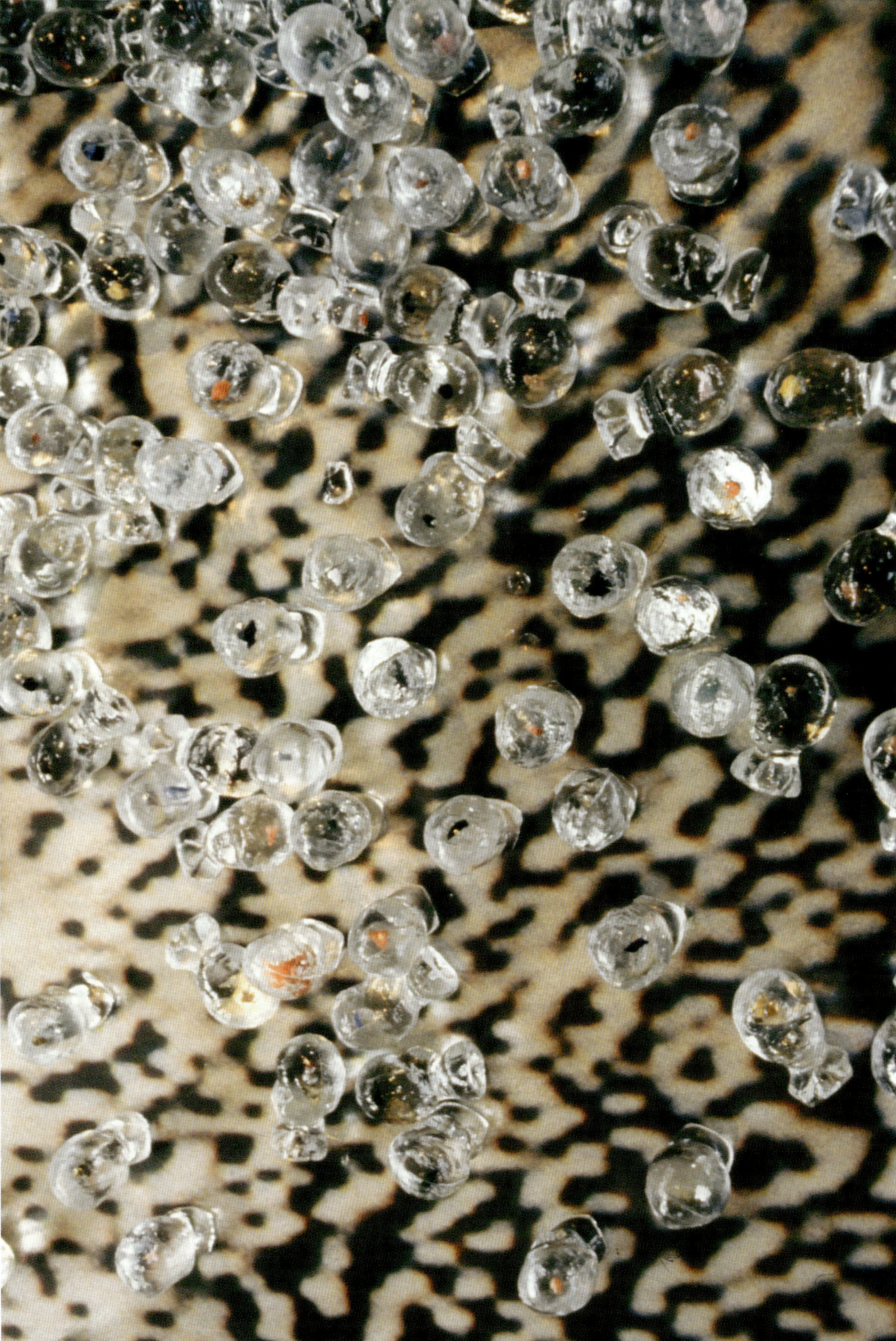

Avalanche, 1993. Installation.
Kunstlerhaus Bethanien,
Berlin, Germany. Detail

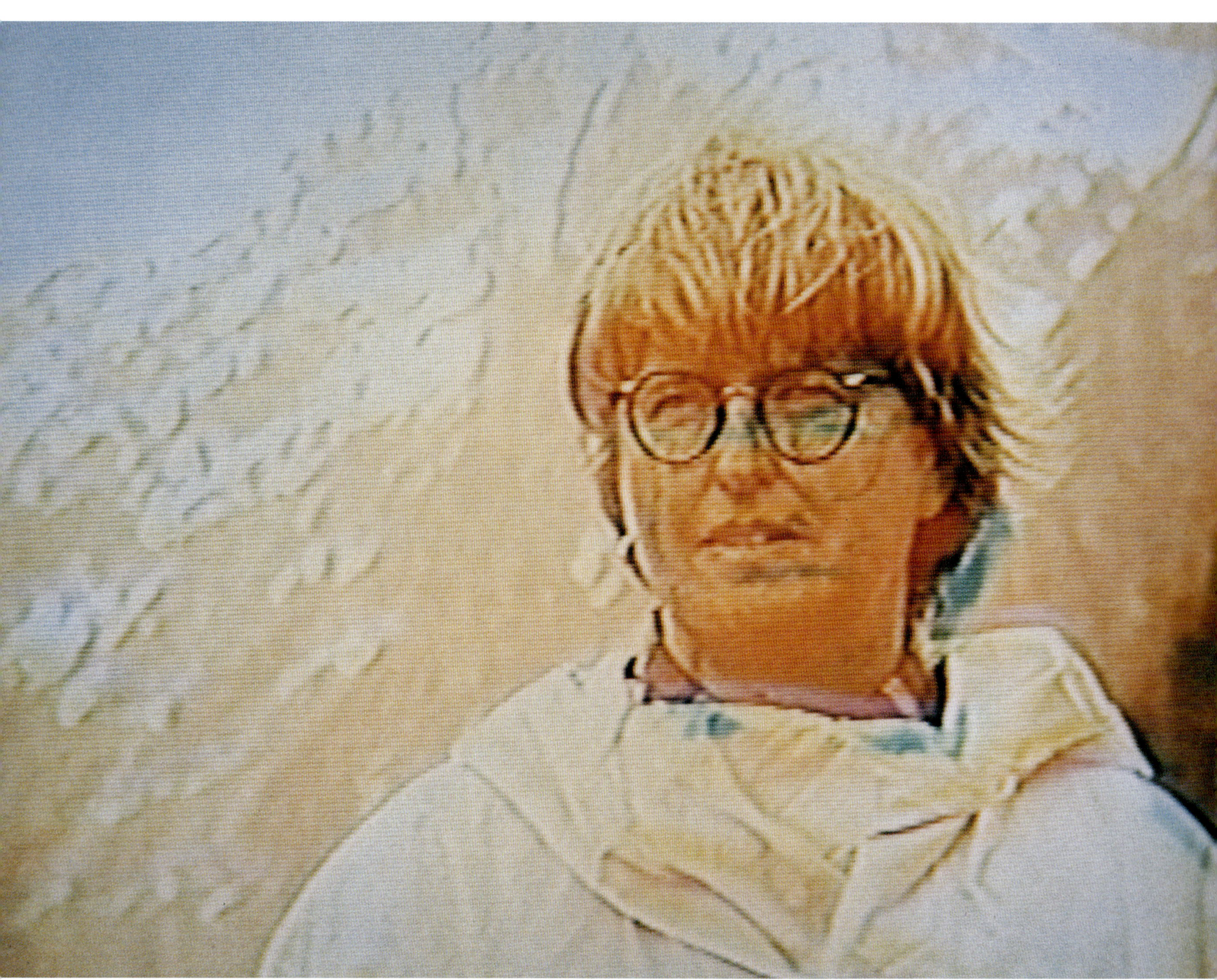

Portrait of the artist at the
fiord in Tafjord.

About the Authors

Nicolas Bourriaud is a French curator and art critic. He co-founded, and from 1999 to 2006 was co-director of Palais de Tokyo, together with Jerôme Sans. He was also founder and director of the contemporary art magazine *Documents sur l'art* (1992–2000), and correspondent in Paris for *Flash Art* from 1987 to 1995. In 2009 Bourriaud was appointed as the Gulbenkian curator of contemporary art at Tate Britain and is among the most widely respected curators in Europe. Bourriaud is internationally renowned for his publications *Relational Aesthetics* (1998) and *Postproduction* (2001). He has curated numerous international exhibitions, including *Courts Métrages Immobiles*, for the 1990 Venice Biennale, *Aperto* for the 1993 Venice Biennale, *Traffic*, CAPC Bordeaux, 1996, *Touch*, San Francisco Art Institute, 2002, *GNS (Global Navigation System)*, Palais de Tokyo, 2003, *Playlist*, Palais de Tokyo, 2004, *The Moscow Biennale* 2007 and *Altermodern* for the Fourth Tate Biennial, Tate Britain, 2009.

Jon Fosse is a Norwegian playwright and author. In addition to critically acclaimed plays he has also published novels, collections of poetry and essays and books for children. He currently lives in Bergen and was born and raised in Hardanger on the west coast of Norway. Fosse debuted as a writer in 1983 and has written extensively ever since. His first play was published in 1994, and since then Fosse has written more than thirty plays. His work has been translated into more than twenty languages, and his plays have been produced on more than 115 stages in most European countries and other places around the world. In 2010 he was awarded the International Ibsen Award.

Ken Friedman is a well-known artist and art theorist associated with the Fluxus movement. He works at the intersection of three fields; design, management and art. Friedman is Professor and Dean of Design at Swinburne University, Melbourne. He has done extensive research in the philosophy of science, the philosophy of design, and doctoral education in design. He also works with national design policy projects in Estonia, Latvia, Lithuania, and Wales. Friedman is editor of the journal *Artifact*, book reviews editor of Design Research News, and communications secretary of the Design Research Society. He co-chaired the La Clusaz Conference on Doctoral Education in Design in 2000, the 2006 conference of the European Academy of Management in Oslo, and the 2006 conference of the Design Research Society in Lisbon.

Hans Ulrich Obrist is a Swiss curator, art critic and art historian. He currently works as co-director of Exhibitions and Programmes and director of International Projects at The Serpentine Gallery in London. In 1996 he co-curated the first edition of *Manifesta*. Obrist is a contributing editor of the magazines *Abitare*, *Artforum* and *Paradis* and also writes frequently for other prestigious art journals. He is widely respected for his inclusive approach to curatorial practice and for his book *A Brief History of Curating*. In 2007 Hans Ulrich co-curated *Il Tempo del Postino* with Philippe Parreno for the Manchester International Festival, also presented at Art Basel, 2009. Also in 2007, The Van Alen Institute awarded him the New York Prize Fellowship for 2007–2008. In 2008 he curated *Everstill* at the Lorca House in Granada. More recently, Obrist has initiated a series of "marathons". The first in the series, the *Interview Marathon* at The Serpentine Gallery involved interviews with leading figures in contemporary culture over 24 hours, conducted by Obrist and architect Rem Koolhaas.

Lorella Scacco is an Italian art critic, journalist and independent curator. She graduated with a degree in The History of Contemporary Art and Aesthetics and is a member of SIE, the Italian Aesthetics Society. She has curated numerous exhibitions and edited catalogues for contemporary art exhibitions in public and private spaces in Italy and abroad, including *Artesto* at Palazzo del Triennale, Milan, *Mobile Journey*, an official collateral event for the 52nd Venice Biennale in 2007 and *The Hot Season – Italian Art Now* for The Stenersen Museum in 2008. She contributes regularly to art magazines and has specialized in Scandinavian contemporary art and in new media art. She recently published the book *Northwave – A Survey of Video Art in the Nordic Countries*.

Selene Wendt is a Norwegian art historian, curator and writer. She currently works as director of The Stenersen Museum in Oslo. She has curated numerous exhibitions of international contemporary art, including Shirin Neshat, *Beyond Orientalism*, Ghada Amer, *Reading Between the Threads*, Liza Lou, *Leaves of Glass*, Maria Magdalena Campos-Pons, *Mil Maneras Para Decir Adios*, Daniele Buetti, *Will Beauty Save the World?*, Magne F, *Payne's Gray*, Abbas Kiarostami, *Shadows in the Snow*, Siri Hermansen, *Bipolar Horizon*, Ulf Nilsen, *Inside Out*, and Crispin Gurholt, *Live Photo*, in addition to major group exhibitions such as *Art Through the Eye of the Needle*, which addressed the breakdown of barriers between art and fashion, *A Doll's House*, which included artists whose works are influenced by doll symbolism, and *Equatorial Rhythms*, which featured visual artists whose works are influenced by music. She has written and edited numerous exhibition catalogues and books, including *Crispin Gurholt Live Photo II*, also published by Skira.

La poupée aux pensées trop
dangereuses, 1975.
Lithograph.

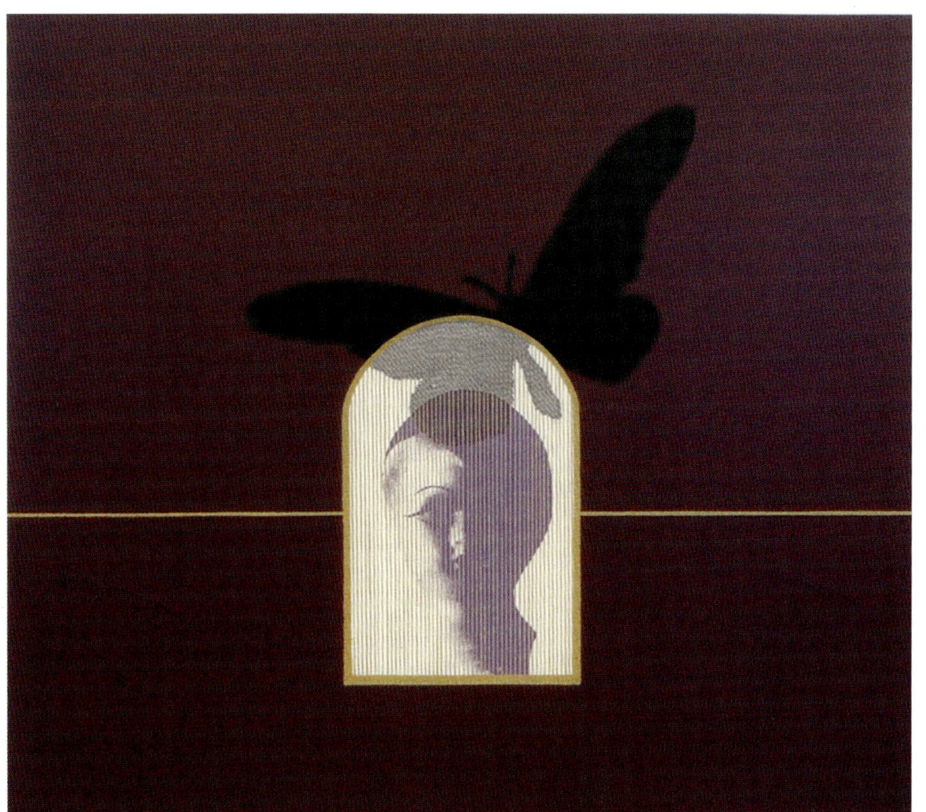